Microsoft® Word 2000
Introductory Edition

INTERACTIVE COMPUTING SERIES

Kenneth C. Laudon
Kenneth Rosenblatt

with Michael W. Domis

Azimuth Interactive, Inc.

Boston   Burr Ridge, IL   Dubuque, IA   Madison, WI   New York   San Francisco   St. Louis
Bangkok   Bogotá   Caracas   Lisbon   London   Madrid   Mexico City   Milan   New Delhi   Seoul
Singapore   Sydney   Taipei   Toronto

McGraw-Hill Higher Education

*A Division of The **McGraw-Hill** Companies*

MICROSOFT WORD 2000 INTRODUCTORY EDITION
Copyright © 2000 by The McGraw-Hill Companies, Inc. All rights reserved. Printed in the
United States of America. Except as permitted under the United States Copyright Act of 1976, no
part of this publication may be reproduced or distributed in any form or by any means, or stored
in a data base or retrieval system, without the prior written permission of the publisher.

 This book is printed on recycled, acid-free paper containing 10% postconsumer waste.
RECYCLED

1 2 3 4 5 6 7 8 9 0 QPD/QPD 9 0 9 8 7 6 5 4 3 2 1 0 9

ISBN 0-07-234936-0

Vice president/Editor-in-Chief: *Michael W. Junior*
Sponsoring editor: *Trisha O'Shea*
Developmental editor: *Kyle Thomes*
Senior marketing manager: *Jodi McPherson*
Project manager: *Carrie Sestak*
Production supervisor: *Michael R. McCormick*
Senior freelance design coordinator: *Laurie Entringer*
Supplement coordinator: *Matthew Perry*
Compositor: *Azimuth Interactive, Inc.*
Typeface: *10/12 Sabon*
Printer: *Quebecor Printing Book Group/Dubuque*

Library of Congress Catalog Card Number: 99-64064

http://www.mhhe.com

Microsoft®
Word 2000
Introductory Edition

INTERACTIVE COMPUTING SERIES

Kenneth C. Laudon
Kenneth Rosenblatt

with Michael W. Domis

Azimuth Interactive, Inc.

At **McGraw-Hill Higher Education**, we publish instructional materials targeted at the higher education market. In an effort to expand the tools of higher learning, we publish texts, lab manuals, study guides, testing materials, software, and multimedia products.

At **Irwin/McGraw-Hill** (a division of McGraw-Hill Higher Education), we realize technology will continue to create new mediums for professors and students to manage resources and communicate information with one another. We strive to provide the most flexible and complete teaching and learning tools available and offer solutions to the changing world of teaching and learning.

Irwin/McGraw-Hill is dedicated to providing the tools necessary for today's instructors and students to navigate the world of Information Technology successfully.

Seminar Series - Irwin/McGraw-Hill's Technology Connection seminar series offered across the country every year, demonstrates the latest technology products and encourages collaboration among teaching professionals.

Osborne/McGraw-Hill - A division of the McGraw-Hill Companies known for its best-selling Internet titles *Harley Hahn's Internet & Web Yellow Pages* and the *Internet Complete Reference*, offers an additional resource for certification and has strategic publishing relationships with corporations such as Corel Corporation and America Online. For more information, visit Osborne at www.osborne.com.

Digital Solutions - Irwin/McGraw-Hill is committed to publishing Digital Solutions. Taking your course online doesn't have to be a solitary venture. Nor does it have to be a difficult one. We offer several solutions, which will let you enjoy all the benefits of having course material online. For more information, visit www.mhhe.com/solutions/index.mhtml.

Packaging Options - For more about our discount options, contact your local Irwin/McGraw-Hill Sales representative at 1-800-338-3987, or visit our Web site at www.mhhe.com/it.

Preface

Interactive Computing Series

Goals/Philosophy

The *Interactive Computing Series* provides you with an illustrated interactive environment for learning software skills using Microsoft Office. The Interactive Computing Series is composed of both text and multimedia interactive CD-ROMs. The text and the CD-ROMs are closely coordinated. *It's up to you. You can choose how you want to learn.*

Approach

The *Interactive Computing Series* is the visual interactive way to develop and apply software skills. This skills-based approach coupled with its highly visual, two-page spread design allows the student to focus on a single skill without having to turn the page. A running case study is provided through the text, reinforcing the skills and giving a real-world focus to the learning process.

About the Book

APPROVED COURSEWARE
Level 1
Microsoft® Office User Specialist
Word 2000 Exam

The Interactive Computing Series offers *two levels* of instruction. Each level builds upon the previous level.

Brief lab manual - covers the basics of the application, contains two to four chapters.

Introductory lab manual - includes the material in the Brief textbook plus two to four additional chapters. The Introductory lab manuals prepare students for the *Microsoft Office User Specialist Proficiency Exam (MOUS Certification).*

Each lesson is organized around **Skills**, **Concepts**, and **Steps (Do It!)**.

Each lesson is divided into a number of Skills. Each **Skill** is first explained at the top of the page.
Each **Concept** is a concise description of why the skill is useful and where it is commonly used.
Each **Step (Do It!)** contains the instructions on how to complete the skill.

About the CD-ROM

The CD-ROM provides a unique interactive environment for students where they learn to use software faster and remember it better. The CD-ROM is organized in a similar approach as the text: The **Skill** is defined, the **Concept** is explained in rich multimedia, and the student performs **Steps (Do It!)** within sections called Interactivities. There are at least <u>45 Interactivities per CD-ROM</u>. Some of the features of the CD-ROM are:

Simulated Environment - The Interactive Computing CD-ROM places students in a simulated controlled environment where they can practice and perform the skills of the application software.
Interactive Exercises - The student is asked to demonstrate command of a specific software skill. The student's actions are followed by a digital "TeacherWizard" that provides feedback.
SmartQuizzes - Provide performance-based assessment of the student at the end of each lesson.

Using the Book

In the book, each skill is described in a two-page graphical spread (Figure 1). The left side of the two-page spread describes the skill, the concept, and the steps needed to perform the skill. The right side of the spread uses screen shots to show you how the screen should look at key stages.

Figure 1

Skill: Each lesson is divided into a number of specific skills

Concept: A concise description of why the skill is useful and where it is commonly used

Running case: A real-world case ties the skill and the concept to a practical situation

Do It!: Step-by-step directions show you how to use the skill

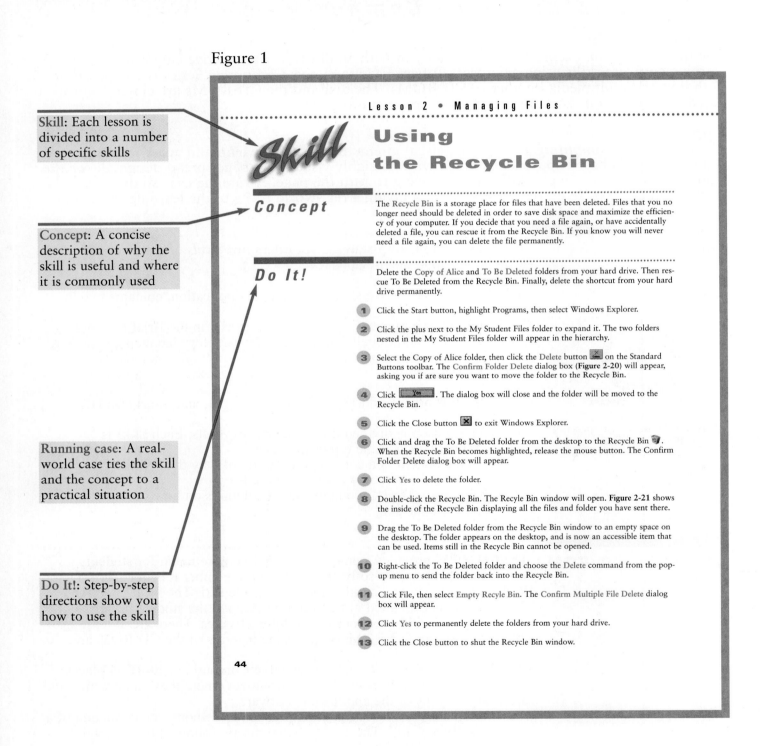

Skill Using the Recycle Bin

Concept

The Recycle Bin is a storage place for files that have been deleted. Files that you no longer need should be deleted in order to save disk space and maximize the efficiency of your computer. If you decide that you need a file again, or have accidentally deleted a file, you can rescue it from the Recycle Bin. If you know you will never need a file again, you can delete the file permanently.

Do It!

Delete the Copy of Alice and To Be Deleted folders from your hard drive. Then rescue To Be Deleted from the Recycle Bin. Finally, delete the shortcut from your hard drive permanently.

1. Click the Start button, highlight Programs, then select Windows Explorer.

2. Click the plus next to the My Student Files folder to expand it. The two folders nested in the My Student Files folder will appear in the hierarchy.

3. Select the Copy of Alice folder, then click the Delete button on the Standard Buttons toolbar. The Confirm Folder Delete dialog box (**Figure 2-20**) will appear, asking you if are sure you want to move the folder to the Recycle Bin.

4. Click . The dialog box will close and the folder will be moved to the Recycle Bin.

5. Click the Close button to exit Windows Explorer.

6. Click and drag the To Be Deleted folder from the desktop to the Recycle Bin . When the Recycle Bin becomes highlighted, release the mouse button. The Confirm Folder Delete dialog box will appear.

7. Click Yes to delete the folder.

8. Double-click the Recycle Bin. The Recycle Bin window will open. **Figure 2-21** shows the inside of the Recycle Bin displaying all the files and folder you have sent there.

9. Drag the To Be Deleted folder from the Recycle Bin window to an empty space on the desktop. The folder appears on the desktop, and is now an accessible item that can be used. Items still in the Recycle Bin cannot be opened.

10. Right-click the To Be Deleted folder and choose the Delete command from the pop-up menu to send the folder back into the Recycle Bin.

11. Click File, then select Empty Recycle Bin. The Confirm Multiple File Delete dialog box will appear.

12. Click Yes to permanently delete the folders from your hard drive.

13. Click the Close button to shut the Recycle Bin window.

44

End-of-Lesson Features

In the book, the learning in each lesson is reinforced at the end by a quiz and a skills review called Interactivity, which provides step-by-step exercises and real-world problems for the students to solve independently.

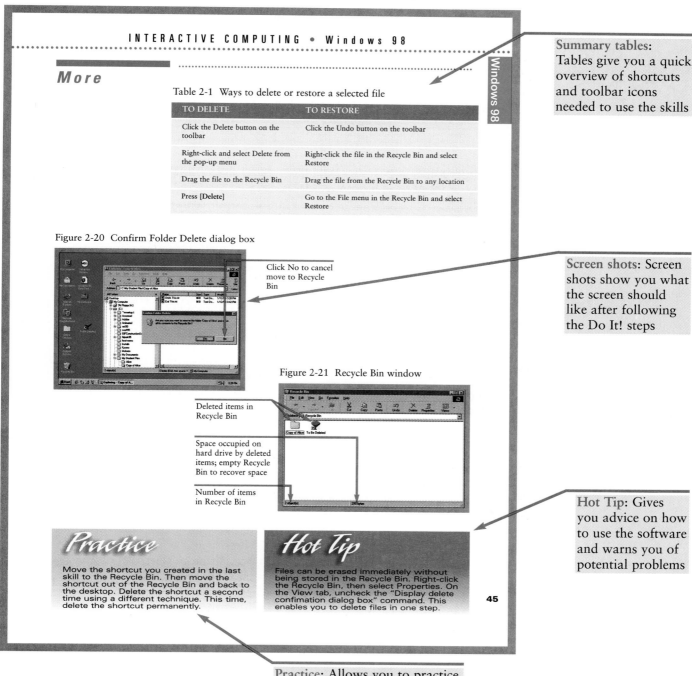

Summary tables: Tables give you a quick overview of shortcuts and toolbar icons needed to use the skills

More

Table 2-1 Ways to delete or restore a selected file

TO DELETE	TO RESTORE
Click the Delete button on the toolbar	Click the Undo button on the toolbar
Right-click and select Delete from the pop-up menu	Right-click the file in the Recycle Bin and select Restore
Drag the file to the Recycle Bin	Drag the file from the Recycle Bin to any location
Press [Delete]	Go to the File menu in the Recycle Bin and select Restore

Figure 2-20 Confirm Folder Delete dialog box

Click No to cancel move to Recycle Bin

Screen shots: Screen shots show you what the screen should like after following the Do It! steps

Figure 2-21 Recycle Bin window

Deleted items in Recycle Bin

Space occupied on hard drive by deleted items; empty Recycle Bin to recover space

Number of items in Recycle Bin

Hot Tip: Gives you advice on how to use the software and warns you of potential problems

Practice

Move the shortcut you created in the last skill to the Recycle Bin. Then move the shortcut out of the Recycle Bin and back to the desktop. Delete the shortcut a second time using a different technique. This time, delete the shortcut permanently.

Hot Tip

Files can be erased immediately without being stored in the Recycle Bin. Right-click the Recycle Bin, then select Properties. On the View tab, uncheck the "Display delete confimation dialog box" command. This enables you to delete files in one step.

45

Practice: Allows you to practice the skill with a built-in exercise or directs you to a student file

Using the Interactive CD-ROM

The Interactive Computing multimedia CD-ROM provides an unparalleled learning environment in which you can learn software skills faster and better than in books alone. The CD-ROM creates a unique interactive environment in which you can learn to use software faster and remember it better. The CD-ROM uses the same lessons, skills, concepts, and Do It! steps as found in the book, but presents the material using voice, video, animation, and precise simulation of the software you are learning. A typical CD-ROM contents screen shows the major elements of a lesson (see Figure 2 below).

Skills list: A list of skills allows you to jump directly to any skill you want to learn or review, including interactive sessions with the TeacherWizard

Figure 2

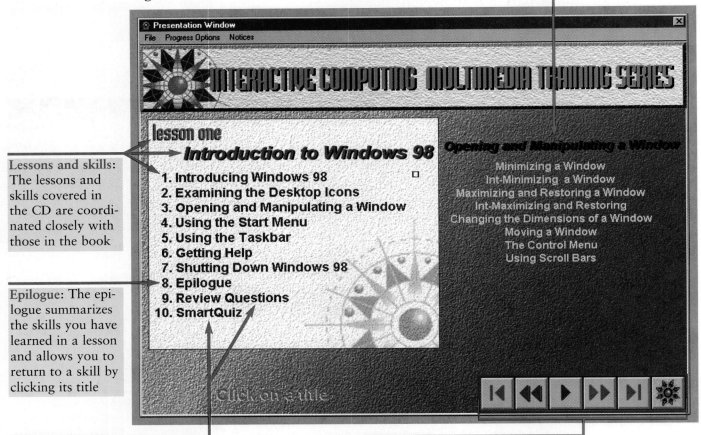

Lessons and skills: The lessons and skills covered in the CD are coordinated closely with those in the book

Epilogue: The epilogue summarizes the skills you have learned in a lesson and allows you to return to a skill by clicking its title

Review Questions and SmartQuiz: Review Questions test your knowledge of the concepts covered in the lesson; SmartQuiz tests your ability to accomplish tasks in a simulated software environment

User controls: Precise and simple user controls permit you to start, stop, pause, jump forward or backward one sentence, or jump forward or backward an entire skill. A single navigation star takes you back to the lesson's table of contents

Unique Features of the CD-ROM: TeacherWizard™ and SmartQuiz™

Interactive Computing: Software Skills offers many leading-edge features on the CD currently found in no other learning product on the market. One such feature is *interactive exercises* in which you are asked to demonstrate your command of a software skill in a precisely simulated software environment. Your actions are followed closely by a digital TeacherWizard that guides you with additional information if you make a mistake. When you complete the action called for by the TeacherWizard correctly, you are congratulated and prompted to continue the lesson. If you make a mistake, the TeacherWizard gently lets you know: "No, that's not the right icon. Click on the Folder icon on the left side of the top toolbar to open a file." No matter how many mistakes you make, the TeacherWizard is there to help you.

Another leading-edge feature is the end-of-lesson SmartQuiz. Unlike the multiple choice and matching questions found in the book quiz, the SmartQuiz puts you in a simulated digital software world and asks you to show your mastery of skills while actually working with the software (Figure 3).

Figure 3

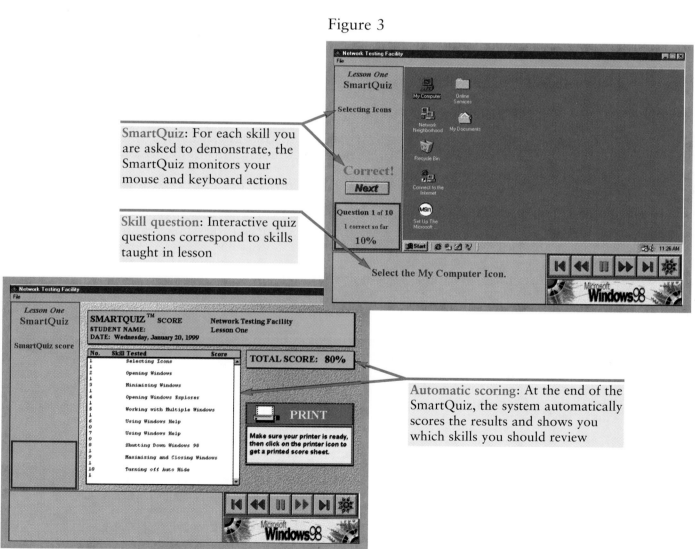

SmartQuiz: For each skill you are asked to demonstrate, the SmartQuiz monitors your mouse and keyboard actions

Skill question: Interactive quiz questions correspond to skills taught in lesson

Automatic scoring: At the end of the SmartQuiz, the system automatically scores the results and shows you which skills you should review

Teaching Resources

The following is a list of supplemental material available with the Interactive Computing Series:

Skills Assessment
Irwin/McGraw-Hill offers two innovative systems, ATLAS and SimNet, which take testing beyond the basics with pre- and post-assessment capabilities.
ATLAS (Active Testing and Learning Assessment Software) – available for the *Interactive Computing Series* – is our live-in-the-application Skills Assessment tool. ATLAS allows students to perform tasks while working live within the Office applications environment. ATLAS is web-enabled and customizable to meet the needs of your course. ATLAS is available for Office 2000.
SimNet (Simulated Network Assessment Product) – available for the *Interactive Computing Series* – permits you to test the actual software skills students learn about the Microsoft Office applications in a simulated environment. SimNet is web-enabled and is available for Office 97 and Office 2000.

Instructor's Resource Kits
The Instructor's Resource Kit provides professors with all of the ancillary material needed to teach a course. Irwin/McGraw-Hill is dedicated to providing instructors with the most effective instruction resources available. Many of these resources are available at our Information Technology Supersite www.mhhe.com/it. Our Instructor's Kits are available on CD-ROM and contain the following:

Network Testing Facility (NTF) - Tests acquired software skills in a safe simulated software environment. NTF tracks a student score and allows the instructor to build screens that indicate student progress.
Diploma by Brownstone - is the most flexible, powerful, and easy-to-use computerized testing system available in higher education. The diploma system allows professors to create an Exam as a printed version, as a LAN-based Online version, and as an Internet version. Diploma includes grade book features, which automate the entire testing process.
Instructor's Manual - Includes:
-Solutions to all lessons and end-of-unit material
-Teaching Tips
-Teaching Strategies
-Additional exercises
Student Data Files - To use the Interactive Computing Series, students must have Student Data Files to complete practice and test sessions. The instructor and students using this text in classes are granted the right to post the student files on any network or stand-alone computer, or to distribute the files on individual diskettes. The student files may be downloaded from our IT Supersite at www.mhhe.com/it.
Series Web Site - Available at www.mhhe.com/cit/apps/laudon.

Digital Solutions
Pageout Lite - is designed if you're just beginning to explore Web site options. Pageout Lite is great for posting your own material online. You may choose one of three templates, type in your material, and Pageout Lite instantly converts it to HTML.
Pageout - is our Course Web site Development Center. Pageout offers a Syllabus page, Web site address, Online Learning Center Content, online exercises and quizzes, gradebook, discussion board, an area for students to build their own Web pages, and all the features of Pageout Lite. For more information please visit the Pageout Web site at www.mhla.net/pageout.

OLC/Series Web Sites - Online Learning Centers (OLCs)/Series Sites are accessible through our Supersite at www.mhhe.com/it. Our Online Learning Centers/Series Sites provide pedagogical features and supplements for our titles online. Students can point and click their way to key terms, learning objectives, chapter overviews, PowerPoint slides, exercises, and web links.

The McGraw-Hill Learning Architecture (MHLA) - is a complete course delivery system. MHLA gives professors ownership in the way digital content is presented to the class through online quizzing, student collaboration, course administration, and content management. For a walk-through of MHLA visit the MHLA Web site at www.mhla.net.

Packaging Options - For more about our discount options, contact your local Irwin/McGraw-Hill Sales representative at 1-800-338-3987 or visit our Web site at www.mhhe.com/it.

Visit www.mhhe.com/it
THE ONLY SITE WITH ALL YOUR CIT AND MIS NEEDS.

Acknowledgments

The Interactive Computing Series is a cooperative effort of many individuals, each contributing to an overall team effort. The Interactive Computing team is composed of instructional designers, writers, multimedia designers, graphic artists, and programmers. Our goal is to provide you and your instructor with the most powerful and enjoyable learning environment using both traditional text and new interactive multimedia techniques. Interactive Computing is tested rigorously in both CD and text formats prior to publication.

Our special thanks to Trisha O'Shea and Kyle Lewis, our Editors for computer applications and concepts. Both Trisha and Kyle have poured their enthusiasm into the project and inspired us all to work closely together. Kyle Thomes, our Developmental Editor, has provided superb feedback from the market and excellent advice on content. Jodi McPherson, marketing, has added her inimitable enthusiasm and market knowledge. Finally, Mike Junior, Vice-President and Editor-in-Chief, provided the unstinting support required for a project of this magnitude.

The Azimuth team members who contributed to the textbooks and CD-ROM multimedia program are:

Ken Rosenblatt (Textbooks Project Manager and Writer, Interactive Writer)
Raymond Wang (Interactive Project Manager)
Russell Polo (Programmer)
Michele Faranda (Textbook design and layout)
Jason Eiseman (Technical Writer, layout)
Michael Domis (Technical Writer)
Larry Klein (Contributing Writer)
Thomas Grande (Editorial Assistant, layout)
Stefon Westry (Multimedia Designer)

Contents

Word 2000 Introductory Edition

Preface..v

1 Introduction to Word..........................WD 1.1
Starting Word...WD 1.2
Exploring the Word Screen...........................WD 1.4
Creating a Document and Entering Text............WD 1.6
Saving and Closing a Document....................WD 1.8
Opening an Existing Document.....................WD 1.10
Deleting and Inserting Text.........................WD 1.12
Formatting Text.......................................WD 1.14
Previewing and Printing a Document..............WD 1.16
Shortcuts..WD 1.18
Quiz..WD 1.19
Interactivity...WD 1.21

2 Editing Documents............................WD 2.1
Searching for Files...................................WD 2.2
Selecting Text and Undoing Actions...............WD 2.4
Cutting, Copying, and Moving Text................WD 2.6
Copying and Moving Text with the Mouse.........WD 2.8
Using the Office Assistant..........................WD 2.10
Other Word Help Features..........................WD 2.12
Using Templates and Wizards.....................WD 2.14
Shortcuts..WD 2.18
Quiz..WD 2.19
Interactivity...WD 2.21

Contents

Continued

3 Advanced Editing .... WD 3.1

Setting Up a Page .... WD 3.2
Inserting Page Numbers .... WD 3.4
Inserting Footnotes and Endnotes .... WD 3.6
Applying Indents .... WD 3.8
Changing Line Spacing .... WD 3.10
Inserting Page Breaks .... WD 3.12
Working with Multiple Documents .... WD 3.14
Using the Format Painter .... WD 3.16
Checking Spelling and Grammar .... WD 3.18
Using AutoCorrect .... WD 3.22
Using the Word Thesaurus .... WD 3.26
Finding and Replacing Text .... WD 3.28
Shortcuts .... WD 3.30
Quiz .... WD 3.31
Interactivity .... WD 3.33

4 Tables and Charts .... WD 4.1

Creating Tables .... WD 4.2
Editing Tables .... WD 4.6
Inserting and Deleting Rows, Columns, and Cells ... WD 4.8
Sorting Data in a Table .... WD 4.10
Calculating Data in a Table .... WD 4.12
Formatting a Table .... WD 4.16
Creating a Chart .... WD 4.18
Editing a Chart .... WD 4.20
Drawing a Table .... WD 4.22
Adding Borders and Shading .... WD 4.26
Shortcuts .... WD 4.30
Quiz .... WD 4.31
Interactivity .... WD 4.33

Contents

Continued

5 Advanced Formatting...........................WD 5.1

Formatting Text with Columns.............................WD 5.2
Making Bulleted and Numbered Lists.....................WD 5.4
Adding Borders and Shading to Text......................WD 5.6
Working with Section Breaks..............................WD 5.8
Inserting the Date and Time..............................WD 5.10
Inserting Headers and Footers............................WD 5.12
Shrinking a Document to Fit..............................WD 5.14
Modifying Page Numbers...................................WD 5.16
Changing Page Orientation................................WD 5.18
Using Special Formatting Effects.........................WD 5.20
Shortcuts..WD 5.22
Quiz...WD 5.23
Interactivity..WD 5.25

6 Using Character Styles and AutoFormat...WD 6.1

Applying a Character Style...............................WD 6.2
Creating Your Own Character Style........................WD 6.4
Applying an AutoFormat...................................WD 6.8
Using the Style Gallery..................................WD 6.10
Editing a Style..WD 6.12
Applying Styles on the Paragraph Level...................WD 6.14
Displaying a Style Report................................WD 6.16
Browsing by Style..WD 6.18
Finding and Replacing a Style............................WD 6.20
Using the Tabs Command...................................WD 6.22
Using Click and Type.....................................WD 6.24
Shortcuts..WD 6.26
Quiz...WD 6.27
Interactivity..WD 6.29

Contents

Continued

7 Merging Documents............................WD 7.1

Creating a Main Document...........................WD 7.2
Creating a Data Source...............................WD 7.4
Adding Information to the Data Source.................WD 7.6
Adding Merge Fields to a Main Document..............WD 7.8
Editing Individual Merged Documents..................WD 7.10
Printing Merged Documents...........................WD 7.12
Preparing and Printing Labels........................WD 7.14
Preparing and Printing Envelopes.....................WD 7.18
Shortcuts..WD 7.22
Quiz...WD 7.23
Interactivity...WD 7.25

8 Creating Web Pages and Graphics..........WD 8.1

Creating a Web Page with a Template..................WD 8.2
Saving a Document as a Web Page.....................WD 8.4
Inserting Clip Art....................................WD 8.6
Formatting Clip Art..................................WD 8.8
Drawing AutoShapes..................................WD 8.10
Formatting Drawn Objects.............................WD 8.12
Inserting a Picture from a File........................WD 8.14
Using WordArt.......................................WD 8.16
Inserting Hyperlinks..................................WD 8.20
Previewing and Editing a Web Page....................WD 8.22
Shortcuts..WD 8.24
Quiz...WD 8.25
Interactivity...WD 8.27

Glossary...WD 1

Index..WD 11

▶ **Starting Word**

▶ **Exploring the Word Screen**

▶ **Creating a Document and Entering Text**

▶ **Saving and Closing a Document**

▶ **Opening an Existing Document**

▶ **Deleting and Inserting Text**

▶ **Formatting Text**

▶ **Previewing and Printing a Document**

L E S S O N

1

INTRODUCTION TO WORD

Microsoft Word 2000 is a word processing software program designed to make the creation of professional-quality documents fast and easy. Unlike a typewriter, Word allows the user to edit, move, and copy text that has been written, providing enormous flexibility in how the finished product will appear.

Among many other features, Microsoft Word will let you:

- Copy, move, and change the appearance of text within a document with a click of the mouse
- Create documents using ready-made templates
- Automatically add page numbers and footnotes to documents
- Automatically find and correct spelling and grammatical errors
- Include tables and charts of data or text
- Request help while you are using the program
- Search for specific pieces of text within a document
- See how your document will appear before you print it on paper

Microsoft Word keeps each document (letter, report, or other piece of written work) in the computer's memory while you are working with it. In order to keep a document permanently, you must save it as a file on your computer's storage device (either floppy or hard disk). Word documents can contain just a few words or thousands of words and images.

Case Study:
Sabrina Lee, a graduating senior from Indiana University, is learning to use Microsoft Word to create a cover letter that she will include with her resume when she sends it to a prospective employer.

Starting Word

Concept

To use the Microsoft Word program, or application, the user must open it. You can use a variety of techniques to launch Word. When you install the program, a short-cut is automatically placed on the Windows Start menu. You can also use My Computer or Windows Explorer to locate Word's executable file.

Do It!

Sabrina wants to open the Microsoft Word application so she can write a cover letter.

1 Make sure the computer, monitor, and any other necessary peripheral devices are turned on. The Windows screen should appear on your monitor, as shown in **Figure 1-1**. Your screen may differ slightly from the one shown.

2 Click the ▓Start button on the Windows taskbar at the bottom of your screen. This will bring up the Windows Start menu.

3 Move the mouse pointer ▹ up the Start menu to the Programs folder. The Programs submenu will appear (See **Figure 1-2**).

4 Position the pointer over Microsoft Word, highlighting it, and click the left mouse button to open the application (if Word is not there, try looking under Microsoft Office on the Programs submenu). Word will open with a blank document in the window.

More

When you started Word you may have noticed a small window containing the Office Assistant. If the assistant is not in your Word window it can be accessed by clicking the Microsoft Word Help button 🔲 found at the right side of the Standard toolbar. Part of the Microsoft Office Help facility, the Assistant offers tips, advice, and help on most Word functions. The Assistant has the ability to guess the help topic you desire based on the actions you are performing, and it can also answer queries by accepting full questions rather than being limited to keyword searches. The Assistant will become active when you use a wizard, walking you through the steps, offering advice and suggestions. When the Assistant feels that you need help with a particular feature it will produce a light bulb in its window, or on the Office Assistant button. Clicking this light bulb will cause a help tip to materialize in the window. Clicking on the Assistant brings up a balloon with various options, Help topics, and a space in which you can type your question.

With your Word or Office 2000 CD-ROM inserted in the appropriate disk drive, you can change the appearance of the Assistant by clicking the Options button in the Assistant's dialog balloon. The Office Assistant dialog box also offers choices for customizing the Assistant's behavior and functionality. To hide the Assistant, choose the Hide Assistant command on the Help menu. If you are working with a freshly installed copy of Word, you will have to click the Start using Microsoft Word option in the Assistant's dialog balloon in order to begin working with the program.

Figure 1-1 Windows screen

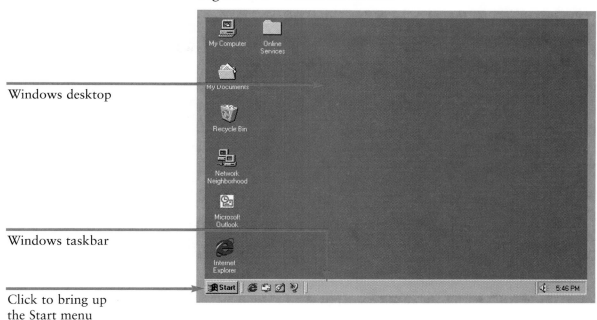

Windows desktop

Windows taskbar

Click to bring up
the Start menu

Word 2000

Figure 1-2 Opening Word from the Start menu

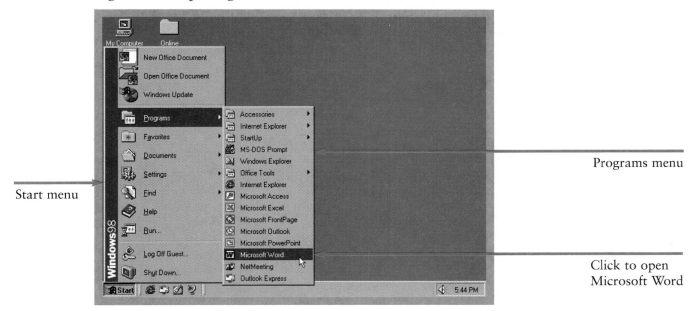

Start menu

Programs menu

Click to open
Microsoft Word

Practice

Click File, then click Exit to close Word.
Then open Word again.

Hot Tip

Each computer can vary in its setup
depending on its hardware and software
configurations. Therefore, your Word
StartUp procedure may be slightly different
from that described above.

Exploring the Word Screen

Concept

When Word is opened, it will present a window with many common Windows features including a title bar, a menu bar, and toolbars. In addition to these, there are many features unique to Word that are designed to make document production fast, flexible, and more convenient.

The Microsoft Word screen, or application window, contains the following components, as shown in **Figure 1-3**:

The title bar shows the name of the application and the name of the active document. A new document is automatically called Document1, Document2, etc., until it is saved with a new name.

The menu bar shows the names of menus containing Word commands. Clicking one of these names will make its menu appear, listing the commands you may choose from. When you open a menu in Word 2000, or in any Office 2000 application, only a few commands will appear at first. These are the commands that have been deemed most popular by the designers of the software. If you do not click one of these commands, the menu will expand to reveal more commands after a few seconds. You can expedite this expansion by clicking on the down arrow button at the bottom of the menu. As you use Word more and more, the program will sense which commands you use most often. These commands will then be the first to appear when you open a menu.

The Standard toolbar contains buttons with icons illustrating commonly used commands. When you position the mouse pointer over a button on a toolbar, the button becomes raised and a small box called a ScreenTip will appear below the button naming its function. Using toolbar buttons is faster than pulling down menus. You can position toolbars in any order, and in various screen locations.

The Formatting toolbar contains the Style, Font, and Size boxes along with buttons for common formatting commands.

The horizontal ruler shows paragraph and document margins and tab settings. In print layout view, the horizontal ruler also shows column widths and a vertical ruler appears.

The insertion point is the blinking vertical bar that marks the place where text will appear as it is entered.

The document window is the open space in which your document appears. When the mouse pointer enters the document window it changes from an arrow to an I-beam I so you can more accurately position it in text.

The positions of the scroll bar boxes in the scroll bars show where the text on the screen is located in relation to the rest of the document. You can move quickly through a document by clicking the scroll bar arrows at either end of the bars to move the scroll box, or you can click and drag the box itself. The horizontal scroll bar also contains the four View buttons. These allow you to view your document in different ways, which you will learn about in Lesson 3.

The left-hand section of the status bar tells you what page and section of your document is currently displayed and the total number of pages. The next section shows the distance (in inches) from the insertion point to the top of the page and its current position given as coordinates of Line and Column number. The remaining portion of the bar is dedicated to showing whether certain options such as Overtype mode or Grammar and Spell Checking are currently active.

Word 2000

Figure 1-3 Components of the Word application window

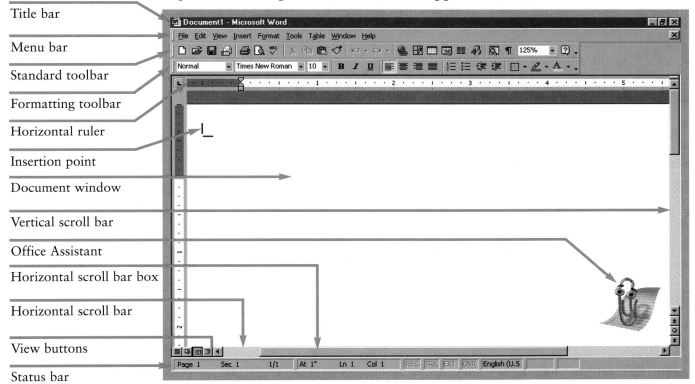

Title bar
Menu bar
Standard toolbar
Formatting toolbar
Horizontal ruler
Insertion point
Document window
Vertical scroll bar
Office Assistant
Horizontal scroll bar box
Horizontal scroll bar
View buttons
Status bar

Familiarize yourself with the tools in the toolbar by positioning the mouse pointer over each button and reading its ScreenTip.

Hot Tip

By default, your Standard and Formatting toolbars may be positioned in a single row in the Word window. In the figure above, the toolbars have been positioned in separate rows allowing more buttons to be visible on each at once.

Creating a Document and Entering Text

Concept

Just as a new sheet of paper must be put into a typewriter before you can type, you must create a new document before you can enter information into Microsoft Word.

Do It!

Sabrina wants to open a new document in Microsoft Word and enter text.

1 When you opened Word, a new document should have appeared with Document1 in the title bar. You can also create a new document once Word is open by clicking the New Blank Document button ▯ on the left end of the Standard toolbar.

2 Using the blank document you just opened, type in the following address, pressing [Enter] after each line:

> Sabrina Lee
> 12 Oakleigh Ave.
> Indianapolis, IN 46202

The text will appear at the insertion point as you are typing it. When you are finished, your document should resemble **Figure 1-4**.

More

In this example, you pressed [Enter] after each line of text to begin a new one because an address consists of short, distinct lines. When writing in a document that does not require abbreviated lines, you do not have to press [Enter] to begin a new line, as Word uses a feature known as Word Wrap to continue on the next line when you run out of space in the line you are on. If a word is too long to be added to the end of the current line, it is placed at the beginning of the line below, allowing you to type without interruptions or guesswork.

A new document may also be made by clicking File, then clicking New. As shown in **Figure 1-5**, the New dialog box will appear, giving you several options to create new documents. For now you will learn to use general blank documents. Other kinds of documents and methods of document creation will be covered in Lesson 2.

You may have noticed that some words have wavy red lines beneath them. If Automatic Spell Checking is active, Word checks your spelling automatically as you type and in this fashion points out words it does not recognize. These lines will not appear when the document is printed. You will find out more about Word's spell-check options in Lesson 3. You may also have noticed dots appearing in spaces and a ¶ at the end of every paragraph and blank line. These are called nonprinting characters and, as the name implies, they do not affect the final appearance of your document. Nonprinting characters can be turned on and off with the Show/Hide button ¶ on the Standard toolbar. A ¶, or paragraph mark, is created every time [Enter] is pressed.

Figure 1-4 Sabrina's name and address

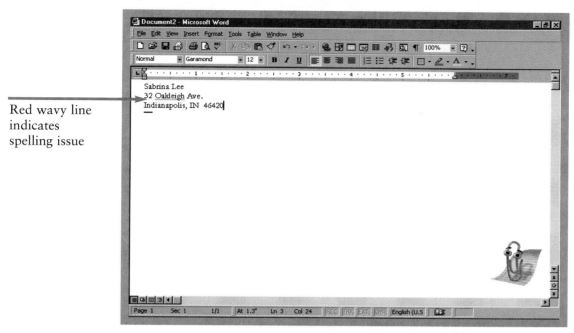

Red wavy line
indicates
spelling issue

Figure 1-5 New dialog box

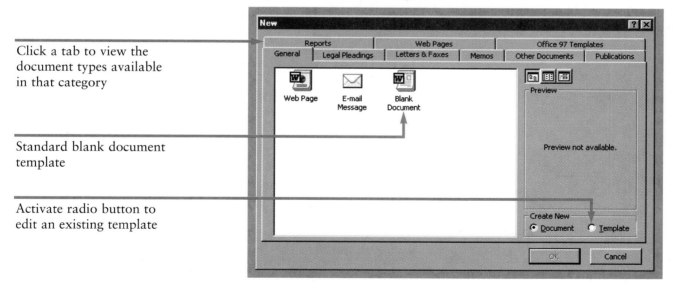

Click a tab to view the
document types available
in that category

Standard blank document
template

Activate radio button to
edit an existing template

Hot Tip

Some commands on a menu have shortcut
keys next to them. Pressing these key combinations is the same as using the menu
commands. Clicking a command with an
ellipsis (...) after it opens a dialog box with
options for that command.

Saving and Closing a Document

Concept

When using a computer, it is essential to Save documents by giving them unique names and storing them on a floppy disk or hard drive. Otherwise, work will be lost when you exit Word or when the computer is shut down. It is also a good idea to save documents as they are modified so that work will not be lost due to power or computer failures. Closing a document removes it from the screen and "files it away" until it is needed again.

Do It!

Save Sabrina's name and address as a file called address.doc and close it.

1. You should still have Sabrina's address on your screen from the previous Skill. Click File, then click Save As to bring up the Save As dialog box, shown in **Figure 1-6.**

2. Word will automatically name your document based on its first few words. In this case, the file name (displayed in the File name: box) is not acceptable, so you must type in another in its place. Notice that the default file name is highlighted. This selected text will be replaced as soon as you begin to type.

3. Type the file name Address into the File name box (remember, the dialog box opens with the File name box already activated and ready to receive text). If you choose not to add the .doc extension to the end of the file name, Word will do it for you automatically when it saves the file. An extension identifies a file's data type for the computer. The extension .doc identifies a Word file.

4. Word needs to be told where your document should be stored in the computer. The left side of the dialog box contains buttons you can click to access some of the most common save locations directly. This includes the My Documents folder, the desktop, and even Web servers. Click the Save in: box to select a location. You will be saving it on your student disk unless your instructor tells you to save the file in a different drive and folder.

5. Click [Save] to save your document to the selected location.

6. Click File, then click Close. The document will disappear from the screen.

More

If you modify a document and do not save the changes before you close it, Word will ask you if you want to save it in one of two ways. If the Office Assistant is open, it will prompt you to save changes via a button in its balloon. If the Assistant is not open, Word will open a dialog box asking if you wish to save changes. These are equivalent methods of saving a file. If you do not save, any changes you have made since the last time you saved will be lost. You can create a new folder in which to save your document by clicking the Create New Folder button 🖼 in the Save As dialog box. In addition to using the Close command, a document can be closed by clicking the document Close button ✖ at the right end of the menu bar. The application Close button in the Word title bar is grouped with the sizing buttons 🔲 🔲, called the Minimize and Maximize buttons, respectively. Minimizing the window reduces it to a program button on the taskbar; click on this button to bring the document back into view. Clicking the Maximize button expands the window so that it fills the entire screen. When the Word window is maximized, the Maximize button will be replaced by the Restore button 🔲, which reduces the window to its previous size. When you have multiple Word documents open at the same time, each one will have its own application window. This is a change from previous versions of Word in which one application window held multiple document windows. Clicking the Application Window Control icon 📝 opens a menu that contains commands equivalent to those executed with the sizing buttons.

Word 2000

Figure 1-6 Save As dialog box

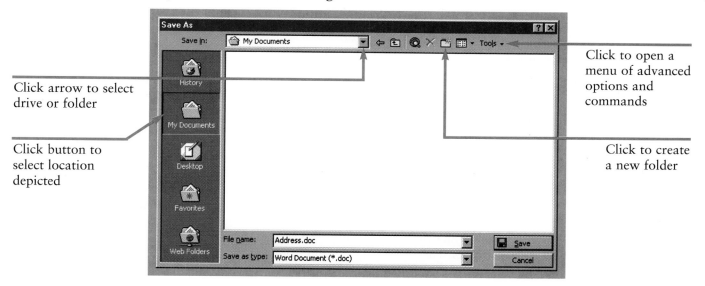

Click arrow to select drive or folder

Click button to select location depicted

Click to open a menu of advanced options and commands

Click to create a new folder

Opening an Existing Document

Concept

To view or edit a document that has been saved, you must open it from the location in which it was stored. Furthermore, you must open it with the application in which it was created, or a comparable one.

Do It!

Sabrina needs to open her cover letter so she can continue to work on it. The file is saved under the name Doit1-6.doc.

1 Click File, then click Open. The Open dialog box will appear, letting you choose which document to open.

2 Click the Look in: box to select the drive that contains your document. A list of folders and drives will appear, as shown in **Figure 1-7**. The drives and directories on your screen may be different from those in the figure. Clicking on a drive or folder will list the documents and/or folders it contains in the contents window below the Look in: box. Double-clicking documents or folders in the contents window will open them. Ask your instructor where to locate the student files and select the appropriate drive and folder.

3 Click Doit1-6 to select it. It will be highlighted in the contents window.

4 Click Open to open the selected file.

More

Word can open word processing documents in a variety of file formats. That is, files created with other programs can be opened and edited by Word. To open a file of a different format from the Open dialog box, just click the Files of type: box and select All Files (*.*). This allows all files in the selected folder to appear in the contents window, available for opening.

If you click the arrow on the right edge of the Open button in the Open dialog box, a menu appears that offers three commands for opening a document in addition to the basic Open command. If you select Open Read-Only, Word will not allow any permanent changes to be made to the document during that particular work session. You can edit the text on your screen, but you will not be able to save the changes. The Open as Copy command creates a new copy of your document, allowing you to keep the old version and edit the new one. The Open in Browser command becomes active when you have selected an HTML document in the contents window. Executing this command opens the selected document in your default Web browser rather than in Word.

Figure 1-7 Open dialog box

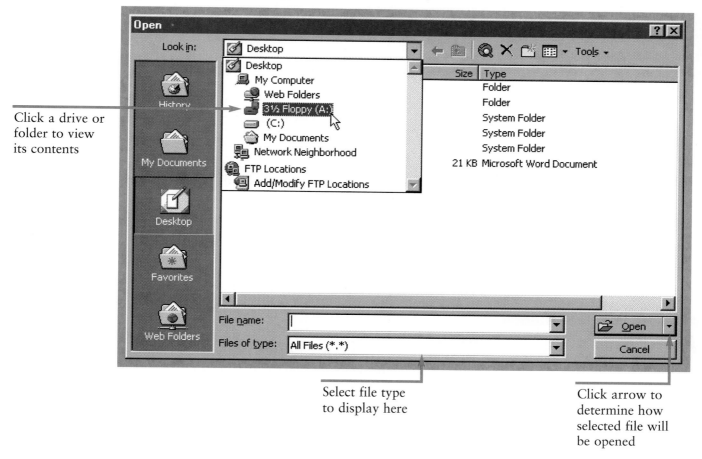

Click a drive or folder to view its contents

Select file type to display here

Click arrow to determine how selected file will be opened

Practice

To practice opening a document, open the student file **Prac1-6**. Leave the file Doit1-6 open, as you will be using it in the next Skill.

Hot Tip

You can also access the Open dialog box by clicking the Open button 🖅 on the Standard toolbar.

 # Deleting and Inserting Text

Concept

One of the fundamental advantages of word processing is the ease it provides in changing content that has been entered previously. Word makes it easy to edit, replace or delete unwanted text.

Do It!

Sabrina wants to modify her street address by changing Oakleigh Ave. to Oakleigh Avenue.

1 Make sure that Doit1-6 (which was opened in the previous Skill) is still in the active window.

2 Move the insertion point to the immediate right of the period in Ave. in Sabrina's address by moving the mouse pointer there and clicking.

3 Press [Backspace] once to erase the period.

4 Type nue to correct the address. Sabrina's address should resemble the one in the final stage of **Figure 1-8**.

5 Save the file to your student disk as Letter.doc.

More

As you just saw, the [Backspace] key erases the character immediately to the left of the insertion point. To erase the character to the right of the insertion point, press [Delete]. Word inserts text at the insertion point; that is, it moves nearby text to the right instead of typing over it. To type over existing text without moving it, double-click the Overtype button OVR on the status bar to enter Overtype mode.

You can move the insertion point one character at a time to the left or right and one line at a time up or down with the arrow keys on the keyboard. This is especially helpful when you are moving the insertion point only a short distance. More ways to move the insertion point using the keyboard are shown in **Table 1-1**. If you will be using the [Home], [End], [Pg Up], and [Pg Dn] keys on the numeric keypad, as required for some of the movement techniques in the table, you must first make sure that Num Lock is disabled. Some keyboards include separate keys for these functions.

Figure 1-8   Changing Ave. to Avenue in Sabrina's address

Place the insertion point

Erase the period

Complete the word

Table 1-1   Moving the Insertion Point with the Keyboard

TO MOVE THE INSERTION POINT	PRESS
Left or right one word	[Ctrl]+[←] or [Ctrl]+[→]
Up or down one paragraph	[Ctrl]+[↑] or [Ctrl]+[↓]
Up or down one screen	[Pg Up] or [Pg Dn]
To the beginning or end of a line	[Home] or [End]
To the beginning or end of a document	[Ctrl]+[Home] or [Ctrl]+[End]

Practice

To practice deleting and modifying text, open the student file **Prac1-7**.

Hot Tip

Clicking the **Undo** button 🔄 on the Standard toolbar allows you to reverse the last command you used. Clicking the arrow next to the Undo button opens a menu that lists all of your previous actions, allowing you to undo several actions at once.

Formatting Text

Concept

Word allows the user to easily change the font, font size, and alignment of text in a document, as well as many other text and document characteristics. Formatting text serves to improve the presentation of your document. You can format text for both stylistic and organizational purposes.

Do It!

Sabrina wants to make her name bold and change the font size of her document.

1 Make sure that Letter.doc is still in the active window.

2 Select Sabrina's name by clicking before the S in Sabrina and dragging (moving the mouse with the button held down) to the end of her last name. The selected text will be highlighted (white text on a black background).

3 Click the Bold button **B** on the Formatting toolbar. The letters in her name will become heavier.

4 Deselect the text by clicking once anywhere in the document window.

5 Select the entire document by clicking before the S in Sabrina and dragging down to the last line and releasing the mouse button after the period in enc. at the end of the document.

6 Click the Font Size arrow ▐10 ▼▌ on the Formatting toolbar and then click 11 (see **Figure 1-9**). The text in the document will increase slightly in size. Do not close the document, as you will be using it in the next Skill.

More

There are several text attributes that the Formatting toolbar allows you to change. The font, or typeface, refers to the actual shape of each individual letter or number as it appears on the screen or in a printed document. Text size is usually measured in points. For example, the text in a newspaper is ordinarily printed in 10 point. Sabrina changed her name to 11 point from Word's default of 10. Other Formatting toolbar options include Bold **B** , Italic **I** , Underline **U** , and Highlight **🖉** . Alignment refers to the manner in which text follows the margins of your document (see **Figure 1-10**). Knowing how to format text for maximum effect is an essential skill that will make your documents appear crisp and professional. Notice how the text on this page is used; different fonts and sizes are used for headings and subject matter, and important terms are bold or colored for added emphasis. To format an entire document, as above, you must select it first. You can select an entire document without dragging the mouse pointer over it by clicking Edit, and then clicking the Select All command. You can also change the color of your font by clicking the Font Color button **A▼** . Click the button itself to apply the current color to the selected text. Clicking the arrow on the right edge of the button opens a color palette from which you can choose a different color.

Figure 1-9 Adjusting font size

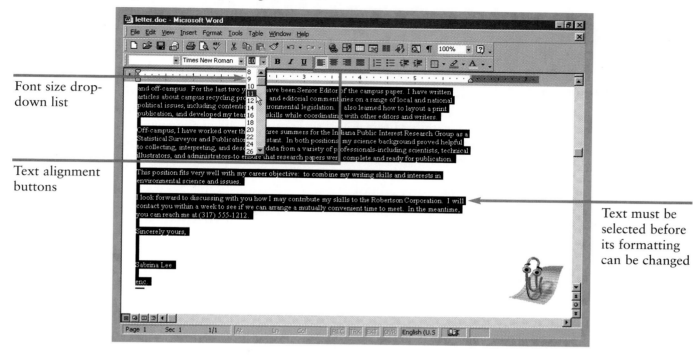

Font size drop-
down list

Text alignment
buttons

Word 2000

Text must be
selected before
its formatting
can be changed

Figure 1-10 Text alignment

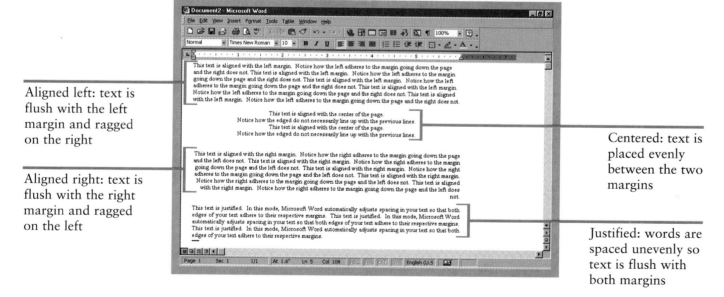

Aligned left: text is
flush with the left
margin and ragged
on the right

Aligned right: text is
flush with the right
margin and ragged
on the left

Centered: text is
placed evenly
between the two
margins

Justified: words are
spaced unevenly so
text is flush with
both margins

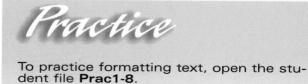

Practice

To practice formatting text, open the student file **Prac1-8**.

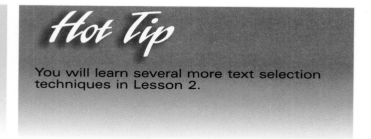

Hot Tip

You will learn several more text selection
techniques in Lesson 2.

Previewing and Printing a Document

Concept

While today's offices are becoming more and more electronic, many people still like to work with hard copies of their documents. If your computer is properly connected to a printer, you can print a paper copy of a document with a click of a button. Or, if you desire more flexibility in printing, Word provides more comprehensive options, including a Print Preview that allows the user to see the document as it will appear when printed.

Do It!

Sabrina wants to print her document.

1. Confirm that your computer is properly connected to a printer (ask your instructor or network administrator if necessary).

2. Click File, then click Print to open the Print dialog box (**Figure 1-11**).

3. Click [OK] to print. (Clicking the Print button 🖨 on the Standard toolbar skips the dialog box and prints automatically.)

4. Save and close the document.

More

You can also view your document as it will appear when printed by clicking File, and then clicking Print Preview. The Print Preview screen (**Figure 1-12**) will appear. A miniature version of your document will be in the window and the mouse pointer will change to the magnification tool 🔍 when it is in the document window. The Standard and Formatting toolbars are replaced with the Print Preview toolbar, and the vertical ruler appears. The Zoom selection box displays how much the document has been shrunk or magnified. To view a particular portion of your document up close, simply click it to display it at 100% of normal size. The mouse pointer will then change to 🔍 and clicking will reverse the magnification. To edit in Print Preview mode, click the Magnifier button 🔍 to change the mouse pointer to an I-beam, then edit and enter text as you normally would. When you are finished editing, click the Magnifier button again to look at other parts of the document. If the document appears correct, you can print it by clicking the Print button at the left end of the Print Preview toolbar. To exit the Print Preview screen and return to your document, click Close.

Figure 1-11 Print dialog box

Specify the printer you are using here

Additional printer options

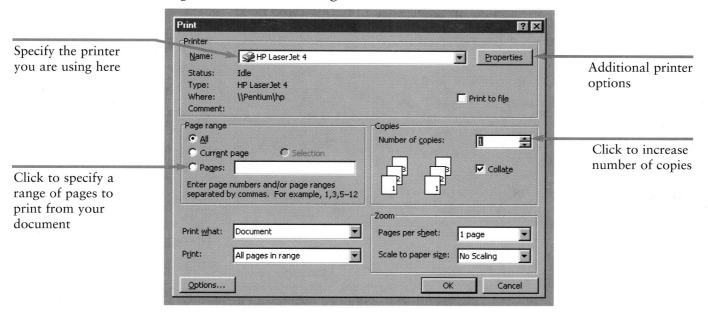

Click to specify a range of pages to print from your document

Click to increase number of copies

Figure 1-12 Print Preview screen

Magnifier toggle button

Print Preview toolbar

Current magnification level

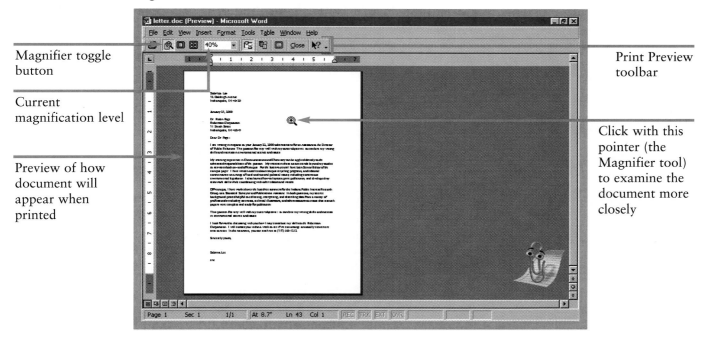

Click with this pointer (the Magnifier tool) to examine the document more closely

Preview of how document will appear when printed

Practice

To practice previewing a document, open the student file **Prac1-9**.

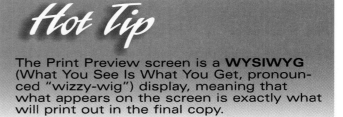

Hot Tip

The Print Preview screen is a **WYSIWYG** (What You See Is What You Get, pronounced "wizzy-wig") display, meaning that what appears on the screen is exactly what will print out in the final copy.

Shortcuts

Function	Button/Mouse	Menu	Keyboard
Create a new document	🗋	Click File, then click New	[Ctrl]+[N]
Show/Hide nonprinting characters	¶	Click Tools, then click Options, then click the View tab; Choose All	[Ctrl]+[Shift]+[*]
Save the active document	🖫	Click File, then click Save	[Ctrl]+[S]
Close the active document	✕	Click the control menu icon, then click Close	[Alt]+[F4]
Open a document	📂	Click File, then click Open	[Ctrl]+[O]
Bold selected text	**B**	Click Format, then click Font; Choose Bold	[Ctrl]+[B]
Italicize selected text	*I*	Click Format, then click Font; Choose Italic	[Ctrl]+[I]
Underline selected text	U	Click Format, then click Font; Choose Underline	[Ctrl]+[U]
Highlight selected text	🖉		
Print Preview	🔍	Click File, then click Print Preview	
Print the active document	🖨	Click File, then click Print	[Ctrl]+[P]

Identify Key Features

Name the items indicated by callout arrows in **Figure 1-13**.

Figure 1-13 Identifying components of the Word screen

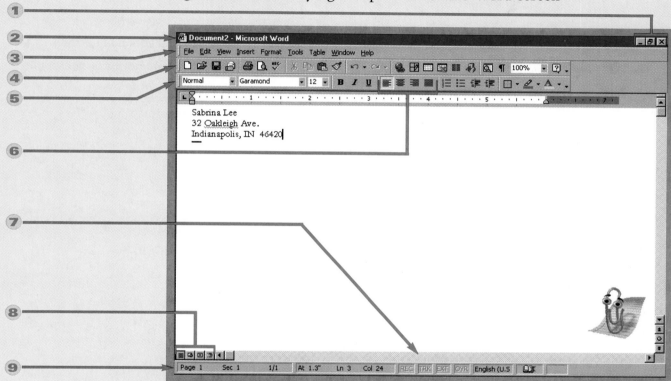

Select the Best Answer

10. The exact location where text appears when entered

11. The shape of letters and numbers

12. Reduces a window to a button on the Windows taskbar

13. The way in which text relates to the left and right margins

14. A window that appears allowing access to specialized commands

15. Allows you to see how your document will appear when printed

16. Offers tips, advice, and help on most Word functions

17. The unit of measurement for font size

a. Office Assistant

b. Alignment

c. Print Preview screen

d. Insertion point

e. Points

f. Dialog box

g. Minimize button

h. Font

Quiz (continued)

Complete the Statement

18. In order to change the formatting of a section of text, you must first:

    a. Click one of the formatting buttons

    b. Save the document

    c. Select the text to be changed

    d. Click the Start button

19. Clicking the 🖫 button:

    a. Ejects the floppy disk

    b. Saves the document

    c. Searches for a file on the hard drive

    d. Selects text

20. Clicking the 🔍 button on the Standard Toolbar:

    a. Searches the document for errors

    b. Magnifies part of the document

    c. Opens the Print Preview window

    d. Brings up the Document Detective window

21. The file extension for Word files is:

    a. .txt

    b. .jpg

    c. .doc

    d. .htm

22. An ellipsis (...) after a command in the command menu means that:

    a. That command has a dialog box

    b. That command is unavailable

    c. The shortcut for that command is the [...] key

    d. The whole name could not fit on the menu

23. The elements of text formatting do NOT include:

    a. Font size

    b. Justification

    c. Style

    d. Delete

24. Text that is justified is:

    a. Carefully edited

    b. Adjusted to meet both margins

    c. Centered

    d. Bold

25. To type over existing text instead of displacing it:

    a. Click the Undo button

    b. Double-click the Highlight button

    c. Double-click the Overtype button

    d. Disable Num Lock

Interactivity

Test Your Skills

1. Identify a job that interests you and determine what the employer is looking for:

   a. Go to the classified section of a newspaper or to an online job listing and find a specific listing that you think might suit you.

   b. Think about what skills and experience might be necessary to successfully apply. You may wish to call the employer or agency in the advertisement to identify more precisely the qualifications of the job.

2. Open Word and write a brief letter applying for the job:

   a. Launch Word using the Start menu.

   b. Enter your name and address at the top of the page.

   c. Skip a line and enter the address and name (if available) of the prospective employer.

   d. Skip a line and enter today's date.

   e. Write the body of the letter, beginning with a salutation and continuing with four short paragraphs, one each for your educational background, prior job experience, any other relevant experience, and the reasons for your interest in this particular job.

3. Format the letter text to more effectively present the letter:

   a. Make all the text in the letter 12 pt Times New Roman.

   b. Format your name at the top of the letter with Bold type.

   c. Align your name and address with the right margin by selecting the appropriate lines and clicking the Align Right button on the Formatting toolbar.

4. Print the letter, then save and close the document and exit Word:

   a. Use Print Preview to examine your letter and then make any changes you think are necessary. Exit Print Preview mode.

   b. After making sure your computer is properly connected to a working printer, click the Print button on the Standard toolbar to print the letter.

   c. Save the letter to your student disk as Test 1.

   d. Close the document and exit Word by clicking the application Close button at the right end of the title bar.

5. Open, edit, and save an existing document:

   a. Open Test 1 from your student disk.

   b. Change the color of the document's text to red and italicize your name.

   c. Save the changes as a new file on your student disk called Test 1-Red.

Interactivity (continued)

Problem Solving

1. Using the skills you learned in Lesson 1, open a new document and write your name, address, and today's date on it as a heading, then add a few sentences about yourself. Adjust the text's formatting so that it matches the example in **Figure 1-14** below. Then conduct a Print Preview to check and print the document. Save it on your student disk as Solved 1.

Figure 1-14 Problem Solving

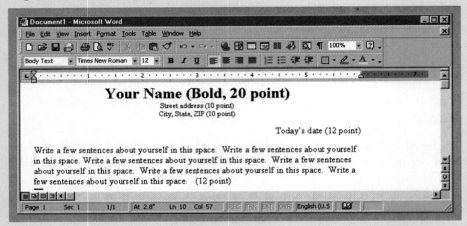

2. As the Assistant Technical Director at VER Recovery Corp., a collection agency, you have been asked to research various word processing programs to determine which is the best for your company. After testing several products, you have decided that the company would benefit most from adopting Microsoft Word 2000. Use Word to write a memo to your boss that details this decision.

3. Due to your outstanding performance as Assistant Technical Director at VER, you have been promoted to Associate Technical Director. As your first act in your new capacity, you have proposed an expansion of the Information Technology department. Your proposal has been improved. Using Word, write a press release to announce the good news. Take advantage of Word's formatting features to make your document lively.

Searching for Files

Selecting Text and Undoing Actions

Cutting, Copying, and Moving Text

Copying and Moving Text with the Mouse

▷ **Using the Office Assistant**

▷ **Other Word Help Features**

▷ **Using Templates and Wizards**

L E S S O N

2

EDITING DOCUMENTS

O nce text has been entered into a Word document, it may be manipulated and edited to suit the requirements of the user. Text may be selected in several different ways so that particular portions can be modified without affecting the rest of the document. Selected text can be copied, moved, or deleted altogether.

Word has a powerful file search function that allows the user to find documents based on a wide variety of search criteria, and a help facility that provides many types of information and assistance with various word processing tasks and special features of the application. This help facility includes the Office Assistant, who acts as a liason between the user and the help files.

In addition to the general blank document template on which Word bases its standard new document, there are a multitude of other templates for document types that can be created with Word. In addition, programs called wizards guide the user through the steps necessary to create various complex documents.

Case Study:
In this lesson, Sabrina will edit her cover letter and create a résumé to go with it, as well as search for a document and explore Word's help facility.

Searching for Files

Concept

There are so many locations in a computer's storage devices in which data may be saved that documents are sometimes difficult to locate. Word's Open dialog box contains powerful search tools that you can use to locate and open misplaced files.

Do It!

Sabrina would like to open the Windows Frequently Asked Questions (FAQ) file. She knows Word can read the file, but does not know where it is located.

1. Click the Open button 📂 on the Standard toolbar. The Open dialog box appears.

2. Click the Files of type: drop-down list arrow and select Text Files.

3. Click the Tools button Tools ▾. The Tools menu will open.

4. Click the Find command. The Find dialog box appears, as shown in **Figure 2-1**. The top section of the dialog box shows the search criterion you have chosen so far, which instructs Word to search for the file type Text Files. The second section of the dialog box allows you to provide additional search criteria. Leave the Property: selection box set to File name, and the Condition: selection box set to includes.

5. Click inside the Value: text-entry box to place the insertion point there. Then type faq as the search value.

6. Click the Look in: drop-down list arrow and select your main hard drive (most likely C:) as the search location.

7. Click the Search subfolders check box to activate it. The Find dialog box is now set to search your hard drive and all its subfolders for a text file whose name includes the letters faq.

8. Click the Find Now button Find Now. Word will ask if you want to add the File name property you specified to the search. Click Yes.

9. The Find dialog box closes and the results of your search are displayed in the Open dialog box's contents window. The file Faq.txt should be selected (see **Figure 2-2**), ready for you to open if you wish. If you do open this file, Word will have to convert it from its text format because it is not a Word document. Do not save changes when you close the file.

More

It is worthwhile to examine the list of properties by which you can search for a file in the Find dialog box. You can use everything from the number of words in a document to the date it was created as a search property. Each search property has its own customized list of conditions from which you can choose when setting your search criteria. You can even save a search and run it whenever you need to find the file with which it is associated.

Figure 2-1 Find dialog box

Chosen in
Open dialog box

Click to make your search
sensitive to uppercase and
lowercase letters (does not
apply to File name property)

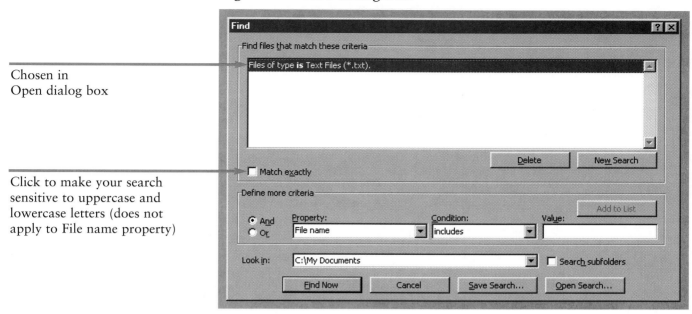

Word 2000

Figure 2-2 Result of file search

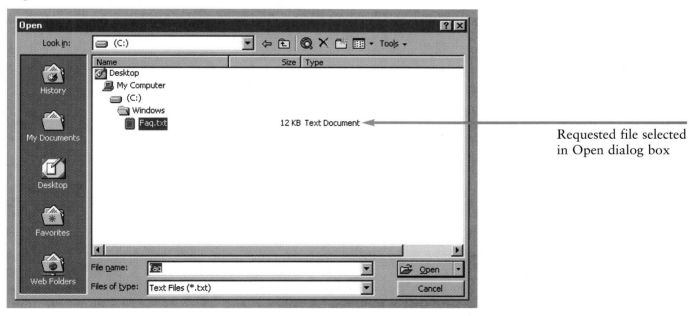

Requested file selected
in Open dialog box

Practice

To practice finding files in Word, open the
student file **Prac2-1**.

Hot Tip

Being as restrictive as possible in your
search criteria will make the search process
faster and reduce the number of unwanted
files found.

Selecting Text and Undoing Actions

Concept

Sections of text must be selected before they can be modified. Selected text acts as a single unit that can moved, modified, or formatted. When text is selected, it appears highlighted on the screen. That is, text that normally appears black on a white screen will be white on a black background. It is important to be careful when working with selected text as it is possible to erase an entire document by pressing a single key. The Undo command can be used to correct such errors by reversing previous commands or actions.

Do It!

Sabrina wants to select a paragraph using two different techniques.

1. Open the student file Doit2-2 and save it to your student disk as Cover Letter.

2. Scroll down to the paragraph that begins My training and experience....

3. Select the paragraph by clicking just before the first letter and dragging the mouse pointer to the end of the paragraph. If the Office Assistant is in the way it will automatically move to another location.

4. Type the letter X. The selected text will be replaced by the text you entered.

5. Click the Undo button 🔄 on the Standard toolbar to bring back the missing paragraph.

6. Deselect the paragraph by clicking once anywhere in the document window.

7. Now select the same paragraph by triple-clicking any portion of it.

More

Once text is selected, it can be replaced by typing in new text; the new entry will take the place of what was selected. When clicking and dragging to select text, the selected area will follow the mouse pointer letter by letter in the first word; subsequent words will be added to the selected area all at once. To select a single line or multiple lines of text, use the Selection bar, a column of space beneath the **L** in the horizontal ruler (see **Figure 2-3**). When the mouse pointer enters this area, it will appear reversed ⬧. Clicking here selects the entire line to the right of the pointer. Dragging up or down will select additional lines. More ways to select text are shown in **Tables 2-1 and 2-2**. Keep in mind that Num Lock must be disabled in order to use the [Home], [End], and arrow keys on the numeric keypad.

You can select large sections of text by placing the insertion point at the beginning, moving to the other end, and pressing [Shift] while you click there.

The Undo command is an essential tool that easily corrects many of the worst mistakes you will make when using Word. The Undo and Redo buttons are grouped on the Standard toolbar. Clicking the Undo drop-down list arrow 🔄▾ opens the Undo drop-down list, which lets you undo one or more of several recently completed actions and commands by simply clicking on the item you wish to undo. The Redo command and its drop-down list work in a similar fashion, but instead reverse past Undo commands.

Figure 2-3 Using the Selection bar

Selection bar

Selection bar
mouse pointer

Selected text

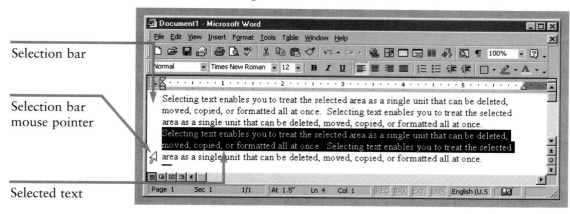

Word 2000

Table 2-1 Mouse selection shortcuts

DESIRED SELECTION	ACTION TO TAKE
A single word	Double-click the word
A sentence	Click the sentence while pressing [Ctrl]
A paragraph	Triple-click the paragraph or double-click next to it in the selection bar
A line of text	Click next to it in the selection bar
A vertical block of text	Click and drag while pressing [Alt]
The entire document	Triple-click in the selection bar

Table 2-2 Keyboard selection shortcuts

DESIRED SELECTION	ACTION TO TAKE
A single character	[Shift]+[←] or [Shift]+[→]
A single word	[Ctrl]+[Shift]+[←] or [Ctrl]+[Shift]+[→]
A paragraph	[Ctrl]+[Shift]+[↑] or [Ctrl]+[Shift]+[↓]
To the beginning or end of a line	[Shift]+[Home] or [Shift]+[End]
To the beginning or end of a document	[Ctrl]+[Shift]+[Home] or [Ctrl]+[Shift]+[End]
A vertical block of text	[Ctrl]+[Shift]+[F8] and move with arrow keys
The entire document (Select All)	[Ctrl]+[A]

Practice

To practice selecting text and using the Undo command, open the student file Prac2-2.

Hot Tip

When you choose an action to undo from the Undo drop-down list, all actions that took place after the selected action will be undone as well.

Cutting, Copying, and Moving Text

Concept

Sections of text can be moved easily within a Word document, deleted or copied from one place, and reapplied in another. Word offers two ways to move text: the drag-and-drop method, which involves the mouse and will be discussed in the next Skill; and Cut-and-Paste, which utilizes the Office Clipboard.

Do It!

Sabrina wants to move a paragraph in her cover letter using the Cut-and-Paste method.

1. Select the entire paragraph that begins with This position..., as shown in **Figure 2-4** (the file Cover Letter should still be in the active window).

2. Click the Cut button 🔗 on the Standard toolbar. The selected text disappears, leaving an extra blank line between the remaining paragraphs.

3. Press [Backspace] once to remove the extra blank line.

4. Place the insertion point to the left of the first letter in the second paragraph in the message section, the one that begins My training and experience....

5. Click the Paste button 📋 on the Standard toolbar. The text you cut earlier reappears at the insertion point.

6. Press [Enter] to add a blank line to separate the paragraphs.

7. Close the file, saving changes when prompted.

More

The Cut, Copy, and Paste commands use the Office Clipboard, a temporary holding area for data. The Office Clipboard can hold up to twelve items simultaneously, unlike the Windows Clipboard, which holds only one. The Cut command removes selected data to the Clipboard, while the Copy command leaves selected text where it is and sends a copy of it to the Clipboard. The Paste command inserts data stored in the Clipboard at the insertion point. If you have more than one item stored on the Office Clipboard when you use the Paste command, Word will paste the item that was sent there most recently. To paste an item that you sent to the Clipboard earlier, open the View menu, highlight the Toolbars command, and click Clipboard to activate the Clipboard toolbar. The Clipboard toolbar, shown in **Figure 2-5**, displays each item currently being stored as an icon, allowing you to choose exactly which item or items you want to paste.

The Clipboard can also be used to move data between documents or even between different Office programs. The last item you sent to the Office Clipboard will also be stored on the Windows Clipboard, allowing you to share the data with any Windows program for which it is appropriate. Clearing the Office Clipboard removes the contents of the Windows Clipboard as well. Both Clipboards are erased when you shut down your computer.

Figure 2-4 Selected paragraph

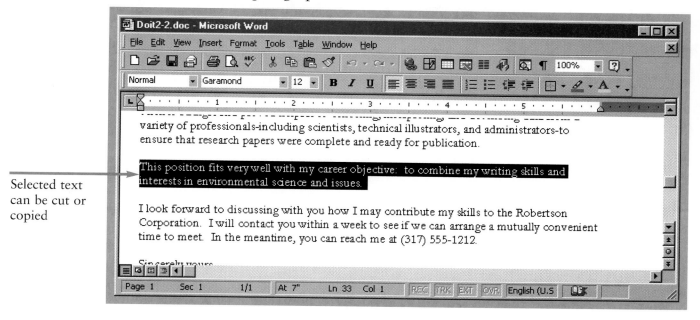

Selected text can be cut or copied

Figure 2-5 Clipboard toolbar

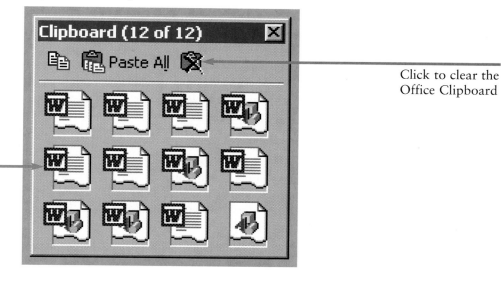

Click to clear the Office Clipboard

Each icon represents an item that has been cut or copied to the Office Clipboard

Practice

To practice cutting, copying, and pasting text, open the student file **Prac2-3**.

Hot Tip

Though pressing [Delete] removes selected text just as using the Cut command does, it does not save it to the Clipboard, and thus the text cannot be reinserted elsewhere.

 # Copying and Moving Text with the Mouse

Concept

The drag-and-drop method of copying and moving text is quick and convenient for moving text a short distance within a Word document. In many instances it is preferable to using the Clipboard with the Cut, Copy, and Paste commands.

Do It!

Sabrina wants to move a paragraph in her cover letter using the drag-and-drop method.

1. Open the student file Doit2-4 and save it to your student disk as Cover Letter 2.

2. Select the entire paragraph that begins with This position including the blank line beneath it, as shown in **Figure 2-6**.

3. Click on a portion of the selected area without releasing the mouse button. The mouse pointer will change into the drag-and-drop pointer, indicating that there is text loaded and ready to be inserted.

4. Position the dotted insertion point ⌶ to the left of the first letter in the second paragraph in the message section, the one that begins My training and experience....

5. Release the mouse button. The text will disappear from its previous location and reappear at the insertion point.

More

Dragging-and-dropping text moves it from its previous location. To copy the text to another area while leaving the original intact, press [Ctrl] before dropping the dragged text. The drag-and-drop pointer will appear with a small plus in a box at the bottom to signify that it will make a copy of the selected text. When the mouse button is released, the selected text will appear in its original place as well as at the insertion point. You can drag and drop single words, sentences, paragraphs, and multiple paragraphs so long as they are selected. The ability to drag-and-drop text is an option that can be turned on and off from the Edit tab of the Options dialog box, which you can access by clicking the Options command on the Tools menu.

Word 2000

Figure 2-6 Moving text with the mouse

Selected text will be inserted here

Drag-and-drop pointer indicates that text is being moved

Selected text being moved

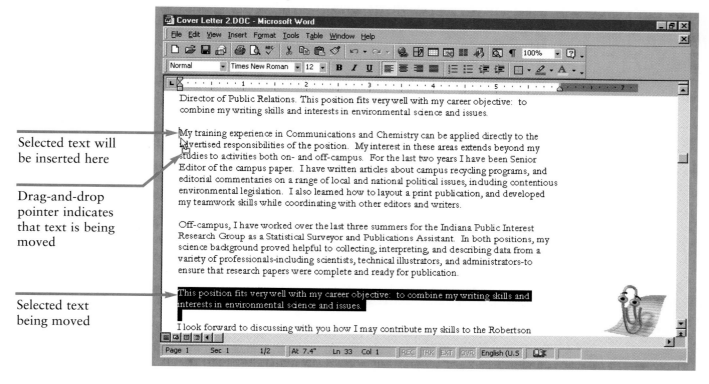

Hot Tip

If you are copying or moving text over a long distance in a document, it might be easier to use the Clipboard instead of the drag-and-drop method. It can be difficult to stop the screen's scrolling accurately when you drag beyond the current screen.

Using the Office Assistant

Concept

The Office Assistant provides several methods for getting help in Word. You can choose from a list of topics that the Assistant suggests based on the most recent functions you have performed. You can also view tips related to your current activity. Or, you can ask a question in plain English.

Do It!

Sabrina wants to ask the Office Assistant about using ScreenTips.

1. Click the Office Assistant. A balloon will pop up with suggested topics related to the actions you have most recently completed.

2. In the text box type What are ScreenTips?, then click the Search button ⟨Search⟩. The Office Assistant peruses the Word Help files and presents a selection of topics (**Figure 2-7**) relating to your question.

3. Position the pointer over the bullet labeled Show or hide toolbar ScreenTips and click. A window will appear, as shown in **Figure 2-8**, displaying the help topic.

4. Read the help topic's explanation. You can leave the window on-screen to refer to while you work. When you are finished reading about ScreenTips, click the Help window's close button to remove it from the screen.

More

From time to time the Assistant will offer you tips on how to use Word more efficiently. The appearance of a small light bulb, either in the Assistant's window or on the Office Assistant button, indicates that there is a tip to be viewed. To see the tip, just click the light bulb or Office Assistant button if the Assistant is hidden.

The Office Assistant's behavior and appearance can be customized to conform to your needs and preferences. Clicking ⟨Options⟩ opens the Office Assistant dialog box. This dialog box has two tabs: Gallery and Options. The Gallery tab contains different Assistants you can install from your Office or Word CD-ROM, and scrolling through the characters offers you a preview of each one. From the Options tab, shown in **Figure 2-9**, you can control when the Assistant will appear, and what kinds of tips it will provide.

Figure 2-7 ScreenTip help topics

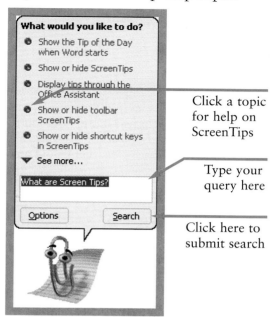

Click a topic for help on ScreenTips

Type your query here

Click here to submit search

Figure 2-8 Microsoft Word Help window

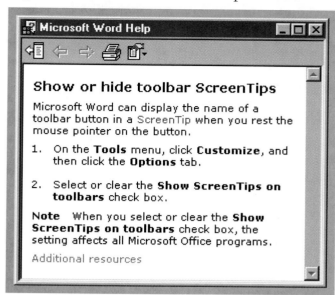

Figure 2-9 Office Assistant dialog box

Remove this check to disable the Office Assistant

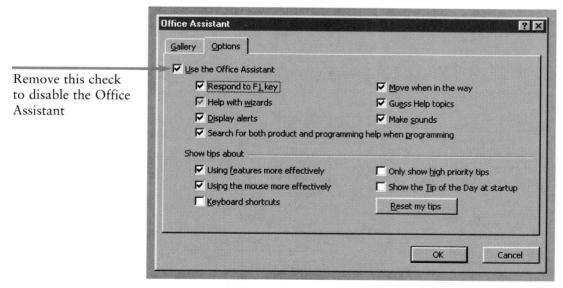

Practice

Use the Office Assistant's ability to answer questions to get help on using the Office Assistant.

Hot Tip

The Office Assistant is common to all Office 2000 applications. Therefore, any of the Assistant's options that you change will affect it in all Office programs.

Other Word Help Features

Concept

Working with new software can be confusing, and, at times, even intimidating. Fortunately, Microsoft Word offers a number of built-in help features in addition to the Office Assistant that you can use when you encounter problems or just have a question about a particular aspect of the program. The What's This? command and the Help tabs are two such features.

Do It!

Sabrina will use Word's What's This? command to get information about the Save command, and the Help tabs to find out more about the status bar.

1 Click Help, then click What's This? The pointer will now appear with a question mark ▶? attached to it indicating that help has been activated.

2 Click the Save button 🖫 with the modified mouse pointer. A ScreenTip will appear, as shown in **Figure 2-10**, describing the command. Click the mouse to erase the ScreenTip.

3 Click the Office Assistant and select any help topic or tip offered to open a Microsoft Word Help window.

4 Click the Show button 🔲. The window will expand to a two-paneled format. The left panel consists of three tabs while the right panel displays help files.

5 Click the Index tab to bring it to the front of the window if it is not already there.

6 Click in the text-entry box labeled Type keywords:, and then type status. Notice that the list box in the middle of the tab scrolls automatically to match your entry.

7 Click the Search button [Search]. Word searches its help files for the word status and displays the topics it finds in the list box at the bottom of the tab.

8 Click the help topic titled Items that appear in the status bar. The help file is loaded into the right panel, as shown in **Figure 2-11**.

9 Read about the status bar, and then close the Help window.

More

The Index tab organizes Word's help topics alphabetically in one continuous list. If this type of search does not suit your needs, you can search the help files using the Contents tab or the Answer Wizard tab. The Contents tab is organized like an outline or the table of contents you might find in a book. It begins with broad topics, symbolized by book icons, each of which can be expanded to reveal more specific subtopics. Once you have revealed a general topic's subtopics, you can select a subtopic in the left panel to display it in the right panel, just as on the Index tab. The Answer Wizard tab replicates the Office Assistant, allowing you to request help topics by entering questions in your own words. Once you have clicked the Show button to display the Help tabs in a Help window, the button changes to the Hide button. Click the Hide button to collapse the window back to a single panel.

Figure 2-10 Save button ScreenTip

Save (File menu)

Saves the active file with its current file name, location, and file format.

Figure 2-11 Getting help with the Index tab

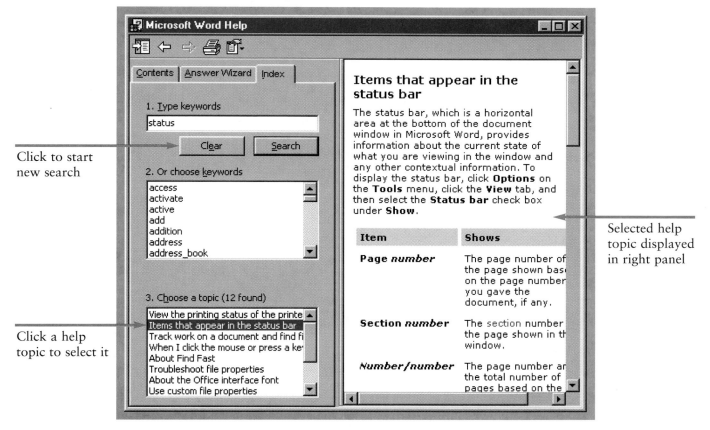

Click to start
new search

Click a help
topic to select it

Selected help
topic displayed
in right panel

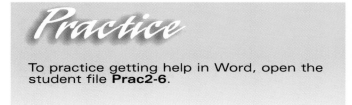

Practice

To practice getting help in Word, open the student file **Prac2-6**.

Hot Tip

When working in a dialog box, click the ? button to get help on features in that dialog box. A question mark will be attached the mouse pointer, just as if you had selected the What's This? command.

Using Templates and Wizards

Concept

When a new document is created, its font and text layout characteristics are based on a collection of previously saved settings. Together, the settings associated with this document are called a template. Word provides templates in many categories, including letters, faxes, brochures and Web pages, and styles, such as contemporary, professional, and elegant. When you opened Word, the new document that appeared was based on the Blank Document template, also known as the Normal template. A wizard is a template that walks the user through the creation of a specific type of document, such as a résumé or newsletter, further automating the process. Templates and wizards serve as a great launching pad for creating items that seem too complicated to start from scratch. Documents created with these tools may be freely edited and changed to meet a user's specifications.

Do It!

Sabrina wants to create a résumé with the Résumé Wizard.

1. Click File, then click New to open the New dialog box.

2. Click the Other Documents tab to bring it to the front of the dialog box. Several icons representing various templates and wizards appear.

3. Click the Résumé Wizard icon. A preview of its output will appear in the Preview box, as shown in **Figure 2-12**.

4. Click `OK` to open the Résumé Wizard. The Résumé Wizard dialog box will appear at the Start step, as shown in **Figure 2-13**. The green square next to Start indicates which step of the wizard you are currently on.

5. Click `Next >` to advance to the Style step.

6. Click the Elegant radio button to select this style of résumé, then click `Next >`.

7. At the Type step, click `Next >` to use the default résumé type, Entry-level, and advance to the next phase in the wizard. The following step allows you to enter your name, address, phone and fax numbers, and e-mail address. Word automatically enters the name of the registered user in the name text box, and any other information that was provided during the install in the other boxes.

8. Enter Sabrina Lee, 32 Oakleigh Ave., Indianapolis, IN 46202 in the name and address text boxes respectively, replacing and deleting any extraneous information that may be entered. Your Résumé Wizard text boxes should resemble those in **Figure 2-14**. Click `Next >`.

Word 2000

Figure 2-12 Templates and wizards in the New dialog box

Other tabs containing different types of templates and wizards

Note:
Your installation of Microsoft Word may include a different selection of templates and wizards

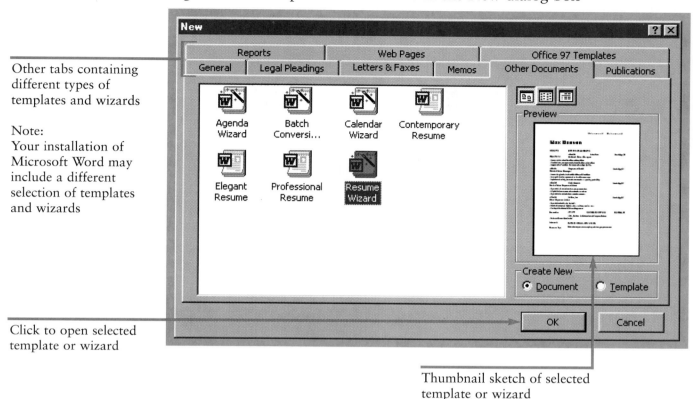

Click to open selected template or wizard

Thumbnail sketch of selected template or wizard

Figure 2-13 Résumé Wizard: Start

Outline tracks your progress through the wizard

Figure 2-14 Résumé Wizard: Address

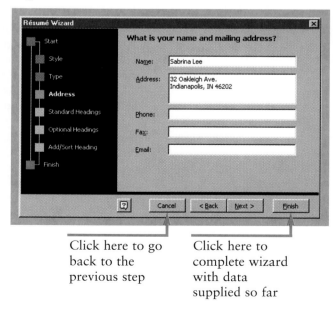

Click here to go back to the previous step

Click here to complete wizard with data supplied so far

Using Templates and Wizards (continued)

Do It!

9 At the Standard Headings step, use the check boxes to select Objective, Education, Interests and Activities, and Work Experience as the only headings in your résumé. Click Next >.

10 No additional headings will be included in your résumé; so click Next > to advance the wizard.

11 The Add/Sort Headings step allows you to insert a heading that was not included in the wizard's choices, delete a heading that you decide you do not wish to include on your résumé, or change the order or selected headings. Click Work experience to select it, then click Move Up to place it before Interests and activities in your résumé, as shown in **Figure 2-15**. Then click Next >.

12 On the outline of the wizard's steps, at the left side of the dialog box, click the box next to Style to go back to that step.

13 Click the Contemporary radio button to use this style rather than the previously selected Elegant, then click Finish. A résumé will appear in Print Layout view with instructions and space to fill in the rest of the necessary details, and the Assistant will open, as shown in **Figure 2-16**, asking if you would like to do more with your résumé.

14 Click ⊙ Cancel, then close the document when you are finished viewing it.

More

Templates vary in the type and amount of formatting information that they contain. Some look like finished documents because Word inserts Placeholders, or text used to show you where to correctly place specific kinds of information. To add text to these templates, simply select the text you want to replace and type in your own. Other templates, such as the Professional Report template, contain less pre-formatting, and instead offer instructions on how to use the template to create the various elements of your document. And wizards, as shown above, automate document production by asking you questions in dialog boxes. By answering these questions, you make the decisions necessary to create the document, and the wizard inserts the information and formats it automatically. Some wizards even include premade examples, in which you need only change certain text variables such as names and addresses to complete the document. Below the Preview box in the New dialog box are two radio buttons that allow you either to create a document based on a template or to directly alter a template's settings. You can create or alter a template and then save the new template to be used for future documents.

Figure 2-15 Résumé Wizard: Add/Sort Headings

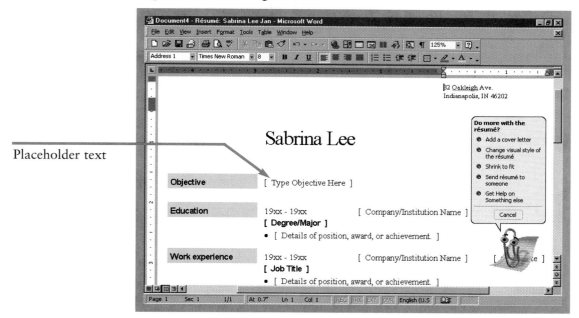

Current order of
résumé headings

Click buttons to move
selected heading up or
down one line at a time

Figure 2-16 Completed résumé

Placeholder text

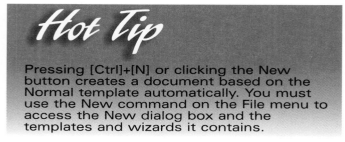

Practice

To practice using a template to create a
document, open the student file Prac2-7.

Hot Tip

Pressing [Ctrl]+[N] or clicking the New
button creates a document based on the
Normal template automatically. You must
use the New command on the File menu to
access the New dialog box and the
templates and wizards it contains.

Shortcuts

Function	Button/Mouse	Menu	Keyboard
Undo last action	↩	Click Edit, then click Undo	[Ctrl]+[Z]
Redo last undone action	↪	Click Edit, then click Redo	[Ctrl]+[Y]
Cut a selection and place it on the Clipboard	✂	Click Edit, then click Cut	[Ctrl]+[X]
Copy a selection and place the copy on the Clipboard	📋	Click Edit, then click Copy	[Ctrl]+[C]
Paste the contents of the Clipboard into the active document	📋	Click Edit, then click Paste	[Ctrl]+[V]
Call up the Office Assistant	?	Click Help, then Click Microsoft Word Help	[F1]
Get a ScreenTip for an item		Click Help, then click What's This?, then click item	[Shift]+[F1], then click item

Quiz

Identify Key Features

Name the items indicated in the figures.

Figure 2-17 Features associated with editing

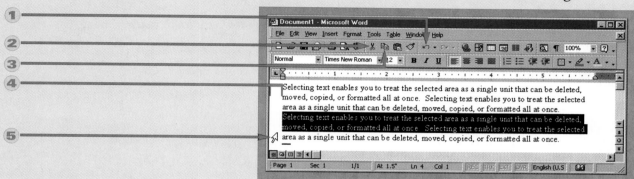

Figure 2-18 Features associated with editing

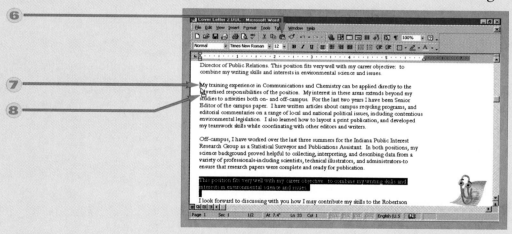

Select The Best Answer

9. An invisible column along the left edge of the text on a page

10. A option that instructs Word to look more thoroughly for a file

11. A menu of recently used commands and actions

12. Observes your work and offers suggestions

13. A program that walks you through the steps of document creation

14. Selects an entire paragraph

15. A temporary storage area for data

16. One of Word's three Help tabs

a. Clipboard

b. Triple-clicking text

c. Search subfolders

d. Index

e. Selection Bar

f. Undo drop-down list

g. Office Assistant

h. Wizard

Quiz (continued)

Complete the Statement

17. The dialog box where Word's file-searching capabilities are used is:

    a. The Find dialog box

    b. The Save dialog box

    c. The Save As dialog box

    d. The Cross-reference dialog box

18. Word bases the formatting of a new document on:

    a. The last document used

    b. The buttons on the Formatting toolbar

    c. The Blank Document template

    d. The Résumé Wizard

19. To copy selected text to another location with the mouse:

    a. Drag-and-drop the selected text

    b. Double-click the desired location

    c. Print the document and photocopy it

    d. Drag-and-drop the selected text while pressing [Ctrl]

20. A template differs from a wizard in that:

    a. A template contains no graphic items

    b. A wizard creates the document for you based on answers you give

    c. Documents created with a template cannot be changed

    d. A wizard doesn't allow you to enter information

21. To select the text from the insertion point to the end of the line:

    a. Click the paragraph mark

    b. Press [Ctrl]+[Home]

    c. Click in the Selection bar

    d. Press [Shift]+[End]

22. Double-clicking in the Selection bar:

    a. Opens the New dialog box

    b. Selects the entire document

    c. Selects the adjacent paragraph

    d. Minimizes the document window

23. Pressing [Ctrl] while dragging-and-dropping text allows you to:

    a. Delete the text

    b. Paste the text

    c. Make a copy of the text

    d. Add the text to the Office Clipboard, but not the Windows Clipboard

24. The 🔲 button:

    a. Inserts the last item placed on the Clipboard at the insertion point

    b. Copies selected text to the clipboard

    c. Opens a note pane

    d. Displays the contents of the Clipboard

Interactivity

Test Your Skills

1. Find a file and open it:

   a. Make sure your student files are installed on your hard drive or your student disk is inserted in the appropriate disk drive.

   b. In Word, go to the Open dialog box.

   c. Using the Find command in the Open dialog box, find the student file SkillTest2.

   d. Open the file and save it to your student disk as Test 2.

2. Select portions of the document and delete them:

   a. Select the last sentence in the second paragraph (the one that begins He was really great...) by clicking it while pressing [Ctrl].

   b. Delete the selected sentence.

   c. Select the postscript at the end of the document by triple-clicking it.

   d. Add the text that extends from the selected paragraph to the end of the document to the selection by pressing [Ctrl]+[Shift]+[End].

   e. Delete the selection.

3. Select paragraphs in the document and move them:

   a. Select the third paragraph (the one that begins On a slightly different note...) by double-clicking next to it in the Selection bar.

   b. Drag the selected paragraph to the blank line following the next paragraph and drop it there.

   c. Select the first paragraph by triple-clicking it.

   d. Cut the selected paragraph and send it to the Clipboard by using the Cut command.

   e. Paste the copy at the end of the final paragraph of the document, before the signature.

4. Use Word's Help facility:

   a. Ask the Office Assistant about selecting text.

   b. Choose the help topic called Select text and graphics. Then click the subtopic in the Microsoft Word Help window called Selecting text and graphics using the keyboard.

   c. Expand the Help window so that it shows the Help tabs.

   d. Use the Index tab to display help topics based on the word view. Read the help file titled Different ways to view a Word document.

   e. Use the Contents tab to read the help files under the heading Customizing with Shortcut Keys.

Interactivity (continued)

5. Create a document using a wizard:

   a. Open the New dialog box.

   b. Start the Memo wizard.

   c. Create a Contemporary memo with the title Word 2000 Memo.

   d. When you finish the wizard, save the document as TYS2 Memo.

   e. Print a copy of your memo.

Problem Solving

1. Using the skills you learned in Lesson 2, use the Résumé Wizard to create a Professional, Entry-level résumé to accompany the letter you wrote at the end of Lesson 1. Be sure to include your current address, career objectives, education, job experience, other relevant experience, and interests and activities. When the wizard has created the résumé, use the Cut and Paste commands and the drag-and-drop method to rearrange the order of the résumé headings. Then print out a copy of the finished résumé and save the file to your student disk as Solved2-Résumé.

2. You are satisfied with the résumé you created above, but realize that it may not be appropriate for every job opening. Create a new résumé without using the wizard, but with all of the content from the first résumé. This will require you to copy text from one Word document to another.

3. As the owner and CEO of a rapidly expanding financial consulting firm, you are very proud to have had your best recruiting season ever. You have hired six outstanding recent college graduates from this year's recruiting class. Use the Letter wizard to write them a letter that welcomes them to the company. Preview and print your letter. Then save it as Solved2-Letter.

4. While at a conference in Chicago, you have been introduced to some startling technological advances in voice-recognition software. Use the Elegant Fax template to create a fax cover letter that you can send to your boss at The Software Train, Inc. The template includes a section in which you can add text so that your fax will only require this one page. Comnplete the cover letter, including your findings at the conference. Save the document as Solved2-Fax, and print a paper copy.

▶ Setting Up a Page

▶ Inserting Page Numbers

▶ Inserting Footnotes and Endnotes

▶ Applying Indents

▶ Changing Line Spacing

▶ Inserting Page Breaks

▶ Working with Multiple Documents

▶ Using the Format Painter

▶ Checking Spelling and Grammar

▶ Using AutoCorrect

▶ Using the Word Thesaurus

▶ Finding and Replacing Text

L E S S O N

ADVANCED EDITING

Word allows you to add many different types of formatting to a document. These can be broken down into three major divisions: text-level formatting, paragraph-level formatting, and document-level formatting.

Text-level formatting, which was covered in Lesson 1, refers to all formatting that applies to individual characters in a document, such as size, font, and such options as bold and italics. No matter where text appears, these characteristics can be applied to single letters or entire sections of text.

Paragraph-level formatting covers the characteristics that can be applied to a paragraph or group of paragraphs. These include alignment, indents, line spacing, line numbers, and other aspects that cannot be applied to a single character.

Document-level formatting includes such options as margins and headers and footers, which are items set to appear on every page of a document, including page numbers and the document title.

Once the document has been completed and formatted to meet your needs, Word offers several proofreading aids to assure the quality of the finished product. In addition to a spelling checker that spots misspelled words throughout the document, Word has a feature called AutoCorrect that can actually fix common typing and spelling mistakes automatically, as they are made. Word also contains a built-in thesaurus that makes finding the perfect word both simple and fast. And if you decide to change a word or phrase that occurs in several places in a long document, Word can search your document for all instances of the item and replace them with something you prefer.

Case Study:
In this lesson, Sabrina will add formatting to a research paper that she has written and will add data that has been collected by her research partner, Juan. She and Juan will then proofread the document and make corrections.

Setting Up a Page

Concept

Word gives you control over many aspects of formatting at the document level. These include margins, paper size, and layout. Changing document level formatting allows you to control how a document will appear both on the screen and when it is printed.

Do It!

Sabrina wants to reduce the left and right margins of a research paper she has been writing.

1 Open the student file Doit3-1 and save it to your student disk as Report.doc.

2 Click File, then click Page Setup. The Page Setup dialog box appears.

3 Click the Margins tab to bring it to the front if it is not already foremost in the dialog box, as shown in **Figure 3-1**.

4 Click the downward-pointing arrow on the side of the Left box three times to reduce the Word default setting from 1.25 inches to 1 inch. The Preview box reflects the change you made to the left margin.

5 Triple-click the Right box to select it.

6 Type the number 1 to replace the selected value of 1.25. Since inches is the default setting for measurement, you do not need to enter its symbol.

7 Click ⬛ OK ⬛ to apply the changes to the document and close the dialog box. The text of your document may now extend beyond the edge of your screen. You can adjust this by reducing the zoom factor on the Standard toolbar. Do not close the document, as you will be using the same one throughout the next several Skills.

More

The Margins tab of the Page Setup dialog box also enables you to adjust the margins at the top and bottom of your pages as well as the left and right margins of headers and footers, which are items at the top or bottom of a page that remain constant across many pages. These can include such things as page numbers, logos, or the title of the document. If your document utilizes facing pages, you can activate the Mirror margins option which adjusts the margins so that the two inner margins and the two outer margins on facing pages are equal to each other. The Paper Size tab lets you format a document to fit any size medium (such as legal-size paper or an envelope) that your printer can handle. The Paper Source tab tells the printer where to get the right size paper for your document. The Paper Source and Paper Size tabs will offer different options depending upon the current selected printer. The Page Layout tab lets you control the vertical alignment of text on each page and allows you to add line numbers to the document.

Figure 3-1 Margins tab of the Page Setup dialog box

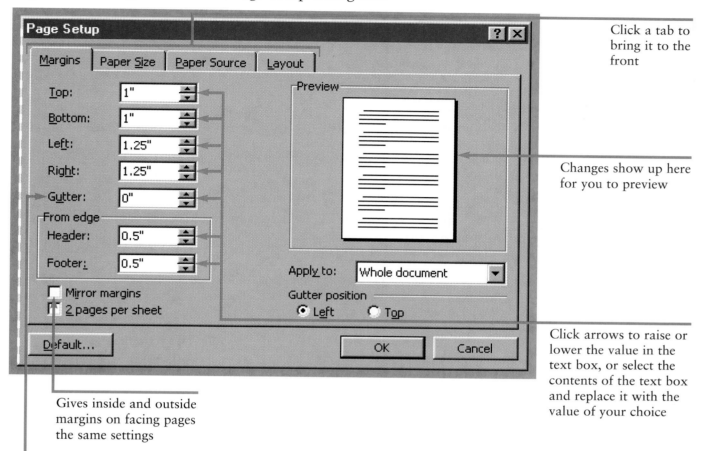

Word 2000

Click a tab to bring it to the front

Changes show up here for you to preview

Click arrows to raise or lower the value in the text box, or select the contents of the text box and replace it with the value of your choice

Gives inside and outside margins on facing pages the same settings

The distance added to the left (or inside, if Mirror margins is selected) margin to allow extra room for binding

Practice

To practice adjusting margins in a document, open the student file **Prac3-1**.

Hot Tip

You can put different kinds of document formatting, such as margins, in one document by changing the setting of the **Apply To** box on the Layout tab of the Page Setup dialog box from Whole Document to This Point Forward.

Inserting Page Numbers

Concept

Word can insert page numbers into documents in a variety of placement locations and styles. Numbers are inserted automatically so you do not have to add a page number to each page individually. You can also add a prefix to each page number to identify chapters or sections, or choose to leave the number of the first page of a document if it is meant to serve as a title page.

Do It!

Sabrina wants to add centered page numbers to the report and view them.

1. Click Insert, then click Page Numbers to bring up its dialog box, as shown in **Figure 3-2**.

2. Click the Alignment box, then click Center to change the horizontal position of each page number from the default right setting to center.

3. Click **Format...** to bring up the Page Number Format dialog box (**Figure 3-3**).

4. Make sure the Number Format box displays Arabic numerals (1, 2, 3...) instead of letters or Roman numerals. If it does not, click the box, then click 1,2,3... to select Arabic numerals.

5. Click **OK** to leave the Format dialog box and return to the Page Numbers dialog box.

6. Click **OK** to confirm and apply the page numbering. Word automatically shifts to Print Layout View so that the page numbers can be seen.

7. Scroll to the bottom of the page to see the inserted page number.

More

The numbers you have added to the document do not appear in Normal View. As you may recall, however, Word allows you to view your document in different ways. For example, the Print Preview screen offers a quick way to see how your document will look when printed, without nonprinting characters but including items not seen in the default Normal View, such as headers, footers, and page numbers. With the View menu, Word offers other ways of looking at your document. Outline View is helpful when you use Word's outlining features to structure your text with headings and subheadings. Like Print Preview, Print Layout View allows you to see your document as it will appear when printed, including page numbers, but retains the Ruler and the Standard and Formatting toolbars and lacks the Print Preview toolbar and magnifying tool. Web Layout View displays your document as it would appear when viewed with a Web browser. You can quickly move between these different views by using the View buttons at the left end of the horizontal scroll bar at the bottom of the window. The current view is indicated by its depressed button next to the horizontal scroll bar or on the View menu. Other view options include Header and Footer, which displays your headers and footers in an editable text box, and Full Screen, which shows only the document window. The Toolbars submenu on the View menu lets you select which toolbars appear on the screen. The Document Map makes moving from location to location in a document easier by letting you click on headings that are linked to your document.

Word 2000

Figure 3-2 Page Numbers dialog box

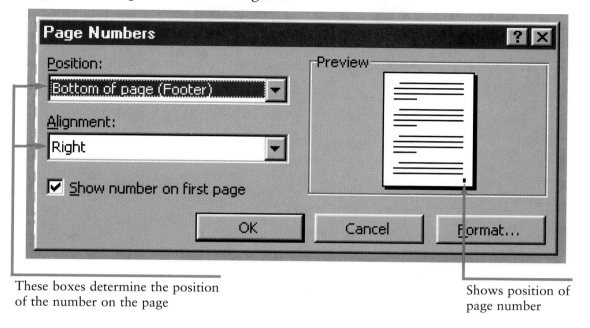

These boxes determine the position
of the number on the page

Shows position of
page number

Figure 3-3 Formatting page numbers

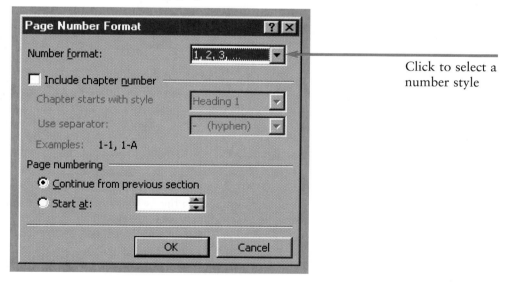

Click to select a
number style

Practice

To practice inserting page numbers, open
the student file **Prac3-2**.

Hot Tip

If you add pages to a document that has
already been formatted with page numbers,
the numbers will be updated automatically.

Inserting Footnotes and Endnotes

Concept

A footnote explains a piece of document text at the bottom of the page on which the text appears. An endnote provides a similar explanation at the end of a document. Both contain two parts: a note reference mark and the note text. Word automates the process of creating and numbering footnotes and endnotes.

Do It!

Sabrina would like to add a footnote to her research paper.

1. Position the insertion point at the end of the first paragraph, after the words their work done. This is where the note reference mark will appear.

2. Click Insert, then click Footnote. The Footnote and Endnote dialog box appears with Footnote (the Word default) selected, as shown in **Figure 3-4.**

3. Click OK to insert the footnote using current settings. Word inserts the note reference mark at the insertion point and opens a note pane at the bottom of the window.

4. Type the following text:
   These "anytime, anywhere" work environments are sometimes called "virtual offices," because work can be performed outside the traditional physical office setting and work schedule.

5. Click Close to leave the note pane and return to the document window.

6. If you are not already in Print Layout View, click View, then click Print Layout. Scroll to the bottom of the page and view the footnote in its proper place (see **Figure 3-5**). Alternatively, you can position the mouse pointer over the reference mark, and the footnote will appear as a ScreenTip.

More

The note pane is a separate part of the document window where footnote text is entered. All footnotes in each document are accessible through the note pane. In the Footnote dialog box, the AutoNumber option is the default setting. With this option selected, Word will automatically renumber the note reference marks if you add or remove some of your footnotes or endnotes, so there will be no break in their continuity. The default formatting for footnote text is 10 point Times New Roman, aligned left. This can be changed just as you would change the formatting of any other text in a document. The Note Options dialog box, accessed by clicking the Options button Options... in the Footnote and Endnote dialog box, offers further flexibility in number format and note placement.

Like page numbers, footnotes and endnotes do not appear as part of the document in Normal View. You can view and edit a footnote by double-clicking its reference mark in the text, which opens the note pane. Switching to Print Layout View shows the footnotes below a horizontal line at the bottom of a page or endnotes at the end of the document as they will appear on the actual page.

Figure 3-4 Footnote and Endnote dialog box

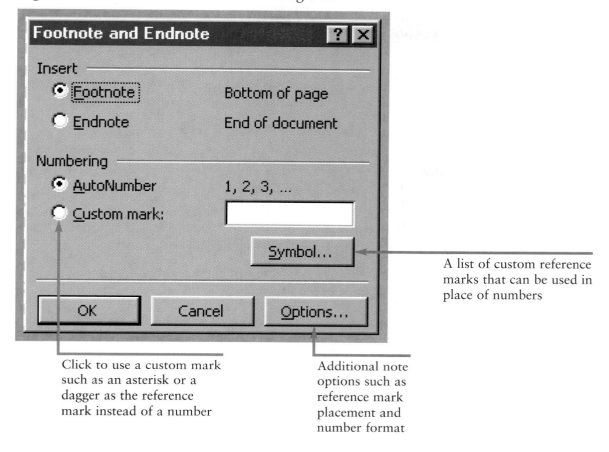

A list of custom reference marks that can be used in place of numbers

Click to use a custom mark such as an asterisk or a dagger as the reference mark instead of a number

Additional note options such as reference mark placement and number format

Figure 3-5 Viewing an endnote on a page

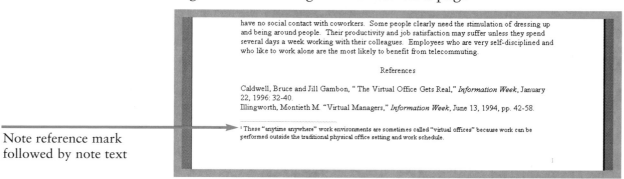

Note reference mark followed by note text

To practice inserting Footnotes into a document, open the student file **Prac3-3**.

Hot Tip

When a note pane is open, you can go to the next pane by pressing **[F6]** or to the previous pane by pressing **[Shift]+[F6]**.

 # Applying Indents

Concept

Paragraph indents may be changed easily using the four indent markers on the ruler, or, for more precise control, the Paragraph dialog box.

Do It!

Sabrina wants to indent the first line of each paragraph in the main text by half an inch and apply a hanging indent to her References section.

1. Select the four paragraphs of main text by clicking before the first word of the first paragraph, scrolling down to the end of the document and holding [Shift] while clicking after the last word of the fourth paragraph. The entire document should be selected between the heading and References sections.

2. Click and drag the First line indent marker in the ruler (see **Figure 3-6**) to the half-inch mark. The first line of each paragraph will move to the right half an inch.

3. Deselect the main text by clicking once anywhere in the document window.

4. Select the entire References section of Sabrina's report, from the word References to the end of the document.

5. Click and drag the Hanging indent marker in the ruler to the half-inch mark (the Left indent marker will move with it). All lines in a paragraph that are not first lines move to the right half an inch. This is called a hanging indent because it leaves the first line hanging at the left margin.

More

All markers on the ruler may be changed by clicking and dragging. The First line indent marker, as seen above, controls the indentation of the first line of selected paragraphs. The Hanging indent marker determines the amount of indentation from the left margin of all lines of a selected paragraph except its first line. The rectangle below the Hanging indent marker is called the Left indent marker and determines the amount of indentation for all lines of a selected paragraph, including the first line. Finally, the Right indent marker at the right end of the ruler regulates the amount of indentation from the right margin for all lines of a selected paragraph. The default settings for all of the indent markers are even with the margins.

You can also indent the first line of paragraphs as you type with the [Tab] key. Each time you press [Tab], the insertion point jumps to the next tab stop. Word's default tab settings are one-half inch. You can also set your own tab stops by clicking the bottom half of the ruler where you want them. After they are set, tab stops can be moved by dragging them along the ruler with the mouse pointer. To remove a tab stop, click and drag it below the ruler. It will vanish when the mouse button is released. Clicking the tab alignment selector at the left end of the ruler selects different tab alignments that can be applied. **Table 3-1** describes the various tab alignments and their properties.

The tab and indent settings can also be adjusted from the Paragraph dialog box, accessible from the Format menu, and shown in **Figure 3-7**. Any indent changes made with the ruler will show up in the indent settings of the dialog box and vice-versa.

Figure 3-6 Horizontal ruler

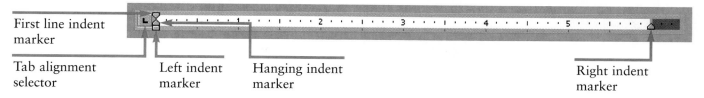

First line indent
marker

Tab alignment
selector

Left indent
marker

Hanging indent
marker

Right indent
marker

Word 2000

Table 3-1 Alignment of Various Tabs

TAB ALIGNMENT	PROPERTIES	BUTTON
Left	Text extends from the tab stop to the right	⌊
Center	Text is centered on the tab stop	⊥
Right	Text extends from the tab stop to the left	⌋
Decimal	The decimal point in the text aligns itself beneath the tab stop; text before the decimal is to the left of the tab stop, text after it is to the right	⊥

Figure 3-7 Adjusting indents from the Paragraph dialog box

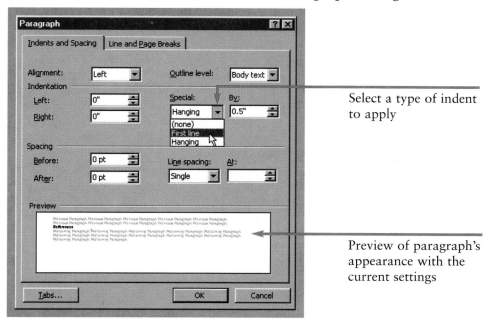

Select a type of indent
to apply

Preview of paragraph's
appearance with the
current settings

 # Changing Line Spacing

Concept

The line spacing, or distance between adjacent horizontal lines of text, can be modified from the Paragraph dialog box. Word also allows the user to change the spacing between paragraphs. Many universities and business organizations require written documents to conform to certain standards, which often include spacing considerations. For example, a professor might demand that research papers be double-spaced, except when text is quoted from another source and should then be single-spaced and indented.

Do It!

Sabrina wants to remove the spaces between paragraphs and double-space her report.

1. Delete each of the blank lines between the four paragraphs of the main text by selecting the blank lines and pressing [Delete].

2. Click Edit, then click Select All to select the entire document.

3. Click Format, then click Paragraph to open the Paragraph dialog box.

4. Click the Line Spacing list box, then click Double (see **Figure 3-8**).

5. Click **OK** to accept the changes you have made. All paragraphs in the document are now double-spaced.

More

The Paragraph formatting dialog box has a Preview box that allows you to see how the changes you are making will affect your text. The Word default setting is single spacing. If the spacing interval you want is not available in the Line Spacing list box, the At box allows you to set your spacing at any interval you enter, such as 1.25 or 0.9. The Before and After boxes refer to the spacing before and after each selected paragraph. This allows you to space paragraphs automatically at any interval without adding blank lines to the document.

Figure 3-8 Adjusting line spacing from the Paragraph dialog box

Paragraph   ? X

Indents and Spacing | Line and Page Breaks

Alignment: [Left ▼]   Outline level: [Body text ▼]

Indentation

Left: [0"] ▲▼   Special: [(none) ▼]   By: [ ] ▲▼

Right: [0"] ▲▼

Spacing

Before: [0 pt] ▲▼   Line spacing: At:

Adjust spacing between paragraphs

After: [0 pt] ▲▼   [Single ▼]   [ ] ▲▼

Single
1.5 lines
Double
At least
Exactly
Multiple

Specify your own spacing interval

Line spacing options

Preview

Tabs...   OK   Cancel

Practice

To practice changing line spacing and paragraph spacing, open the student file **Prac3-5**.

Hot Tip

When formatting the paragraphs in a document, it is often helpful to show nonprinting characters with the  button.

Inserting Page Breaks

Concept

The dotted horizontal line that divides pages in a document in Normal View (or the clear separation between pages in Print Layout View) is called a Soft page break. It will shift position as lines are added or removed from a document. Likewise, when enough text has been entered to fill a page, Word will create another page. A Hard page break, also known as a Manual page break, can be inserted where a page break should always occur, regardless of deletions or additions to previous text. Hard page breaks allow you to define different sections of a document clearly by starting new sections on a separate page.

Do It!

Sabrina wants to put the References section of her report on a separate page.

1 Place the insertion point before the word References at the head of the References section of the report. This will become the first line of the new References page.

2 Click Insert, then click Break. The Break dialog box appears with **Page Break** already selected, as shown in **Figure 3-9**.

3 Click ⟦ OK ⟧ to insert a page break at the insertion point. The References section will now appear at the top of a new page. Word will automatically renumber the pages of the document to account for the new page.

More

A Hard page break looks the same as a Soft page break, except the words Page Break appear in the center of the solid horizontal line dividing the page. You can remove a Hard page break by clicking next to it in the Selection bar to select it and then pressing [Delete]. The Break dialog box also allows you to add Section Breaks. A section is just a distinct part of your document that is separated from the rest. For example, chapters in a book can be manipulated as sections. Inserting a section break ends a section and dictates where the next will begin. When you choose the Next Page section break option from the Break dialog box, Word breaks the page at the section break and the next section begins at the top of the next page. When you click Continuous, Word inserts a section break and starts a new section on the same page. Clicking Odd Page or Even Page begins the new section on the next odd-numbered page or even-numbered page (see **Figure 3-10**).

Figure 3-9 Break dialog box

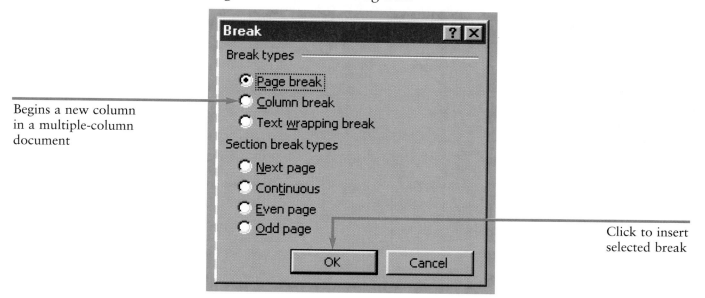

Begins a new column
in a multiple-column
document

Click to insert
selected break

Word 2000

Figure 3-10 Types of section breaks

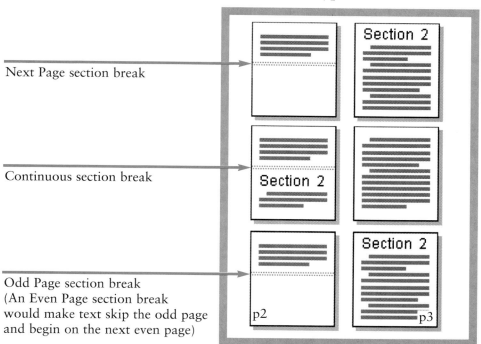

Next Page section break

Continuous section break

Odd Page section break
(An Even Page section break
would make text skip the odd page
and begin on the next even page)

Practice

To practice inserting page and section
breaks, open the student file **Prac3-6**.

Hot Tip

Viewing a page break from Print Layout
View will give you a better idea of how
much space the break leaves behind on the
previous page.

Working with Multiple Documents

Concept

Word, like many other Windows programs, lets the user work with more than one document at a time. You can create a new document or open an existing one without jeopardizing the active document. Document windows can be arranged so that one, two, or all open documents may be seen simultaneously. In addition, text can be copied and moved between open documents by using the Office Clipboard. This can save you from the time-consuming task of having to retype text that you want to use in another document.

Do It!

Sabrina wants to combine text that she and her partner, Juan, have written.

1. Open the student file Doit3-7. This is Juan's contribution to their report. Sabrina's portion, Report.doc will remain open but will be hidden behind the newly opened document.

2. Click Edit, then click Select All to select all of the text in Juan's document.

3. Click the Copy button 📋 on the Standard toolbar to copy Juan's document to the Clipboard.

4. Click Window on the menu bar, then click Report.doc to bring Sabrina's report into view. The Window menu shows all open Word documents, with a check next to the active document.

5. Place the insertion point just before the second paragraph in her report, the one that begins, There are both....

6. Click the Paste button 📋 to insert Juan's text into their report. Notice that his text conforms to the document-wide settings that Sabrina set earlier. Its margins change from 1.25 to 1 inch to match the rest of the document. It remains single-spaced, however, as line spacing is formatted at the paragraph level. The text will be revised in the next Skill.

More

There are several ways to move between various open Word documents. The Window menu shows all open Word documents, and on the File menu there is a list of documents that Word has opened recently. The number of recently opened documents displayed here can be altered from the General tab in the Options dialog box, which you can access by clicking the Options command on the Tools menu. There is also a list of recently opened files on the Documents menu available on the Windows Start menu. Clicking one of these files will open it, or bring it the active document if it is already open. The Clipboard can be used to transfer data between documents in the same way it is used within a single document. The active window is always the one in front. If the active window is not maximized, you may be able to see inactive windows behind it (see **Figure 3-11**).

Figure 3-11 Working with multiple documents

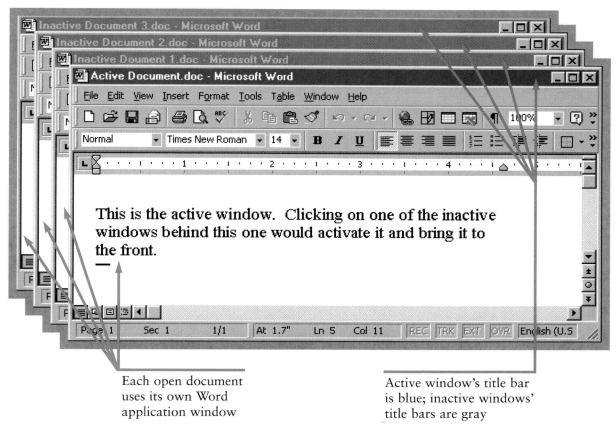

Each open document
uses its own Word
application window

Active window's title bar
is blue; inactive windows'
title bars are gray

To practice moving text between two documents, open the student file **Prac3-7**.

Hot Tip

The **Split** command on the Window menu allows you to divide the active window into two panes so that you can view different portions of the same document simultaneously.

Using the Format Painter

Concept

The Format Painter makes it possible to copy the formatting settings from selected text to another section of text. This feature allows you to unify the formatting in a document without having to apply each formatting change individually.

Do It!

Sabrina would like to format Juan's text like the rest of her document.

1. Select Sabrina's first paragraph by double-clicking next to it in the Selection bar.

2. Click the Format Painter button 🖌 on the Standard toolbar. The mouse pointer will appear as an I-beam with a paintbrush next to it 🖌I as it moves over areas that have formatting differing from that of the selected text. This indicates that the formatting of the selected text has been copied and is ready to be applied to a new area (see **Figure 3-12**).

3. Click Juan's paragraph (not his references) to automatically format it to match Sabrina's text.

4. Select the three lines of Juan's references by clicking next to the first line in the Selection bar and dragging down to select the other two lines as well.

5. Click and drag the selected text to the very end of the document, releasing the mouse button after moving the dotted insertion point to the right of Sabrina's last reference. Now all references are in their proper place in the References section.

6. Select one of Sabrina's references by double-clicking next to it in the Selection bar.

7. Click the Format Painter button to copy her formatting settings.

8. Select the three lines of Juan's references by clicking next to the first line in the Selection bar and dragging down to select the other two lines as well. Now all of the references follow Sabrina's formatting.

9. Click Window, then click Doit3-7.doc to go back to Juan's document.

10. Click File, then click Close to close Juan's document. Do not save changes.

11. Click File, then Close again to close Sabrina's document. This time, save changes when prompted.

Word 2000

More

To format more than one area with the same selected format settings, double-click the Format Painter button. When you have formatted all the text you need, click the button again to turn off the Format Painter. If you only want to copy the character formatting, don't include the paragraph mark ¶ at the end of the text you are formatting. Remember, the paragraph mark is the place in the text where [Enter] was pressed to go to a new line; it can be displayed by clicking the Show/Hide ¶ button on the Standard toolbar. If the text you have selected to format includes the paragraph mark, the paragraph formatting will be copied too. The collection of all formatting characteristics of a document is referred to as its style. The Style command, available on the Format menu, allows you to apply styles from any of Word's templates to the current document. These styles include the margins, text formatting, indents, and other format options existing in the document style you choose.

Figure 3-12 Copying formatting with the Format Painter

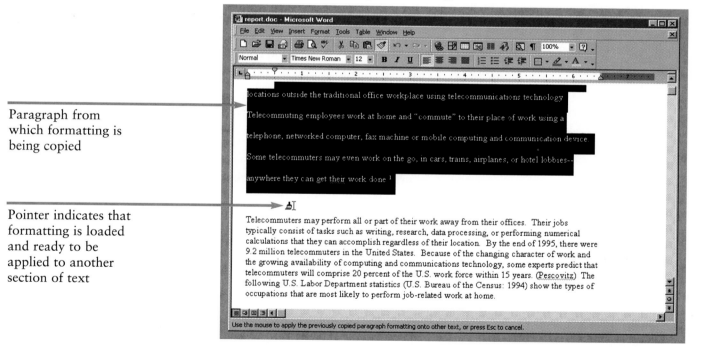

Paragraph from which formatting is being copied

Pointer indicates that formatting is loaded and ready to be applied to another section of text

Practice

To practice using the Format Painter, open the student file **Prac3-8**.

Hot Tip

The Style dialog box allows you to preview the selected template by itself, or as it would appear applied either to your document or to a sample document.

Checking Spelling and Grammar

Concept

Word has the ability to check the spelling and grammar in a document and offer suggestions for how to correct words and phrases that its built-in dictionary does not recognize as correct. Word permits you to check the accuracy of single words, sentences, paragraphs, or the entire document at once. While proofreading your work yourself is still a necessary part of producing professional documents, using Word's automated proofreading features is a good first step. In order to complete this Skill, the Check spelling as you type, Check grammar as you type, and Check grammar with spelling features must be active. These options, which are active by default, can be found by selecting the Options command on the Tools menu and going to the Spelling & Grammar tab in the Options dialog box.

Do It!

Sabrina wants to check a document for spelling and grammar errors.

1. Open the student file Doit3-9 and save it to your student disk as Spelling. This is a sample paragraph with several spelling and grammar errors in it.

2. Right-click (click with the right mouse button) the first word in the paragraph that is underlined with a wavy red line, processer. A pop-up menu appears with several suggested correct spellings. As shown in **Figure 3-13**, move the mouse over the list to select the first choice, processor, and click. Word replaces the misspelled word with the selected alternative.

3. Click Tools, then click Spelling and Grammar. The Spelling and Grammar dialog box will appear, as shown in **Figure 3-14**, with the first error highlighted in red and suggestions for replacing it below.

4. Select the correct word in the Suggestions box, grammar, and click ⬚ Change All ⬚ to correct all occurrences of this spelling mistake throughout the document. Word then highlights a repeated word.

5. Click ⬚ Delete ⬚, which appears in place of the Change button. The second you disappears. Word now detects a grammatical error in the document, noting that the verb provide does not agree with its subject, it.

6. Click ⬚ Change ⬚ to change the highlighted word to provides, thereby creating agreement between subject and verb and clarifying the meaning of the sentence. Next, the Spelling and Grammar checker highlights a proper name, which it does not recognize.

Figure 3-13 Automatic spell checking

Right-click a flagged word to open pop-up menu of correction choices

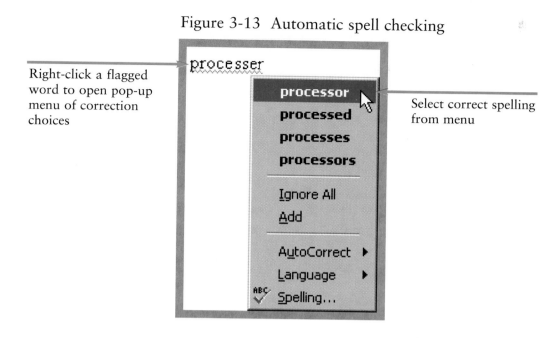

Select correct spelling from menu

Figure 3-14 Spelling and Grammar dialog box

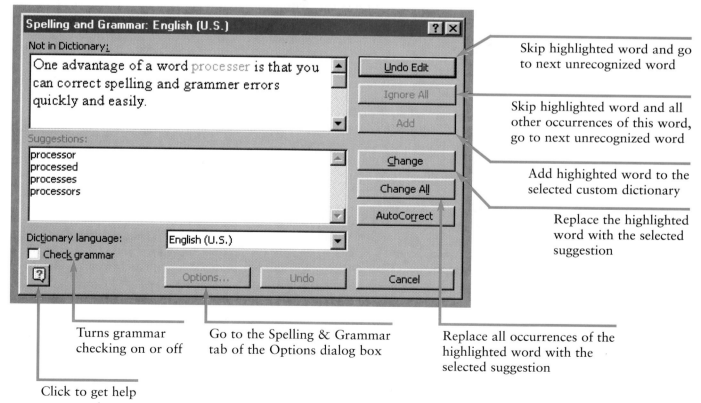

Skip highlighted word and go to next unrecognized word

Skip highlighted word and all other occurrences of this word, go to next unrecognized word

Add highlighted word to the selected custom dictionary

Replace the highlighted word with the selected suggestion

Turns grammar checking on or off

Go to the Spelling & Grammar tab of the Options dialog box

Replace all occurrences of the highlighted word with the selected suggestion

Click to get help

Checking Spelling and Grammar (continued)

Do It!

7　Click [Ignore] to ignore the selected word, which, though Word doesn't recognize it, is spelled correctly. Word now highlights a misspelled word.

8　Click [Change]. Word replaces simpley with the correct spelling, simply, and the Spelling and Grammar dialog box disappears, replaced with a small Microsoft Word message box notifying you that no further errors were found and that the check is complete.

9　Click [OK]. The message box disappears.

10　Save and close the document.

More

In the same way that the Change All button in the Spelling dialog box causes Word to correct all further instances of the selected word, the Ignore All button instructs Word to skip over all instances of an unrecognized word throughout the document. Word takes capitalization into account when checking spelling, so if it was told to ignore Microwaveable, for example, it would still stop on microwaveable if it were to appear elsewhere in the document. The reason that different copies of Word may recognize different words is that words can be permanently added to Word's custom dictionary, a document that is unique to each copy of Microsoft Word. If you click [Add] in the Spelling and Grammar dialog box when the spell checker highlights a word it does not know but that you know is spelled correctly, the word will be added to the custom dictionary and will not be questioned again. You may freely edit the sentence appearing in the Not in Dictionary box just as you would edit it in your document; changes you make to the sentence will take effect when the Spelling and Grammar checker goes on to the next error.

Word's Automatic Spell Checking feature was mentioned briefly in Lesson 1. As you type, Word can underline with a wavy red line words that it does not recognize. Likewise, it underlines with a wavy green line words or phrases that it believes are grammatically incorrect. Right-clicking a word underlined in red in this fashion brings up a pop-up menu that contains a list of suggested alternatives to the underlined word, the Ignore All and Add commands, and a shortcut to the Spelling dialog box. Clicking one of the alternate words on the list will change the underlined word to match it. There is also an AutoCorrect option, which you will learn more about in the next Skill. When a word that is underlined with a green wavy line is right-clicked, a similar pop-up menu appears with a list of suggested alternatives, an Ignore Sentence option, and a shortcut to the Grammar dialog box. The Spelling & Grammar tab in the Options dialog box (**Figure 3-15**) can be reached by clicking the Options button [Options...] in the Spelling and Grammar dialog box.

Word 2000

Figure 3-13 Spelling & Grammar tab of the Options dialog box

Turn Automatic Spell
Checking on and off

Customize Spell
Checking

Click to
select
custom
dictionary

Turn Automatic
Grammar Checking
on and off

Customize
Grammar
Checker's
settings

Spelling & Grammar

| Spelling & Grammar |

Spelling
- ☑ Check spelling as you type
- ☐ Hide spelling errors in this document
- ☑ Always suggest corrections
- ☐ Suggest from main dictionary only
- ☑ Ignore words in UPPERCASE
- ☑ Ignore words with numbers
- ☑ Ignore Internet and file addresses

Custom dictionary:
[CUSTOM.DIC ▼] [Dictionaries...]

Grammar
- ☑ Check grammar as you type
- ☐ Hide grammatical errors in this document
- ☐ Check grammar with spelling
- ☐ Show readability statistics

Writing style:
[Standard ▼]
[Settings...]

[Recheck Document]

[OK] [Cancel]

Practice

To practice using the spell checker, open
the student file **Prac3-9**.

Hot Tip

You can create additional custom
dictionaries, but Word comes equipped
with only one.

Using AutoCorrect

Concept

Word's AutoCorrect feature corrects specified typing mistakes automatically as they are entered and can be programmed to accommodate a wide variety of errors. For example, it can capitalize the first letter of a sentence automatically. AutoCorrect prevents you from having to fix typing errors that you commit frequently, saving you valuable time. AutoCorrect also allows you to format to convert certain characters and character combinations into symbols that represent them better.

Do It!

Sabrina wants to set AutoCorrect to fix a typing mistake she often makes.

1. Open a new blank document by clicking the New button 🗋 on the Standard toolbar.

2. Click Tools, then AutoCorrect. The AutoCorrect dialog box opens to the AutoCorrect tab. An insertion point appears in the Replace: box, as shown in Figure 3-16.

3. Type the word corect in the Replace box, misspelling it intentionally.

4. Press [Tab] to move the insertion point to the With: box.

5. Type the word correct. Word will now replace corect with correct in any document.

6. Click OK to accept the changes you have made and to leave the AutoCorrect dialog box. The blank document that you created in the first step should be in the active window.

7. Type the following sentence exactly as it appears: Word will now corect mistakes i make. Notice that as you typed the sentence, Word fixed the misspelled corect and capitalized the letter i automatically.

Figure 3-16 AutoCorrect dialog box

AutoCorrect options available to you

Turns AutoCorrect on or off

Type common misspelling here

Word converts this character combination into a smiley face

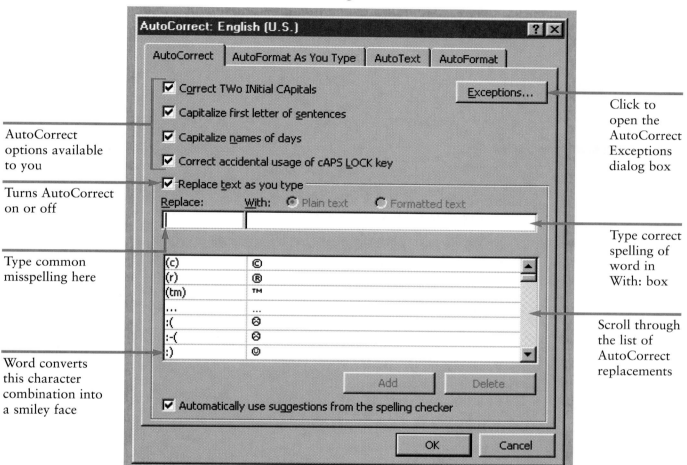

Click to open the AutoCorrect Exceptions dialog box

Type correct spelling of word in With: box

Scroll through the list of AutoCorrect replacements

Using AutoCorrect (continued)

Do It!

8 Press [Space] after the previous sentence, then type the word many (lowercase, as shown) followed by a space. Word recognizes many as the first word of a new sentence, because it is preceded by a period and a space, and therefore capitalizes it.

9 Type misc. mistakes are fixed automatically. Notice that although you typed a period and a space after misc the word mistakes was not capitalized. This is because misc. is on Word's AutoCorrect Exceptions list along with most other common abbreviations.

10 Close the document. Do not save changes.

More

Word's AutoCorrect Exceptions dialog box, shown in **Figure 3-17**, can be accessed by clicking `Exceptions...` in the AutoCorrect dialog box. Word will recognize the period and space after one of the abbreviations on this list as differing from those at the end of a sentence, and will not capitalize the next word. To get rid of an AutoCorrect entry that you don't want, select the entry in the AutoCorrect dialog box and click `Delete`.

While AutoCorrect fixes spelling errors in words you have finished typing, Word's AutoComplete feature recognizes many words and phrases as you are typing them, predicts the outcome, and offers to complete them for you. For example, if you type Dear M, Word will suggest the AutoComplete tip Dear Mom and Dad. Simply press [Enter] to accept the tip, and the remaining text will be inserted for you. If Word recognizes that text you are typing matches a word or phrase contained in its list of AutoText entries, an AutoComplete tip will appear with Word's guess as to what you wish to type. If the suggestion is incorrect, simply continue typing and the tip will disappear. Use the AutoText tab in the AutoCorrect dialog box (shown in **Figure 3-18**) to add to the list of terms that AutoComplete will recognize. You can also see what AutoText entries are available by clicking `All Entries ▾` on the AutoText toolbar. Clicking one of the AutoText entries inserts it into your document at the insertion point. Some AutoText entries automatically include relevant data. If the insertion point is on the fourth page of a ten-page document and you insert the AutoText entry Page X of Y for instance, Word will insert Page 4 of 10.

Figure 3-17 AutoCorrect Exceptions dialog box

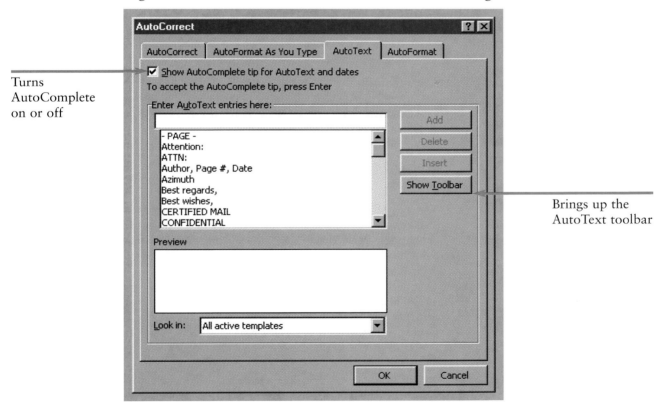

Type abbreviation here to include it on the exceptions list

Click tabs to enter other types of exceptions

Word 2000

Figure 3-18 AutoText tab of the AutoCorrect dialog box

Turns AutoComplete on or off

Brings up the AutoText toolbar

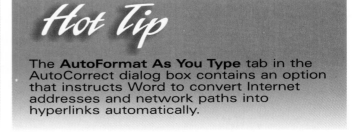

Using the Word Thesaurus

Concept

Word contains a Thesaurus facility that can suggest synonyms and antonyms for words that you select.

Do It!

Sabrina wants to find a more descriptive word than the one she used in one of her sentences.

1. Open the student file Doit3-11 and save it as Report2.doc. It is a copy of Sabrina and Juan's report that has been fully checked for spelling.

2. Select the word hard in the fifth sentence of the third paragraph of the report, the sentence that begins Many telecommuters are not locked into a hard 9-to-5 work schedule....

3. Click Tools, then click Thesaurus on the Language submenu. The Thesaurus dialog box appears with the word hard displayed in the Looked Up box, as shown in Figure 3-19.

4. Click the word inflexible in the Replace with Synonym box to select it.

5. Click **Look Up** to search for synonyms of inflexible.

6. Click the word rigid in the Replace with Synonym box to select it.

7. Click **Replace** to insert rigid in place of hard in the report.

More

The Meanings box in the Thesaurus dialog box shows the various possible meanings of the selected word. Depending on the word, the Meanings box may also have Antonym or Related Words listed, which will show you opposite meanings and words with similar structure, respectively.

Word can also quickly count and display the number of pages, words, characters, paragraphs, and lines in your document. To activate the Word Count dialog box (see **Figure 3-20**) with all the information already calculated for the open document, simply click Tools, and then click Word Count.

Figure 3-19 Thesaurus dialog box

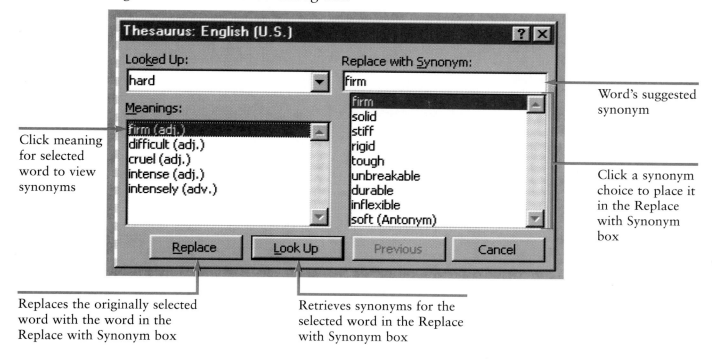

Word 2000

Click meaning for selected word to view synonyms

Word's suggested synonym

Click a synonym choice to place it in the Replace with Synonym box

Replaces the originally selected word with the word in the Replace with Synonym box

Retrieves synonyms for the selected word in the Replace with Synonym box

Figure 3-20 Word Count dialog box

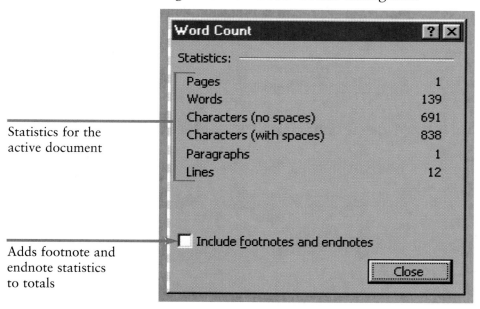

Statistics for the active document

Adds footnote and endnote statistics to totals

Practice

To practice using the Thesaurus, open the student file **Prac3-11**.

Hot Tip

Click the **Looked Up** drop-down list arrow in the Thesaurus dialog box to view all words that have been looked up during the current session, with the original selected word at the bottom.

 # Finding and Replacing Text

Concept

The **Find** command allows you to search a document for individual occurrences of any word, phrase, or other unit of text. The **Replace** command gives you the ability to replace one or all ocurrences of a word that you have found. Together, the Find and Replace commands form a powerful editing tool, capable of making multiple document-wide changes in a matter of seconds.

Do It!

Sabrina and Juan have used both **per cent** and **percent** in their report and, though both spellings are acceptable, they want to spell the word consistently throughout their document.

1 Place the insertion point at the beginning of the document. Word will search the document from the insertion point forward.

2 Click **Edit**, then click **Replace**. The Find and Replace dialog box appears with the Replace tab in front and the insertion point in the **Find What** text box, as shown in **Figure 3-21**.

3 Type **per cent** into the Find What text box.

4 Click in the **Replace With** text box to move the insertion point there.

5 Type **percent** as one word in the Replace With text box.

6 Click **Replace All** to search the document for all instances of **per cent** and replace them with **percent**. A message box appears to display the results. In this case, one replacement was made.

7 Click **OK** to close the message box.

8 Close the Find and Replace dialog box.

9 Save and close the document.

More

You can examine and replace each instance of a word individually instead of automatically by clicking the **Find Next** button instead of **Replace All**. The **Search** drop-down list determines the direction of the search relative to the insertion point; you can search upward or downward through the document or keep the Word default setting of **All**, which checks the entire document including headers, footers, and footnotes. The five check boxes control other Find options, as explained in **Table 3-2**. The **Format** drop-down list contains formatting specifications, such as bold text or a particular indent depth, that Word can search for and replace. The **Special** drop-down list shows special characters that Word can search for, such as paragraph marks, manual page breaks or a particular letter or digit. The **No Formatting** button removes all formatting criteria from your search parameters.

The **Find** tab of the Find and Replace dialog box is identical to the Replace tab except it lacks the replace function and merely searches your document for the items you specify.

Figure 3-21 Find and Replace dialog box

Enter the word you want to search for and replace here

Enter the replacement word here

Use check boxes to activate search options

Find and Replace

Find | Replace | Go To

Find what:

Replace with:

Less ▲ | Replace | Replace All | Find Next | Cancel

Search Options

Search: All

☐ Match case
☐ Find whole words only
☐ Use wildcards
☐ Sounds like
☐ Find all word forms

Replace

Format ▼ | Special ▼ | No Formatting

Word 2000

Click to determine search direction

Table 3-2 Find Options

OPTION	DESCRIPTION
Match case	Finds only text with uppercase and lowercase letters that match exactly the contents of the Find What text box
Find whole words only	Disregards larger words that contain the word that is being searched for
Use wildcards	Searches for wildcards, special characters, or special search operators that are in the Find What box. These can be added from the Special ▼ menu.
Sounds like	Looks for words that sound like the text in the Find What text box but are spelled differently
Find all word forms	Locates all verb forms of a word, such as Do, Doing, Does, and Did

Practice

To practice finding and replacing text, open the student file **Prac3-12**.

Hot Tip

The **Go To** tab in the Find and Replace dialog box provides a quick way to get to a particular place in a long document such as a specific page, footnote, or section.

Shortcuts

Function	Button/Mouse	Menu	Keyboard
Adjust margins		Click File, then click Page Setup, then click the Margins tab	
Indent selected paragraphs	Click and drag indent markers on the horizontal ruler	Click Format, then click Paragraph, then click the Indents and Spacing tab	[Ctrl]+[M] (Normal) [Ctrl]+[T] (Hanging)
Adjust Line Spacing of selected paragraphs		Click Format, then click Paragraph, then click the Indents and Spacing tab	[Ctrl]+[1] (Single) [Ctrl]+[2] (Double) [Ctrl]+[5] (1.5)
Go to the next window (When working with multiple documents)	Click on the part of the next window that is showing, if the active window is not maximized	Click Window, then click the name of the next document	[Ctrl]+[F6]
Go to the previous window (When working with multiple documents)	Click on the part of the previous window that is showing, if the active window is not maximized	Click Window, then click the name of the previous document	[Ctrl]+[Shift]+[F6]
Check for spelling and grammar errors	[ABC ✓]	Click Tools, then click Spelling	[F7]
Find next misspelling (With Automatic Spell Checking active)	Scroll down in the document to the next word with a wavy red underline		[Alt]+[F7]
Open the Word Thesaurus		Click Tools, then click Language, then Thesaurus	[Shift]+[F7]

Identify Key Features

Name the items indicated by callout arrows in **Figure 3-22**.

Figure 3-22 Identifying formatting and editing concepts

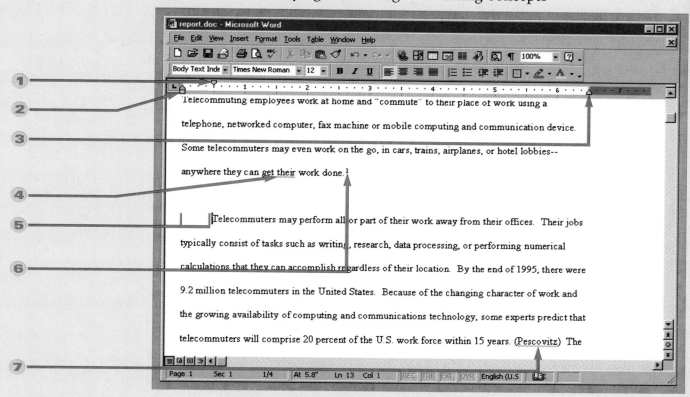

Select The Best Answer

8. Objects that slide along the horizontal ruler and determine text placement

9. A Word feature that fixes common mistakes as they are entered

10. A document where Word places words you "teach" it

11. A line where a new page always begins, regardless of how much space is left on the previous page

12. The place where footnote and endnote text resides

13. The invisible line that marks the boundary between text and the edge of a page

14. Displays the number of words, characters, paragraphs, and lines in your document

a. Hard page break

b. Word Count dialog box

c. AutoCorrect

d. Indent markers

e. Margin

f. Custom dictionary

g. Note pane

Quiz (continued)

Complete the Statement

15. Document-level formatting includes:
    a. Indents
    b. Font
    c. Margins
    d. Footnotes

16. A reference mark is:
    a. A mark in the text referring to a footnote or endnote
    b. Another name for a tab stop
    c. Text that has been highlighted
    d. An encyclopedia buyer

17. When there is no more room on a page and more text is entered, Word automatically creates a:
    a. New document based on the Normal template
    b. Manual page break
    c. Drop-down list
    d. Soft page break

18. AutoCorrect will fix a spelling mistake it recognizes as soon as:
    a. The space bar is pressed
    b. The document is saved
    c. Automatic Spell Checking is turned on
    d. The word matches the first five letters of a spelling mistake on AutoCorrect's list of entries

19. Paragraph-level formatting includes:
    a. Page numbers
    b. Headers and footers
    c. Italics
    d. Line spacing

20. The button:
    a. Adds color to text
    b. Copies formatting from one area to another
    c. Pastes the contents of the Clipboard into the document at the insertion point
    d. Displays or hides the Drawing toolbar

21. To copy text from one document to another, you have to:
    a. Set up File Sharing on the Control Panel
    b. Click while pressing [F11]
    c. Use the Clipboard
    d. Use the Style Gallery

22. To view page numbers, switch to:
    a. Normal View
    b. Print Layout View
    c. Full Screen View
    d. Mirror margins

23. To leave the first line of a paragraph against the margin while indenting the other lines, apply a:
    a. Dangling indent
    b. First line indent
    c. Footer
    d. Hanging indent

Interactivity

Test Your Skills

1. Open a document and format it:

   a. Open the student file **SkillTest 3** and save it to your student disk as **Test 3**.

   b. Open the **Page Setup** dialog box on the File menu.

   c. Set the left and right margins at **1 inch**.

   d. Insert page numbers at the bottom center of the page.

2. Apply indents to the document, change the line spacing, and insert a footnote:

   a. Select all of the text in the document below the title.

   b. From the **Paragraph** dialog box on the Format menu, apply a **first line** indent of .5 inches and change the **line spacing** to **double**.

   c. Insert a footnote after (p. 43) in the fifth line of the second paragraph of the document reading, **All quotes refer to the revised 1862 edition of the book.**

3. Adjust the alignment and text formatting of the document:

   a. Select all of the text in the document below the title and **justify** it.

   b. Select the title and **center** it.

   c. Add **bold** formatting to the title and the author's name.

4. Open another document and copy text into the original document:

   a. Open the student file **SkillTest 3a** and select the paragraph it contains. It is the conclusion to the paper used above.

   b. Copy the selected paragraph to the Clipboard.

   c. Close SkillTest 3a, bringing **Test 3** back as the active window.

   d. Place the insertion point at the very end of the document.

   e. Paste the copied paragraph onto the end of the paper.

5. Use the **Format Painter** to change the formatting of the inserted paragraph to match the rest of the document:

   a. Select the second-to-last paragraph in the document by triple-clicking it.

   b. Click the Format Painter button to copy the formatting of the selected paragraph.

   c. Drag the I-beam (which now has a paintbrush next to it) across the last paragraph in the document to select it and change its formatting to match that of the previous paragraph.

   d. Click once in the paragraph to deselect it.

Interactivity (continued)

Test Your Skills

6. Check for spelling errors and replace all instances of one word with another:

   a. Click Tools, then click Spelling and Grammar to run the Spelling and Grammar checker. Clear the Check grammar check box to check only for spelling errors.

   b. Correct the three misspelled words in the document, ignoring names and unusual words.

   c. Click Edit, then click Replace to open the Replace dialog box.

   d. Use the Replace All command to replace all occurrences of Browne with the correct name, Brown.

   e. Close the document, saving changes if prompted.

7. Add a word to the AutoCorrect Replace text as you type list:

   a. Open a new document.

   b. Open the AutoCorrect dialog box.

   c. Use the AutoCorrect tab to instruct Word to replace occurrences of clcik with click.

   d. Close the dialog box and test your AutoCorrect entry in the blank document.

   e. Return to the AutoCorrect tab and delete clcik from the list.

Problem Solving

1. Using the skills you learned in Lesson 3, open the student file Problem Solving 3 and save it as Solved 3. Change the left and right margins to 1.25", apply a hanging indent of .5" to the document, and change the spacing to 1.5. Add page numbers to the upper-left corner of each page, starting on page 1. Center and boldface the title, and justify the main body text of the document. Insert three footnotes into the paper. The text of the footnotes is contained in the student file Problem Solving 3a. Insert the first footnote at the end of the third paragraph, following the word products. The second footnote follows the word inventory at the end of the fourth paragraph. The final footnote should be placed after the word line at the end of the sixth paragraph. Open the Spell checker and correct all misspellings in the document. Finally, save and close the file.

2. You are applying for a position as a restaurant reviewer for a local magazine. Before your interview, you want to practice your reviewing technique. Review your three favorite restaurants in a three paragraph, one page document. Set up the document with .75" margins. After you enter all of your text, insert a Continuous Section break between the first and second, and second and third paragraphs. Then, format the first paragraph with 14 point, italicized text and a hanging indent. Next, format the second paragraph with a 1.5" first line indent and 11 point, Arial text. Finally, format the third paragraph exactly like the first. Save the document as Solved 3-Reviews.

▷ **Creating Tables**

▷ **Editing Tables**

▷ **Inserting and Deleting Rows, Columns, and Cells**

▷ **Sorting Data in a Table**

▷ **Calculating Data in a Table**

▷ **Formatting a Table**

▷ **Creating a Chart**

▷ **Editing a Chart**

▷ **Drawing a Table**

▷ **Adding Borders and Shading**

L E S S O N

TABLES AND CHARTS

To present information in a document more accurately, it is often helpful to organize data into a table. Word makes it easy to create and modify tables in its documents, and it has the ability to perform many more complex tasks with data, such as sorting and calculating, that are usually found only in complicated spreadsheet programs.

Word can create blank tables in which data may be entered, or transform existing data directly into table form. Once a table has been made, data can be inserted or deleted quickly to meet your needs, or reorganized to get your point across more effectively.

Sometimes, it may be difficult to glean trends or important facts from a table accurately with so much information in text and number form. A chart can be very helpful by presenting the data as a picture that can be more easily grasped and understood.

Case Study:
Juan has accumulated some data for the report that he and Sabrina are working on, and he would like to organize it as a table that will be inserted into the document. Once the table has been finished, he will create a chart based on it and add the chart to the report.

Creating Tables

Concept

A Table consists of information organized into horizontal rows and vertical columns. The intersection of a row and a column is called a cell. A table may be created from scratch or can be assembled from existing text. Tables often utilize row and column headers, which are lables that identify the adjacent data. Data in a table can consist of words, or labels, and numbers, also called values.

Do It!

Juan wants to insert a table into the report he and Sabrina have written.

1   Open the file Report2 from your student disk. This is the copy of Sabrina and Juan's report, which you were working on in the last lesson.

2   Place the insertion point at the end of the second paragraph, after the word home.

3   Insert a Manual page break (there will not be enough room on the page for the table without it). The insertion point will appear just below the new break.

4   Click the Insert Table button 🎛 on the Standard toolbar. A table grid appears, allowing you to choose the number of rows and columns in your table.

5   Move the mouse pointer over the table grid until a 2 x 3 area is selected, as shown in Figure 4-1, and click. A table appears in the document at the insertion point with gridlines delineating the rows and columns, and cell markers showing the end of the text in each cell, as shown in Figure 4-2. If the cell markers are not showing, you can make them appear by clicking ¶ on the Standard toolbar.

Figure 4-1 Using the Insert Table button

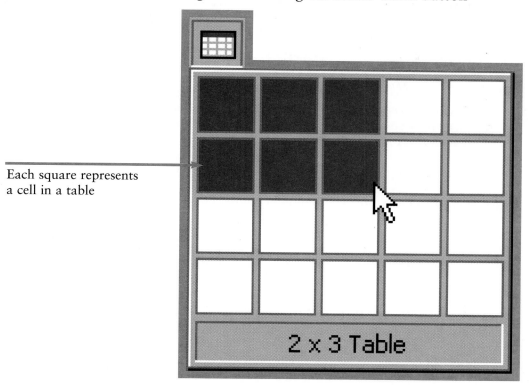

Each square represents
a cell in a table

Figure 4-2 Table inserted in Word document

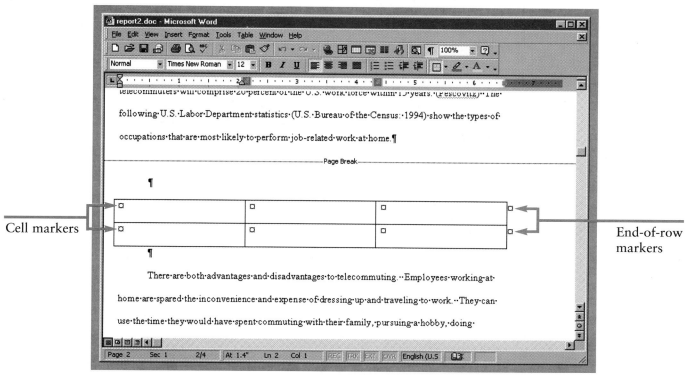

Cell markers

End-of-row
markers

Creating Tables (continued)

Do It!

6   Type the following three pieces of information, pressing [Tab] once after each of the first two headings:

Occupation	Total	Percent at Home

7   Press [Tab] to go to the next row.

8   Type the following three pieces of information, pressing [Tab] once after each of the first two:

Managerial	14.4	5.2

Your table should now resemble the one in **Figure 4-3**.

More

You can also create a table by selecting existing text in your document and clicking the Insert Table button; the cells in the table will be determined by the tabs and paragraphs in the selection. A new table may also be created manually by clicking Table, then clicking Draw Table. The Tables and Borders toolbar (see **Figure 4-4**) will appear, and you can draw a table and its row and column borders using the mouse pointer. If you choose the Insert Table command from the Table menu, you can access the AutoFormat dialog box, which will be explained later in the lesson.

If you wish to insert an existing worksheet into your Word document, you can insert it as a linked object or an embedded object. A linked object will show up in the Word document (its destination file) but will remain linked to its source file. Thus, any changes made to the source file will be reflected in the destination file. If it is inserted as an embedded object, the file will become part of the Word document and can be altered by double-clicking it to open the parent application. This is an excellent example of the way different Microsoft Office applications can be used together productively. For example, if you have an Excel worksheet that is being updated frequently and you would like to insert it into your Word document as a table, insert it as a linked object so that you can be sure that the table will always be up to date. To insert a linked object at the insertion point, click Insert, then click Object, and then click the Create from File tab. Select the file you wish to insert by clicking the Browse button, and activate the Link to file check box (if this box is not checked, the file will be inserted as an embedded object instead). The table will appear in your Word document, and double-clicking it will open an Excel window from which the table can be fully edited. Word's Help facility offers many more tips and methods for fully utilizing these functions.

Figure 4-3 Adding information to a table

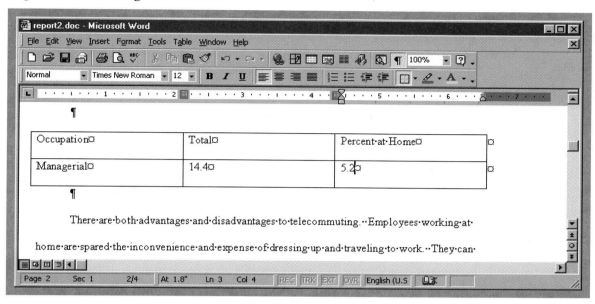

Figure 4-4 Tables and Borders toolbar

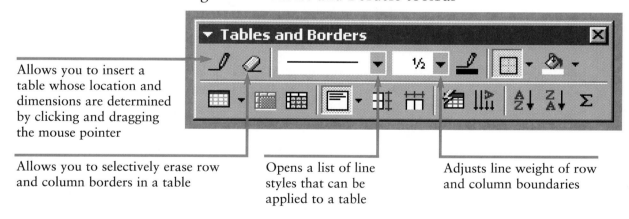

Allows you to insert a table whose location and dimensions are determined by clicking and dragging the mouse pointer

Allows you to selectively erase row and column borders in a table

Opens a list of line styles that can be applied to a table

Adjusts line weight of row and column boundaries

Practice

To practice creating tables, open the student file **Prac4-1**.

Hot Tip

You can create a table in Word using Microsoft Excel by clicking the **Insert Microsoft Excel Worksheet** button on the Standard toolbar. This allows you to use Excel commands within that worksheet as you create your table.

Editing Tables

Concept

A table in a Word document can be edited in much the same way that ordinary text is edited.

Do It!

Juan would like to change the Total heading in his table to Total (in millions) and Percent at Home to Percent Working at Home.

1 Position the insertion point just after the word Total in the table.

2 Type a space, then type (in millions) to complete the heading.

3 Press [Tab] to move to the next cell to the right. All the information in the cell is selected.

4 Click between the words Percent and at to deselect the cell and position the insertion point there.

5 Type Working and press [Space] to complete the cell edit.

More

As you can see, table editing is very similar to editing text in a paragraph. Text may be centered or aligned to either side of a cell by selecting it and clicking the appropriate formatting button. Also, the Selection bar works in much the same way in a table as it does with text. Clicking in the Selection bar next to a row selects the entire row; dragging up or down in the Selection bar adds more rows to the selected area. In addition, there is a miniature selection bar area at the left end of each cell, and clicking it will select the entire cell. A cell may also be selected by triple-clicking it, whereas double-clicking will select an entire word within the cell just as it does in regular text. To select a column, place the mouse pointer over its top border until the mouse pointer changes to a downward arrow ↓, then click to select the column. Cells can be made wider or narrower by clicking and dragging their edges: Place the mouse pointer on the gridline that makes up the edge of a cell until it changes to ◄║►, then click and drag the cell border to the desired distance. If you click and drag the edge of a selected cell, then that cell will be the only one in its column to be affected. To make the whole column's width change, make sure that no cells are selected before you adjust the edges.

The insertion point may be placed anywhere in a table with the mouse pointer. The keyboard may be used in a variety of ways to move through the table and select its contents. **Table 4-1** shows many keyboard movement and selection techniques that will make working with tables much easier. Remember to press [Tab] instead of [Enter] to move to the next cell; pressing [Enter] causes a new line to be created within the cell. When the insertion point is within the boundaries of a table, the ruler will reflect the table's column boundaries (see **Figure 4-5**). Dragging the column boundary markers on the ruler will change the corresponding column widths. When exact precision is required, row and column sizes may be manually entered in the Table Properties dialog box, available on the Table menu.

Table 4-1 Keyboard movement and selection shortcuts

DESIRED ACTION	PRESS THIS
Move to the next or previous cell in a table and select its contents	[Tab] or [Shift]+[Tab]
Move up or down one row	[↑] or [↓]
Move to the first or last cell in a row	[Alt]+[Home] or [Alt]+[End]
Move to the top or bottom cell in a column	[Alt]+[Pg Up] or [Alt]+[Pg Dn]
Select an entire column	[Alt]+Click
Select an entire table	[Alt]+[5] on the numeric keypad (with Num Lock off)

Figure 4-5 Formatting a table using the ruler

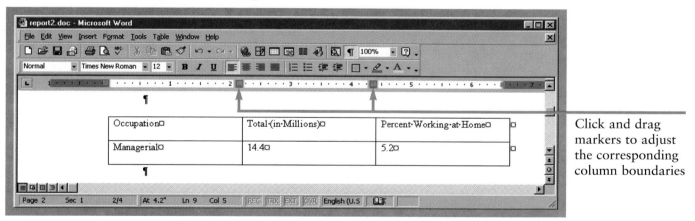

Click and drag markers to adjust the corresponding column boundaries

Practice

To practice editing a table, open the student file **Prac4-2**.

Hot Tip

To insert a tab character into a cell to indent its contents, press **[Ctrl]+[Tab]**, as pressing [Tab] alone will simply move the insertion point to the next cell.

Inserting and Deleting Rows, Columns and Cells

Concept

Word makes it easy to add or delete rows and columns in a table when more or fewer are required.

Do It!

Juan wants to add three rows of new data to the table.

1. Position the insertion point in the last cell in the last row of the table, after the number 5.2.

2. Press [Tab]. The insertion point moves to the first cell of a new row.

3. Type the following nine pieces of information, pressing [Tab] between each:

Professional	15.5	4.9
Sales	13.2	6.2
Service	14.9	3.7

The entered text is automatically formatted to fit into three new rows.

More

To insert additional empty rows or columns, first select the row or column that will be moved down or over to accommodate the new one. Then click the Insert Rows button or the Insert Columns button, which will appear in place of the Insert Table button when a row or column is selected. The number of new rows or columns created is the same as the number selected. For example, if you select two rows and click the Insert Rows button, two new empty rows will appear above the ones you selected. To add a column to the end of a table, select the end-of-column markers in the same way you would select a column, then click the Insert Columns button. To delete a row or column, select it and then right-click it. The Table shortcut menu (**Figure 4-6**) will appear, offering, among other choices, an option to delete your selection. You can also use this menu to insert additional columns or rows. The Table shortcut menu has many of the same commands that are available on the Table menu, as well as shortcuts to several standard formatting options. To delete and individual cell, right-click it and then choose the Delete Cells command from the pop-up shortcut menu that appears. The Delete Cells dialog box, shown in **Figure 4-7**, will open. From this dialog box, you can determine whether the cell is deleted from its column or from its row by shifting the remaining cells up or to the left. You can also use this dialog box to delete an entire row or column. Row and column dimensions may also be adjusted from the Table Properties dialog box (**Figure 4-8**), available on both the menu bar Table menu and the Table shortcut menu.

Figure 4-6 Table shortcut menu

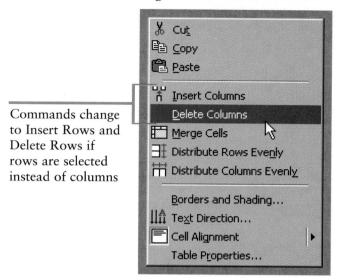

Commands change to Insert Rows and Delete Rows if rows are selected instead of columns

Figure 4-7 Delete Cells dialog box

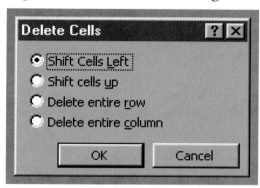

Figure 4-8 Row tab of Table Properties dialog box

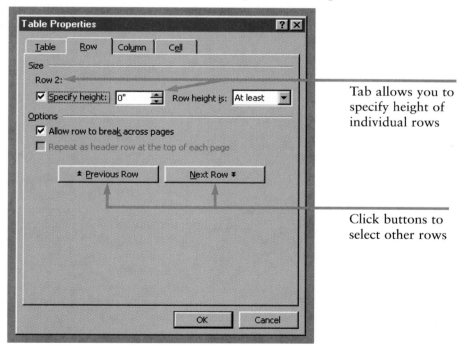

Tab allows you to specify height of individual rows

Click buttons to select other rows

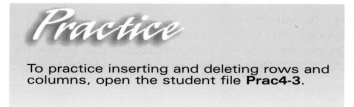

Practice

To practice inserting and deleting rows and columns, open the student file **Prac4-3**.

Hot Tip

To easily delete an entire row or column, select it and then either use the cut command or press **[Shift]+[Delete]**. Just pressing [Delete] will leave the cells intact but erase the contents.

Sorting Data in a Table

Concept

Cells in a Word table can be automatically sorted by various criteria without re-typing them or going through tedious cutting and pasting. For example, Word can automatically alphabetize a long table of names or sort a table of orders by shipping date. Sorting allows you to locate specific data in a table quickly.

Do It!

Juan would like his table to list occupations in order of decreasing Working-at-Home percentage.

1. Make sure the insertion point is positioned inside the table.

2. Click Table, then click Sort. The Sort dialog box appears, as shown in **Figure 4-9**.

3. Click the Sort by drop-down list arrow, then click Percent Working at Home. Word automatically reads all your column headings and includes them in the list, with the first heading as the default choice. When Percent Working at Home was chosen, Word analyzed the kind of data in that column and changed the Type list box from text to number.

4. Click the Descending radio button in the Sort By section to make Word sort the table with the largest values first.

5. Click the Header Row radio button in the My List Has section if it is not already selected.

6. Click [OK] to sort the table. The rows are placed in descending order according to their value in the Percent Working at Home column (see **Figure 4-10**).

More

Word allows you to sort by more than one criterion. For example, if you had a table of names with people's first and last names in separate cells, Word could sort them primarily by last name, then by first name. Thus, if several people had the same last name, Word could sort them by first name as well. Word allows up to three levels of sorting in this fashion. You can set secondary sorting criteria on the Sort dialog box by choosing another criterion in the Sort by text box. In the My List Has section, the default setting is Header Row, meaning the first row of your table explains the contents of the cells below, such as the header "Occupation" in Juan's table. If you select No Header Row, Word will make the first row into labels such as Column 1, Column 2, and so on. Also, if No Header Row is chosen but you do in fact have a header row, your column titles will be sorted with the other rows and may not end up at the top of the table.

Since only one row in Juan's table actually needed to be relocated, he could have moved the row manually. An alternative to the sort feature is to select an entire row and then move it with the pointer, the same way you move regular text. Release the dragged text in the row that you want to end up below the selection being moved.

Figure 4-9 Sort dialog box

Primary sorting criterion

Secondary sorting criterion

Excludes first row when sorting

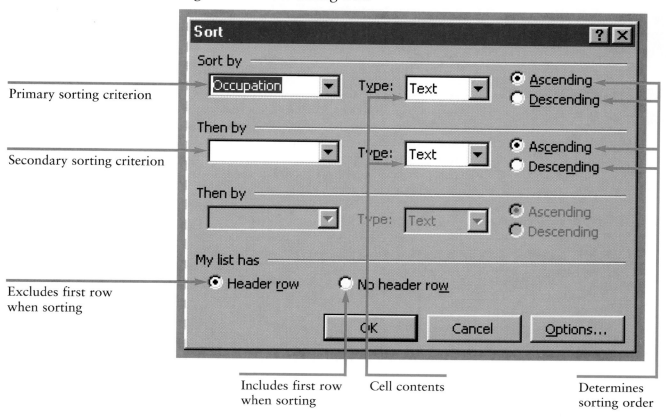

Word 2000

Includes first row when sorting   Cell contents   Determines sorting order

Figure 4-10 Sorted table

Occupation	Total (in Millions)	Percent Working at Home
Sales	13.2	6.2
Managerial	14.4	5.2
Professional	15.5	4.9
Service	14.9	3.7

Practice

To practice sorting data in a table, open the student file **Prac4-4**.

Hot Tip

You can make Word sort uppercase and lowercase letters differently by clicking the Case Sensitive check box in the Sort Options dialog box, available by clicking  in the Sort dialog box.

Calculating Data in a Table

Concept

The Formula command makes it easy to perform calculations with data in a table. Word comes with preprogrammed formulas such as sum, product, and average, but additional formulas may be entered to meet the needs of each user and each table. Using formulas transforms your table from a simple display object into a functional tool. Once you master formulas, you will never have to worry about committing costly mathematical errors.

Do It!

Juan wants Word to automatically average the values in the Percent Working at Home column and insert the average in a new cell.

1. Position the insertion point after the number 3.7 in the last cell of the last row of the table.

2. Press [Tab] to create a new row.

3. Type the word Average into the first cell of the new row.

4. Press [Tab] twice to move the insertion point to the last cell in the row.

5. Click Table, then click Formula. The Formula dialog box appears, as shown in **Figure 4-11**, with the formula =SUM(ABOVE) suggested in the Formula text box.

6. Delete the suggested formula by selecting it and pressing [Delete].

7. Click the Paste function list arrow, then click AVERAGE, as shown in **Figure 4-12**. The AVERAGE formula appears in the Formula text box with the insertion point between parentheses.

8. Type C2:C5, the range of cells you wish to average, inside the parentheses.

Word 2000

Figure 4-11 Formula dialog box

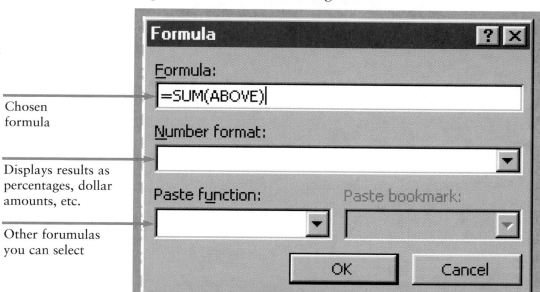

Chosen
formula

Displays results as
percentages, dollar
amounts, etc.

Other forumulas
you can select

Figure 4-12 Selecting a function

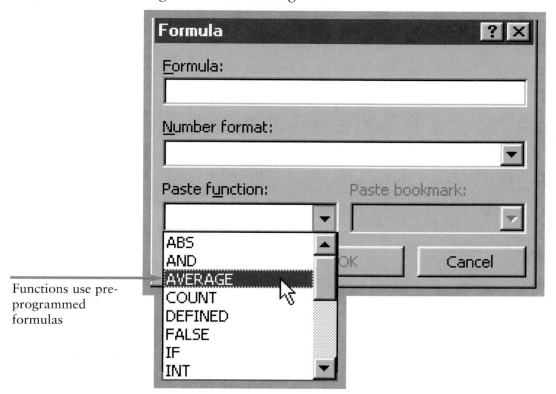

Functions use pre-
programmed
formulas

Calculating Data in a Table (continued)

Do It!

9. Place the insertion point before the word AVERAGE in the Formula text box.

10. Press [=] to place an equal sign before the formula. The equal sign at the beginning tells Word that a formula, rather than a label or a value, is about to be entered.

11. Click [OK] to apply the formula to the column. The average of the values in the column, 5, appears in the last cell of the table, as shown in **Figure 4-13**.

More

Changing data in one of the cells that the calculation is based on does not immediately affect the result seen on the screen. To update the calculation taking the new data into account, select the column that has to be recalculated and press [F9], which is the Update Fields command.

When entering your own formulas into the Formula dialog box you will refer to other cells in the table using cell references, which identify a cell by its position as a function of its column letter and row number. For example, the cell reference for the second cell in the third column is C2. (See **Figure 4-14**.) You can use the Word Formula feature in many ways. In **Figure 4-15**, formulas are used to calculate the total monthly spending for three different people as well as the resulting 12-month projected total cost. The formulas shown are the ones that would be entered into the Formula text box when the Formula dialog box is called up with the insertion point in that particular cell. Each of the formulas in the Monthly Total column (Column E) adds the numbers to the left in their respective rows to arrive at the total. Likewise, the formulas in Column F multiply by 12 the monthly total for the row that was just calculated to arrive at a projected total for the year. The symbol for multiplication is an asterisk (*); division is represented by a slash (/). As they are in **Figure 4-13**, the formulas will result in an unformatted number. To make the calculated result appear with a dollar sign and two decimal places showing, click the Number Format text box in the Formula dialog box, and then click $#,##0.00;($#,##0.00) on the drop-down list. This will be tacked on to the end of the formula in the Formula text box, which will instruct Word to place the result in the correct format.

Figure 4-13 Appearance of table with average calculated

Occupation	Total (in Millions)	Percent Working at Home
Sales	13.2	6.2
Managerial	14.4	5.2
Professional	15.5	4.9
Service	14.9	3.7
Average		5 ←

Average of the values in the four cells above

Figure 4-14 Cell references

	A	**B**	**C**
1	A1	B1	C1
2	A2	B2	C2 ←
3	A3	B3	C3

Cell C2 is in column C, row 2

Figure 4-15 Sample table with formulas in the cells to which they will be applied

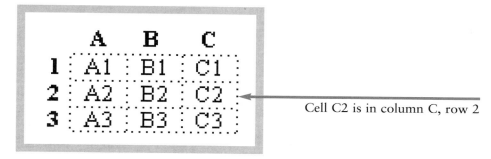

¤	Rent/month¤	Food/month¤	Other/Month¤	Monthly Total¤	Annual Total¤
Margot¤	$450¤	$65¤	$340¤	=SUM(LEFT)¤	=E2*12¤
Bart¤	$625¤	$125¤	$385¤	=SUM(LEFT)¤	=E3*12¤
Diane¤	$900¤	$95¤	$290¤	=SUM(LEFT)¤	=E4*12¤

This formula adds all values to the left in its row to get the monthly total

This formula multiplies the contents of cell E4 by 12 to get the annual total

Practice

To practice calculating data in a table, open the student file **Prac4-5**.

Hot Tip

Word has several different preset formulas and number formats available to you on the drop-down lists in the Formula dialog box, or you can enter your own into the Formula and Number Format text boxes.

Formatting a Table

Concept

A table's appearance can be changed in many ways. Word's table formatting options include, among others, shading, borders, and 3-D effects. You can format individual table elements, or apply en entire set of formatting changes to a table. Both techniques can improve the organization, clarity and appearance of tables.

Do It!

Juan wants to format his table to improve its appearance.

1. Place the insertion point after the space after the word "Total" and press [Enter].

2. Place the insertion point after the space after the word "Working" and press [Enter].

3. Click and drag the column edges to approximately match the column widths in the formatted table in **Figure 4-16**.

4. Select columns B and C.

5. Click the Center alignment button on the Formatting toolbar. Word centers the selected columns.

6. Select the entire table, then press [Ctrl]+[1] (use the number keys above the keyboard, not the numeric keypad) to single-space the text.

7. After deselecting the columns by clicking elsewhere in the table, place the insertion point in the table and click Table, then click Table AutoFormat. The Table AutoFormat dialog box appears with a sample table in its Preview box, as shown in **Figure 4-17**.

8. Scroll down in the Formats list box and click Grid8. The Preview box shows the characteristics of this table format.

9. Click the Last Row check box in the Apply Special Formats To section at the bottom of the Table AutoFormat dialog box. This will visually differentiate your last row from the others, indicating that it contains a different type of information from the other rows.

10. Click ▭ OK to close the dialog box and apply the specified formatting to your table. It changes from a simple line grid enclosing the data to a clean, professional-looking table (see **Figure 4-16**).

More

You can explore the various formatting options available to you in the Table AutoFormat dialog box by selecting various formats and options and viewing the results in the Preview box. If your table spans more than one page and it has a header row to explain the contents of the columns, you can instruct Word to put the heading at the top of each new page of the table. To do so, place the insertion point in the header (first) row. Click Table, then click Heading Rows Repeat.

Figure 4-16 Formatted table

Occupation	Total (in Millions)	Percent Working at Home
Sales	13.2	6.2
Managerial	14.4	5.2
Professional	15.5	4.9
Service	14.9	3.7
Average		**5**

Figure 4-17 Table AutoFormat dialog box

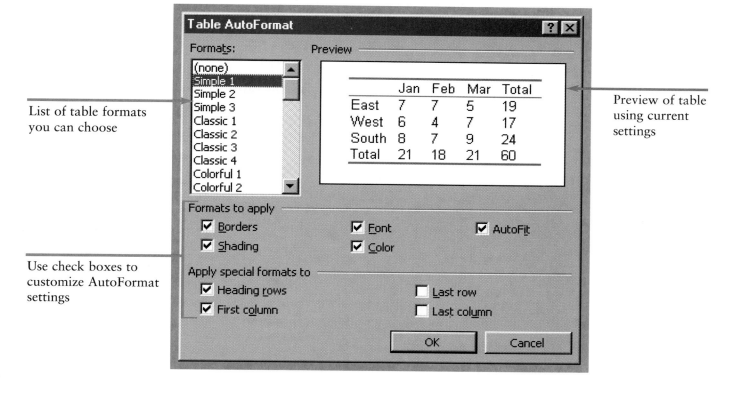

List of table formats you can choose

Use check boxes to customize AutoFormat settings

Preview of table using current settings

Practice

To practice formatting a table, open the student file **Prac4-6**.

Hot Tip

Borders applied to a row are moved with it when rows are sorted. Therefore, you should always sort a table before formatting it with Table AutoFormat, or the table could be formatted incorrectly.

Creating a Chart

Concept

Sometimes a table may be more readily understood if it is presented graphically as a chart. Word allows you to create a chart from scratch, or generate it from an existing table.

Do It!

Juan wants to display his table as a chart.

1. Place the insertion point anywhere within the table.

2. Click Table, then highlight Select, and then click Table to select the entire table.

3. Click Insert, then click Object. The Object dialog box appears.

4. Scroll down through the Object Type box and double-click Microsoft Graph 97 Chart. It opens, turning your table into a Microsoft Graph Datasheet, as shown in Figure 4-18. A preliminary chart appears, based on Juan's data and the program's defaults.

5. Click Chart, then click Chart Options. The Chart Options dialog box appears with the Titles tab on top.

6. Type Home-Based Workers into the Chart title text box. After a brief delay, the title will appear at the top of the preview chart.

7. Press [Tab] to move the insertion point to the the Category (X) text box, then type Occupation. After a brief delay, it will appear at the bottom of the preview chart.

8. Click [OK] to create the chart.

9. Close the Datasheet window. The chart you have created appears below Juan's table in a hatched frame, as shown in Figure 4-16. Some parts of the chart, especially the labels beneath it, appear cramped and cut off. These will be fixed in the next Skill. Notice that when the chart is selected, positioning the mouse pointer over a column of the chart brings up a ScreenTip displaying both what series the column represents and its exact value.

10. Click the blank area on the right-hand side of the page to deselect the chart.

More

The Chart Type dialog box, available on the Chart menu, has an extensive repertoire of formats you can apply to your charts. The Microsoft Graph application automatically suggests the type of graph or chart that seems to most closely match the format of your data, as all formats are not appropriate for all situations. For example, Juan's table could not be expressed accurately or effectively with a pie chart or radar graph.

Figure 4-18 Chart datasheet created from a table

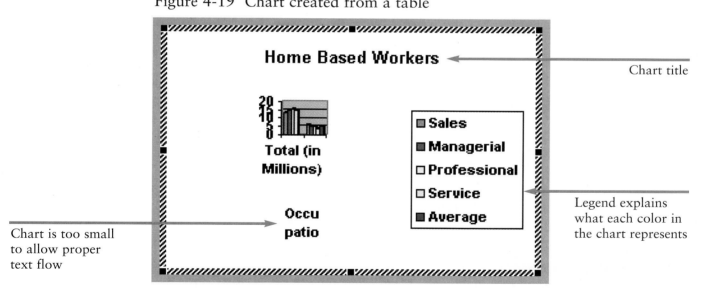

		A	B	C	D	E
	Occupatio	Total (in M	Percent Working at Home			
1	Sales	13.2	6.2			
2	Manageria	14.4	5.2			
3	Profession	15.5	4.9			
4	Service	14.9	3.7			

Shows the color that will be used for each data series in the chart

Figure 4-19 Chart created from a table

Home Based Workers

Total (in Millions)

Occu patio

Sales
Managerial
Professional
Service
Average

Chart title

Legend explains what each color in the chart represents

Chart is too small to allow proper text flow

Practice

To practice creating a chart, open the student file **Prac4-7**.

Hot Tip

If the proper files have been installed on your computer, you can use the **Help** feature of Microsoft Graph 97 Chart to find out more about its various capabilities in the same way that you use Word's Help.

Editing a Chart

Concept

Word treats a chart as a graphic object instead of as text, but it may still be modified by accessing the program that created it. You can edit virtually all aspects of a chart including its size, position, and the characteristics of each individual element.

Do It!

Juan is dissatisfied with the appearance of his chart, especially its size and its column labels. He wants to fix these problems and remove the Average column from the chart entirely.

1 Double-click the chart to open Microsoft Graph. The Microsoft Graph toolbar will replace the Standard and Formatting toolbars at the top of the screen, and a hatched frame will appear around the chart with sizing handles at its corners and at the midpoint of each side.

2 Click the midpoint sizing handle on the bottom of the chart's frame, drag it downward and release it just below the 4 1/2" mark on the vertical ruler. The chart expands vertically, making it possible for more increments to appear along the vertical axis of the chart.

3 Click the midpoint sizing handle on the right side of the frame, then drag the edge of the frame to the right and release it when it is even with the 5 1/2" mark on the horizontal ruler. The chart expands horizontally until it is almost the width of the page, and has room to display the column labels along the bottom without breaking them up awkwardly.

4 Click the Average column on the chart. (It is the column farthest to the right.) Dots appear in the corners to indicate that it is selected.

5 Press [Delete]. The Average column disappears and the chart is automatically updated, removing its reference from the legend and expanding the other columns slightly to make up for the space left behind by its removal. The chart should now look like the one in **Figure 4-20**.

6 Save and close the document.

More

When working with a chart in a Word document, remember that the chart is a foreign element created by another application. To make changes to the chart itself, you must first double-click it to open its parent application. To alter a chart based on changed data in the table that the chart was created from, you must either alter the data sheet for the table, available on the View menu of the Graph program, or recreate the chart. To act upon the chart as an element of your Word document (that is, move it or copy it to another document), only click it once to select it. A box indicated by sizing handles, not the hatched frame that indicates that its parent application has been opened, will appear around it. Then you may cut the chart and paste it, or move it by dragging it and dropping it to another location within the document. Text added during chart creation, such as the title and category, may be changed by selecting it and entering new text. When selected, a frame will appear around it indicating its selection.

Figure 4-20 Properly modified chart

Graph toolbar

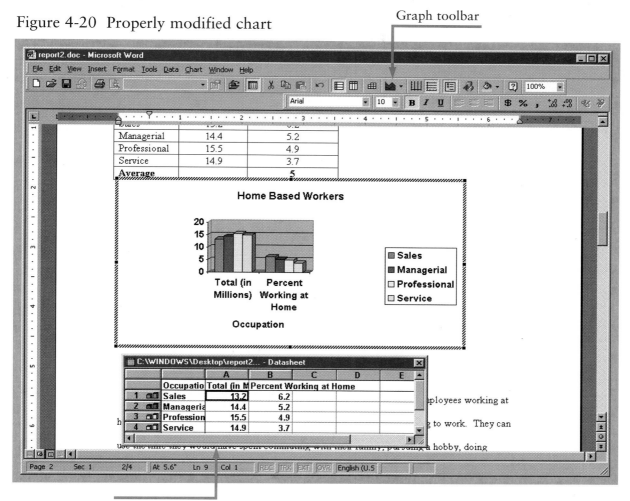

Datasheet will
close when chart
is deselected

To practice changing a chart, open the student file **Prac4-8**.

Hot Tip

To get a better idea of the layout of your page with the chart on it, you can view it from the Print Preview screen. You can still modify the chart there as you would in the regular view.

Drawing a Table

Concept

As you saw earlier in this lesson, Word allows you to create tables with predefined borders using the Insert Table button. Sometimes, you may want to have more control over the construction of a table. Word makes this possible by letting you draw a table gridline by gridline with the Draw Table tool. Therefore, you can create a table customized precisely for your needs as easily as you can create a standard table.

Do It!

Since Juan and Sabrina's report has involved several steps, Juan wants to create a table to make sure he and Sabrina have completed all the steps required.

1. Click ⬜ to open a new blank document.

2. Click the Tables and Borders button 🔲 . The Tables and Borders toolbar will appear, floating on the screen. If the toolbar obscures your view of the document window, you can drag it by its title bar to a better location. The document should now be in Print Layout View.

3. Type Sabrina and Juan's Progress Report on the first line of the document and press [Enter].

4. Click the Draw Table button 🖉 on the Tables and Borders toolbar. The mouse pointer should look like a pencil when it is over the document.

5. Position the mouse pointer just below the word Sabrina. Then click and drag from that point down and to the right. As you drag, a dashed outline will appear. Release the mouse button when the outline reaches 4 inches on the horizontal ruler and 3 inches on the vertical ruler (see **Figure 4-21**). This rectangle will serve as the outside border of the table.

6. Place the mouse pointer on the top border of the table at the 2 inch mark on the horizontal ruler. Then click and drag straight down to the bottom border, drawing a vertical line in the middle of the table.

7. Place the mouse pointer on the left border of the table at the ½ inch mark on the vertical ruler. Then click and drag straight across to the right border, drawing a horizontal line.

8. Repeat the last step to create horizontal lines in the table every ½ inch. The table should resemble the one shown in **Figure 4-22**.

Figure 4-21 Table border drawn by hand

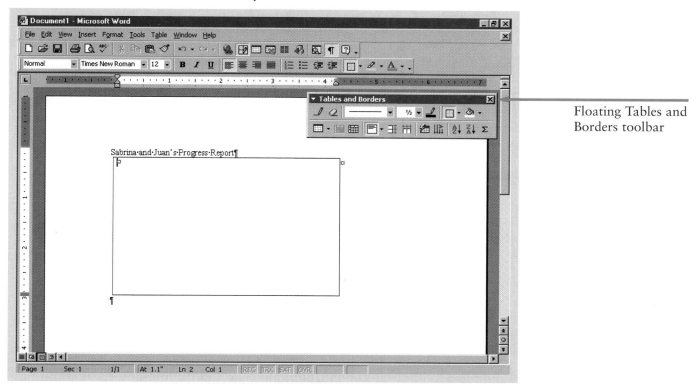

Floating Tables and Borders toolbar

Figure 4-22 Table with gridlines drawn

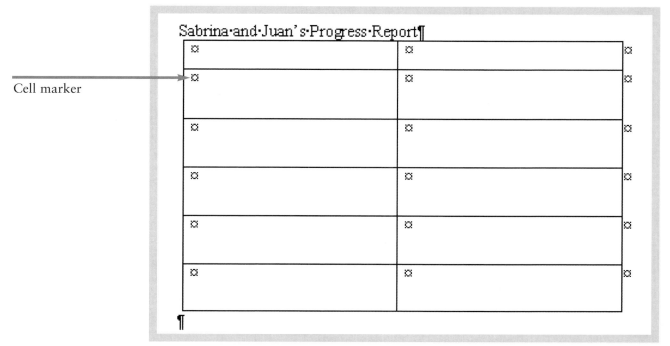

Cell marker

Drawing a Table
(continued)

Do It!

9 Click  to turn off the Draw Table tool.

10 Select the line of text above the table, cut it, and paste it into cell A1.

11 Click next in the Selection bar next to Row A to select cells A1 and B1.

12 Click the Merge Cells button on the Tables and Borders toolbar. Cells A1 and B1 are combined into one cell.

13 With the merged cell still selected, click the Italic button. The text in the selected cell is italicized. Click in cell A2 to place the insertion point there and deselect cell A1. The table should resemble **Figure 4-23**.

14 Type Task in cell A2.

15 Press [Tab] to move the insertion point to cell B2.

16 Type Completed by in cell B2.

17 Use the Selection bar to select Row 2 of the table, and then click the Underline button. A line is placed beneath all text in the row.

18 Consult **Figure 4-24** to fill in the rest of the table, then save it as Progress Table.

More

You can activate the Draw Table tool to add more gridlines to a table at any time. You can also remove gridlines, thereby eliminating rows and/or columns, by clicking the Eraser button on the Tables and Borders toolbar. Simply click on a gridline with the Eraser tool selected to remove the line.

As you have seen, you can apply font formats to text in a table just as you would in a normal document. Most formatting options you have seen applied to text in other scenarios are available in tables as well including alignment, font, font size, and font color. You can even rotate text in a cell by clicking the Text Direction button on the Tables and Borders toolbar.

Figure 4-23 Merged cell with font format applied

Sabrina·and·Juan's·Progress·Report¶		⌧
⌧		
⌧	⌧	⌧
⌧	⌧	⌧
⌧	⌧	⌧
⌧	⌧	⌧
⌧	⌧	⌧

Figure 4-24 Completed table

Sabrina·and·Juan's·Progress·Report¶		⌧
⌧		
Task⌧	Completed·by⌧	⌧
Main·text⌧	Sabrina⌧	⌧
Additional·text/stats⌧	Juan⌧	⌧
Table/chart⌧	Juan⌧	⌧
Editing/formatting⌧	Both⌧	⌧

Practice

Use the Draw Table tool to create a table that will allow you to plot statistics from a survey in which subjects were asked to name their favorite season.

Hot Tip

You can transform an existing table into plain text and vice-versa by using the Convert command on the Table menu.

Adding Borders and Shading

Concept

Previously in this lesson you enhanced the appearance of a table using the AutoFormat command, which allows you to apply a predetermined set of formats to a table. Although the AutoFormat does offer some options, the degree of control it permits is not great. Just as the Draw Table command gives you greater control over the structure of a table, the Table Properties command opens the door to numerous options for enhancing the appearance of a table.

Do It!

Juan would like to add a customized border and shading to his table.

1. Progress Table should still be the active document. Click Table on the menu bar, highlight Select, and then click Table on the submenu. The entire table will be selected.

2. Click Table again, then click Table Properties. The Table Properties dialog box will open to the Table tab.

3. Click the Borders and Shading button [Borders and Shading...] at the bottom of the tab. The Borders and Shading dialog box opens to the Border tab, shown in **Figure 4-25**.

4. In the Setting section of the tab, click the All option.

5. In the Style box, click the third option, tightly spaced dashes.

6. Click the drop-down arrow at the right edge of the Color box to open a color palette. Then click the blue square.

7. Click the drop-down arrow at the right edge of the Width box to open a list of line weights. Then select the 2¼ pt option.

8. Check the Preview on the right side of the tab to see what the border you have created looks like. Click [OK] to close the Borders and Shading dialog box.

9. Click [OK] to close the Tables and Properties dialog box.

10. Click a blank area of the document to deselect the table, which should now appear like the one in **Figure 4-26**.

Figure 4-25 Border tab of Borders and Shading dialog box

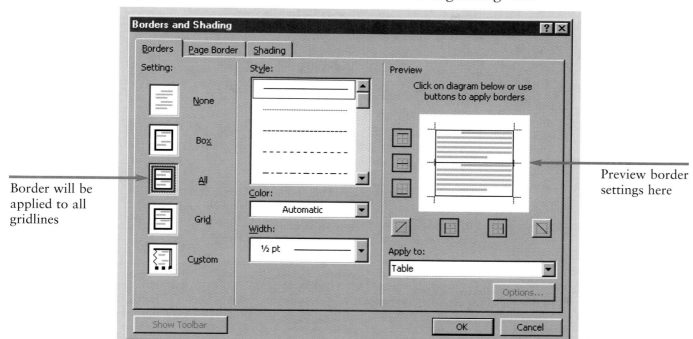

Border will be
applied to all
gridlines

Preview border
settings here

Figure 4-26 Table with border applied

Sabrina and Juan's Progress Report¶ ¤	
Task¤	Completed·by¤
Main·text¤	Sabrina¤
Additional·text/stats¤	Juan¤
Table/chart¤	Juan¤
Editing/formatting¤	Both¤

Adding Borders and Shading (continued)

Do It!

11 Click inside cell A1 to activate the cell.

12 Click the arrow on the right edge of the Shading Color button 🎨▾ on the Tables and Borders toolbar. The Shading Color palette will appear.

13 Click the Gray-30% square (the last square in the first row). Word shades the active cell with the color you selected, as shown in **Figure 4-27**.

14 Click in the Selection bar next to Row 2 to select the entire row.

15 Shade Row 2 with the color Red.

16 Select Row 4.

17 Click Edit, then click Repeat Shading Color to shade the selected row like Row 2. If the Repeat command does not appear right away, leave the Edit menu open for a few seconds until it expands and the command is added.

18 Select Row 6.

19 Press the key combination [Ctrl]+[Y] on the keyboard, which is a shortcut for the Repeat command.

20 Deselect the table, which should now resemble **Figure 4-28**.

21 Save your changes and close the document.

More

The border options you applied in this Skill can also be accessed from the Tables and Borders toolbar. Likewise, you will find the shading options you applied from the toolbar on the Shading tab of the Borders and Shading dialog box. If you choose More Fill Colors on the Shading Color palette, you can create custom colors by changing the intensities of a standard color's components. The Page Border tab, also in the Borders and Shading dialog box, allows you to add a border to the entire page rather than just to a table.

Figure 4-27 Gray-30% shade applied to cell A1

Sabrina·and·Juan's·Progress·Report¶ ¤	
Task¤	Completed·by¤
Main·text¤	Sabrina¤
Additional·text/stats¤	Juan¤
Table/chart¤	Juan¤
Editing/formatting¤	Both¤

Figure 4-28 Red shade applied and repeated

Sabrina·and·Juan's·Progress·Report¶ ¤	
Task¤	Completed·by¤
Main·text¤	Sabrina¤
Additional·text/stats¤	Juan¤
Table/chart¤	Juan¤
Editing/formatting¤	Both¤

Practice

Return to the file PRAC4-6, which includes a table that you AutoFormatted. Change the alternating shaded rows to blue and orange, and the borders around the first and last rows to dashed lines. Save the file as PRAC4-10.

Hot Tip

The listing of the Repeat command on the Edit menu will change to include the action that will be repeated when you execute the command. You can only repeat the action you performed most recently.

Shortcuts

Function	Button/Mouse	Menu	Keyboard
Insert a Table	▦	Click Table, then click Insert Table	
Insert a row above the selected row	Right-click the selected row, then click Insert Rows (Or click ▤)	Click Table, then click Insert Rows	
Insert a column to the left of the selected column	Right-click the selected column, then click Insert Columns (Or click ▦)	Click Table, then click Insert Columns	
Delete the selected row	Right-click the selected row, then click Delete Rows	Click Table, then click Delete Rows	[Shift]+[Delete]
Delete the selected column	Right-click the selected column, then click Delete Columns	Click Table, then click Delete Columns	[Shift]+[Delete]
Align selected text in a cell or paragraph to the left	▤		[Ctrl]+[L]
Align selected text in a cell or paragraph to the right	▤		[Ctrl]+[R]
Center selected text in a cell or paragraph	▤		[Ctrl]+[E]
Justify selected text in a cell or paragraph	▤		[Ctrl]+[J]
Repeat last action		Click Edit, then click Repeat (action name)	[Ctrl]+[Y]

Identify Key Features

Name the items indicated by callouts in Figure 4-29.

Figure 4-29 Identifying components of a table

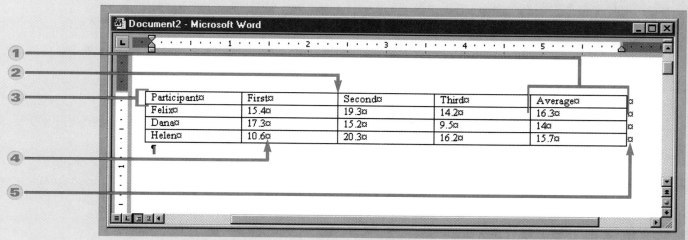

Select The Best Answer

6. Indicates a selected chart
7. An order in which data can be sorted
8. Appears when you right-click a table
9. Explains the symbols and colors being used in a chart
10. Visible boundary between cells in a basic table
11. An existing worksheet that becomes part of Word
12. What Word uses to calculate data
13. The basic unit of a table
14. Enhances the information presented in a table
15. Rearranging data in a table by category
16. A graphic representation of a table

a. Descending
b. Gridlines
c. Table shortcut menu
d. Hatched border
e. Legend
f. Embedded object
g. Formatting
h. Cell
i. Formula
j. Chart
k. Sorting

Quiz (continued)

Complete the Statement

17. The Insert Table command:

    a. Creates a table based on the Normal template

    b. Creates a table based on dimensions you choose

    c. Pastes data from the Clipboard into a table

    d. Replaces the desktop with a tabletop

18. To move the insertion point to the next cell in the current row:

    a. Press [End]

    b. Use the right arrow key on the keyboard

    c. Press [Tab]

    d. Double-click the table

19. D14 refers to:

    a. The fourteenth cell in the fourth column

    b. The fourteenth cell in the fourth row

    c. A formula

    d. A document designation for a Word table

20. Paragraphs and table columns both have:

    a. Page numbers

    b. Selection bars

    c. Gridlines

    d. Cell markers

21. The first step in creating a chart from a selected table is:

    a. Clicking the Chart button

    b. Pressing [Ctrl]+[F8]

    c. Clicking Insert, then clicking Chart

    d. Clicking Insert, then clicking Object

22. The Chart legend:

    a. Is about the ChartWizard

    b. Must be created in Excel and inserted into the Word document containing the chart it belongs with

    c. Contains the Color buttons

    d. Explains the meaning of colors used in the chart

23. An equal sign must be written before a formula or Word will:

    a. Read the data as a label and not perform any calculations

    b. Use the wrong data to perform the calculations

    c. Use the right data, but perform the calculations incorrectly

    d. Do nothing

24. You may delete columns by accessing the:

    a. Table menu

    b. Tools menu

    c. Edit menu

    d. Format menu

25. To sort data in a table you should:

    a. Open the Sort dialog box, and use it to sort the data

    b. Cut and paste all of the information you would use to sort the data

    c. Sort it yourself on a piece of scrap paper before entering the data on the computer

    d. You must access a program other than Word

Interactivity

Test Your Skills

1. Open a new document and create a table:

   a. Open a new Word document.

   b. Click Table, then click Insert Table to open the Insert Table dialog box.

   c. Create a table that is 4 rows by 5 columns.

2. Add data to the table:

   a. Enter a name into each of the lower three cells in the leftmost column.

   b. Insert a number between 1 and 100 into each of the three cells to the right of each name, for a total of nine cells.

   c. Label the cells in the top row as follows: Name, March, April, May, and Average.

3. Average the columns and sort the table:

   a. Position the insertion point in the second cell down in the last column, which is cell E2.

   b. Click Table, then click Formula to open the Formula dialog box.

   c. Enter the formula =AVERAGE(B2:D2) into the Formula text box and press [Enter].

   d. Repeat the last three steps for the other two cells in the Average column, making sure that you are using the correct cell references for the appropriate calculation.

   e. Sort the table in the order of descending Average.

4. Format the table:

   a. Place the insertion point within the table and click Table, then click Table AutoFormat.

   b. Select a table format that you like and check the boxes that you want in the Formats to Apply section of the dialog box.

   c. Make sure that both the Heading Rows and First Column check boxes are checked in the Apply Special Formats To section of your dialog box and press [Enter].

   d. Shade the first row of the table with Gray-15% and apply a green, Box border to the entire table.

   e. Save the document to your student disk as Test 4.

5. Create a chart from an existing table:

   a. Select the table you created above.

   b. Create a chart using an appropriate type for the data.

   c. Edit and format the chart as necessary.

   d. Save the document as Test 4-Chart.

Interactivity (continued)

Problem Solving

1. Using the skills you learned in Lesson 4, create a chart from the table in the document Test 4, which you made in the previous section. Accept the default Chart type, and try to make the chart clear and precise. When you have finished modifying the chart, save the document to your student disk as Solved 4.

2. Create a table to help calculate the grade point averages of the students you have been tutoring over the last two years.

a. Calculate the Grade Point Average for every student, over the two-year period.

b. Calculate the GPA for every semester that you tutored those students.

c. Calculate the overall GPA, including every student, over the two-year period.

Student	Semester 1	Semester 2	Semester 3	Semester 4
Steven	3.6	3.1	4.0	2.7
Sarah	3.3	3.9	3.5	3.0
Donny	2.8	2.3	2.4	3.7
Melanie	3.1	1.4	2.9	2.5
Ray	1.7	2.6	2.0	3.1

3. As the leader of a public relations team, you are responsible for your employees business expenses. Create a table to calculate information about their expenses over the first half of the year. Format all dollar amounts with dollar signs and two decimal places.

a. Figure out the total each employee spent.

b. Figure out the total the entire team spent over the six-month period.

c. Figure out the average amount spent by each employee over the six-month period.

d. Figure out the average amount spent by the team every month.

e. Turn the table you created into a Chart. Use the default Chart type to create a chart representing the table you created. Make any modifications on the chart you feel are necessary to make it as easy to understand as possible.

Employees	Jan	Feb	Mar	Apr	May	June
Kit	213	306	176	314	86	103
Pam	143	94	207	77	289	304
Joe	332	256	317	258	112	128

▶ Formatting Text with Columns

▶ Making Bulleted and Numbered Lists

▶ Adding Borders and Shading to Text

▶ Working with Section Breaks

▶ Inserting the Date and Time

▶ Inserting Headers and Footers

▶ Shrinking a Document to Fit

▶ Modifying Page Numbers

▶ Changing Page Orientation

▶ Using Special Formatting Effects

L E S S O N

ADVANCED FORMATTING

Once you have learned the basic elements of formatting, you can utilize some of Word's more advanced formatting options. With a little practice, you will be able to create documents with columns, stylized lists, headers and footers, and formatted page numbers. Word also allows you to achieve greater flexibility in designing documents by letting you break them up into distinct sections with fundamentally different formatting.

Columns permit you to create professional-looking newsletters and similar documents. By using section breaks, you can format different sections of your text with different numbers of columns. Inserting section breaks also permits you to start page numbers over again at a specific point in a document. The actual text of your documents can be formatted in a number of ways to improve its organization and effectiveness. If you use lists in your document, you can format them with bullets or numbers to demarcate the individual list items. Insert headers and footers to enter text that needs to appear on every page of a document. You can even insert the current date without typing it, and set it to update automatically each time you open the document.

Word also allows you to shrink a document slightly to make it fit on fewer pages. Depending on what type of document you are creating, you may want to change the orientation of a page so that it frames your text more appropriately.

Case Study:
Juan has written the text for a club newsletter, but has not yet formatted it as such. He will use columns, bulleted and numbered lists, section breaks, and various other techniques to format the text into the correct configuration. Then, he will use Word to create an electronic greeting card to send to his friend Sabrina, who was successful in her job search.

 # Formatting Text with Columns

Concept

Some types of documents, whether for traditional or practical reasons, function better on a printed page when organized into columns. Word allows you to start a document with multiple columns, or convert existing text into columns. A Word document may make use of up to thirteen columns, with text flowing freely from one to the next as you add and edit it.

Do It!

Juan wants to format the text he has written for a newsletter into columns.

1. Open the student file Doit5-1 and save it to your student disk as Club News.doc.

2. Click File, then click Select All to select the entire document.

3. Click the Justify button ▦ on the Formatting toolbar. The text is realigned so that each paragraph is flush against both the left and right margins. This is accomplished by adjusting the spaces between words, and it will be carried over so that each paragraph is flush against both borders of each column as in a newspaper.

4. Select all the text in the document by clicking just before the first word, The, and dragging to just after the word scale at the end of the document. The blank lines before and after the text should not be selected.

5. Click Format, then click Columns. The Columns dialog box, shown in **Figure 5-1**, will appear. The dialog box offers several preset column formats.

6. Click the Three option in the Presets box. A blue border will appear around your choice indicating its selection, and the Preview box will reflect the format change.

7. Click the Line between check box so that a solid horizontal line will appear between each column and the one next to it.

8. Click ▭ OK ▭ to apply the column formatting to the document. With the text deselected and scrolled to the top, the document should like **Figure 5-2** (with non-printing characters showing).

More

Selected text can be quickly formatted in up to seven columns by clicking the Columns button ▦ on the Standard toolbar and dragging down and to the right to select the desired number of columns from the menu that appears. When the insertion point is in a part of a document that is in column format, the ruler displays the column boundaries with markers. You can resize columns by dragging these markers on the ruler, or by using the Width and spacing section of the Columns dialog box. In many senses, each column in a document acts like a normal, single column document. For example, columns can be formatted with any of the text alignment options available in a normal document, and text wrapping occurs in columns just as in a normal document. In addition, just as the Selection bar runs down the left side of a single column document, the left side of each column in a multicolumn document has its own Selection bar for selecting lines or paragraphs of text in that column.

Figure 5-1 Columns dialog box

Selected Preset

Use this section to make precise adjustments to column width and spacing

Remove check mark to revise columns individually

Select 1-13 columns

Preview of selected column format

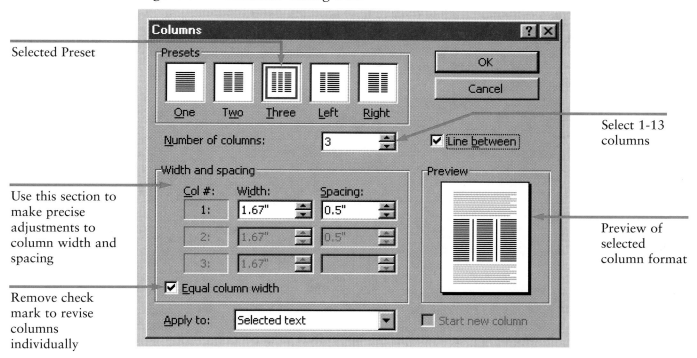

Figure 5-2 Document formatted with three columns

Line between columns

Section break inserted because lines above were not formatted with columns

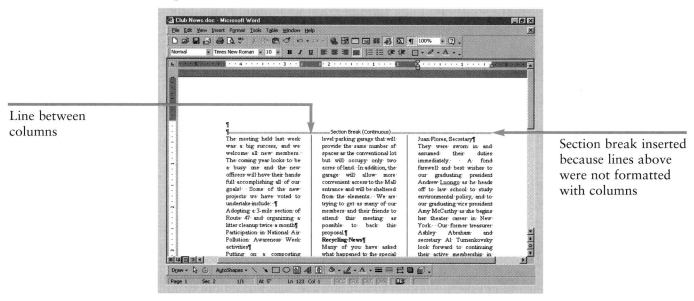

Practice

Open the student file **Prac5-1** to practice formatting text with columns.

Hot Tip

Unless the print is very small, it is usually not a good idea to format text into more than three columns on a vertically oriented page, as the text wrapping becomes erratic and the columns become difficult to read.

Word 2000

Making Bulleted and Numbered Lists

Concept

You can improve the appearance and effectiveness of a list by formatting it with bullets or numbers. A bullet is a dot or other symbol used to separate items in a list when their sequence is unimportant. Numbers can be used in a list when its purpose is to express a sequence of events or rank order.

Do It!

Juan wants to convert one section of his newsletter into a numbered list and another into a bulleted list.

1. Select the second, third, and fourth paragraphs in the first column of Club News, from Adopting a 3-mile section to late this spring., as seen in **Figure 5-3**.

2. Click the Numbering button on the Formatting toolbar. Word indents the three paragraphs and numbers them consecutively (see the right portion of **Figure 5-3**).

3. Select the four lines, split over the second and third columns, that list the club's new officers. Remember that holding down [Shift] allows you to add to a selection of text after you have released the mouse button.

4. Click the Bullets button on the Formatting toolbar. The names are indented and a bullet appears in front of each one.

5. Click to save the changes you have made. Remember, the Save command and button allow you to overwrite the previous version of a file with the new one. Use Save As to create a new version of a file in a different location or with a new name.

More

When text is formatted into a bulleted or numbered list, one bullet or number is assigned to each paragraph. Once inserted, a bullet or number is not part of the text, and cannot be selected. It can, however, be deleted, and in the case of a numbered list, the list will correct itself so that there is no gap in the numbers. For example, if item 7 in a list is deleted, all numbers in the list higher than 7 will decrease by one so that the list does not go from 6 to 8. To remove bullets or numbers from lists you have formatted, select the list and click either the Numbering or Bullets button to remove whichever style has been applied to the text. Word can also create a numbered or bulleted list as you enter the information. If you precede the first item in a list with the number 1, for example, Word will automatically format the list with an indent and start the next line with the number 2 when you press [Enter].This feature is called AutoFormat As You Type, and it also formats such items as common fractions and ordinals (1st, 2nd, 3rd, etc.) automatically.

The Bullets and Numbering dialog box, accessible from the Format menu, gives you more more options for formatting lists. You can choose from several different kinds of bullet and numbering styles on the Bulleted and Numbered tabs, respectively. The Outline Numbered tab, shown in **Figure 5-4**, allows you to create outline style numbered lists, such as those that would appear at the front of a thesis. You can customize these lists so that the headings used in the outline are attached to heading styles used in your document, thereby creating a multileveled outline.

Figure 5-3 Creating a numbered list

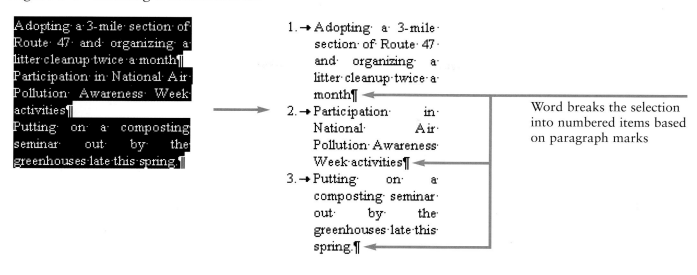

Word breaks the selection into numbered items based on paragraph marks

Figure 5-4 Bullets and Numbering dialog box

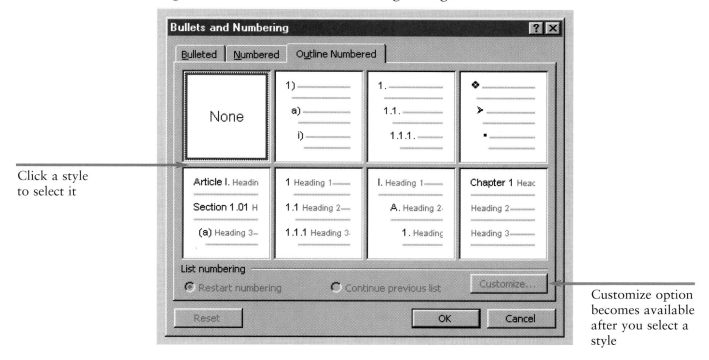

Click a style to select it

Customize option becomes available after you select a style

To practice making bulleted and numbered lists, open the student file **Prac5-2**.

Hot Tip

AutoFormat As You Type options can be controlled from the **AutoFormat** and **AutoFormat As You Type** tabs in the **AutoCorrect** dialog box, which is accessible from the **Tools** menu.

 # Adding Borders and Shading to Text

Concept

Borders and shading can be used to make a document more visually appealing and call attention to important items. Borders are lines that are added on any side or all around selected text to set it apart from surrounding text. Shading is a background color or pattern that is applied behind text to emphasize it.

Do It!

Juan wants to add a title with a border to his newsletter and add shading to the document's topic headings.

1. Place the insertion point on the very top line of Club News.doc, above the section heading and the columns. Then type The Recycled Paper in 20 pt, Times New Roman text.

2. Select the words you just typed, click Format, and then click Borders and Shading. The Borders and Shading dialog box, will open to the Borders tab (see **Figure 5-5**).

3. In the Setting: section of the dialog box, click the Shadow option. Then click the drop-down arrow in the Width: box and select 1 pt.

4. Click ⬛ OK ⬛ to apply the border. The deselected title should look like **Figure 5-6**.

5. Select the bold heading Awareness Update in the first column. Then open the Borders and Shading dialog box again and click the Shading tab.

6. In the Patterns section of the tab, click the drop-down arrow in the Style: box, and then select the 20% option from the drop-down list.

7. Click ⬛ OK ⬛ to apply the shading.

8. Select the bold heading Recycling News in the second column.

9. Press [Ctrl]+[Y], the keyboard shortcut for the Repeat command, to apply the same shading to this selection.

10. Repeat the above step to shade the two remaining bold headings, New Officers! and Meeting Notice. See **Figure 5-7** to confirm that you have shaded correctly.

11. Save the changes you have made to the document.

More

When creating a border, you can choose lines of various weight, color, and style. Once you have become comfortable with applying borders, you may want to work more quickly than the Borders and Shading dialog box will allow. If this is the case, click View, highlight Toolbars, and then click Tables and Borders. The Tables and Borders toolbar permits you to take advantage of many of the options in the Borders and Shading dialog box with the click of a button.

Figure 5-5 Borders and Shading dialog box

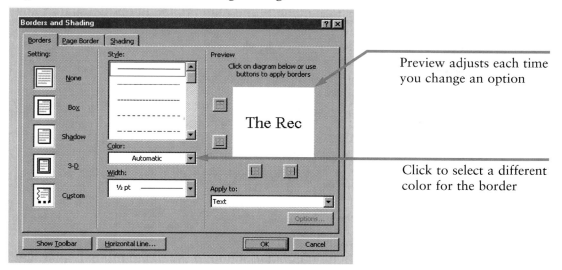

Preview adjusts each time
you change an option

Click to select a different
color for the border

Figure 5-6 Text with border applied

Shadow style border

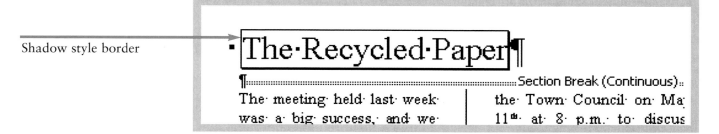

Figure 5-7 Text with shading applied

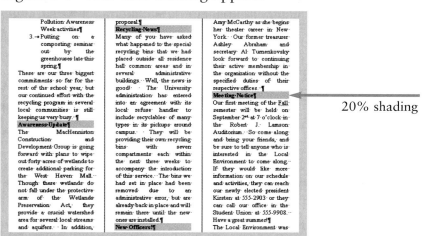

20% shading

Practice

Open the student file **Prac5-3** to practice
appying borders and shading.

Hot Tip

You can also apply borders to a selection
by clicking the arrow on the right edge of
the **Borders** button on the Standard
toolbar.

 # Working with Section Breaks

Concept

A section break is the boundary between two distinct sections of a document. Dividing a document into sections is helpful when two or more parts of it require different formatting, such as a different number of columns. Using a section break is also an effective technique for adding clarity to a document.

Do It!

Juan wants to format the last paragraph of the newsletter so that it stretches across the bottom of the page in a single wide column.

1. Position the insertion point at the beginning of the last paragraph of the document, just before The Local Environment....

2. Click Insert, then click Break. The Break dialog box appears, as seen in **Figure 5-8**.

3. Click the Continuous radio button under the heading Section break types.

4. Click ⬛ OK to insert the break. The last paragraph is now split among the three columns at the bottom of the document (do not worry if your document has spilled over to a second page).

5. Select the entire last paragraph by clicking just before The Local Environment... in the Selection bar and dragging straight down to select the rest of the paragraph and the remaining blank lines in the document.

6. Click the Columns button ⬛ on the Standard toolbar. A menu of columns appears beneath the button. Move the mouse pointer over the leftmost column. It will become highlighted and the words 1 Column will appear below it (see **Figure 5-9**).

7. Click the mouse button to format the selected paragraph into one column.

8. With the paragraph still selected, click the Align Left button ⬛ to change the text from justified to left-aligned.

9. If there are extra blank lines above the paragraph, delete them (there should be one blank line between the three column section and the one column section). Delete unnecessary blank lines below the paragraph as well. The new section, with non-printing characters hidden, should resemble **Figure 5-10**.

10. Save the changes you have made to the document.

More

When you first formatted the newsletter into three columns, a section break should have appeared before and after the selected text, as blank lines at the beginning and end still retained their original single column formatting. Word automatically inserts a section break when column formatting is changed in only part of a document. Different sections in a document do not have to have different formatting. Sometimes treating similarly formatted text as separate sections makes it easier to work with them within the scope of a large document.

Figure 5-8 Break dialog box

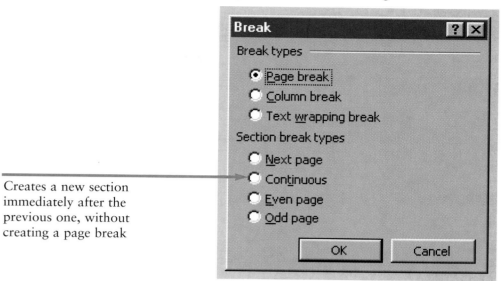

Creates a new section
immediately after the
previous one, without
creating a page break

Figure 5-9 Using the Columns button

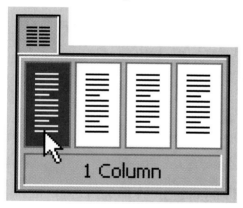

Figure 5-10 New section after a section break

> The Local Environment was founded in 1983 by students who felt a need to express their concerns over the way in which people interact with their surroundings on a daily basis. The organization is dedicated to environmental protection and maintenance on a community scale.

Practice

To practice working with sections and section breaks, open the student file **Prac5-4**.

Hot Tip

If you cannot see a section break or are unsure of exactly where it occurs click the **Show/Hide** button ¶ on the Standard toolbar.

Inserting the Date and Time

Concept

Word allows you to insert the current date and time in a variety of combinations and formats without having to type it yourself. This can be especially helpful if you are required to follow a certain standard when dating documents. Word will let you set this standard as your default expression of the date, time, or both, in a number of short and long formats.

Do It!

Juan will insert the date below the title of his newsletter.

1. Place the insertion point on the blank line between the newsletter's title and the main body text.

2. Click Insert, then click Date and Time. The Date and Time dialog box will appear, as shown in **Figure 5-11**. The available data and time formats are displayed in a list box on the left side of the dialog box.

3. Click the third format listed, which includes the month written in full, the date followed by a comma, and the year written in four digits.

4. Click the Default button Default... . A message box appears asking if you want to change the default date format to the one you selected.

5. Click Yes . From now on, this format will already be selected when you open the Date and Time dialog box, allowing you to insert the date more quickly.

6. Click OK to insert the date. The dialog box closes and today's date appears where you placed the insertion point (see **Figure 5-12**).

7. Click next to the date in the Selection bar to select it.

8. Click B to change the date to bold text.

9. Save the changes you have made to the document.

More

The Symbol command on the Insert menu allows you to insert a wide variety of symbols into a document. On the Symbols tab of the Symbol dialog box, shown in **Figure 5-13**, you can select any of the fonts available on your system. The grid below will then display all of the symbols associated with the selected font. Once you have selected a symbol, you can add it to the AutoCorrect dialog box, assign a keyboard shortcut to it, or simpy insert it. The Special Characters tab of the Symbol dialog box lists a number of common symbols, such as the Registered symbol ®, and their keyboard shortcuts.

Figure 5-11 Date and Time dialog box

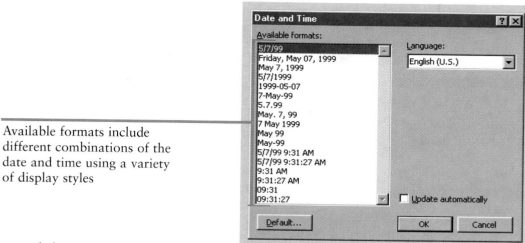

Available formats include different combinations of the date and time using a variety of display styles

Figure 5-12 Inserted date

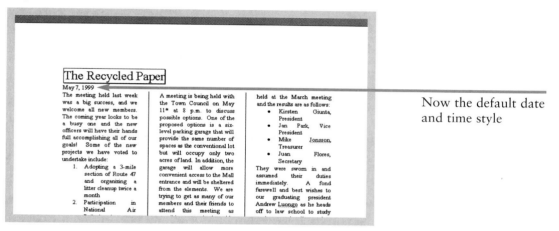

Now the default date and time style

Figure 5-13 Symbol dialog box

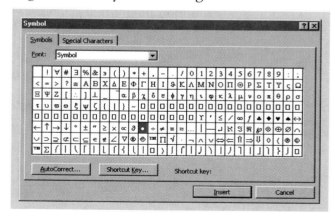

Open the student file **Prac5-5** to practice inserting the date and time.

If you check the **Update automatically** check box in the Date and Time dialog box, the date you insert will change to the current date each time you open the document.

 **Inserting Headers and Footers**

Concept

A header is text that appears above the main text but below the top margin of the document. A footer is similar, but appears at the bottom of the document, just above the bottom margin. Headers and footers are often used to display information that will appear on every page of a document such as the date, page numbers, or the author's name.

Do It!

Juan wants to include the volume and issue number of his newsletter in the header, and place his name in the footer as the author.

1. Click View, then click Header and Footer. The Header text box and the Header and Footer toolbar will appear. The Footer text box is also visible if you scroll to the bottom of the page. The insertion point is in the Header box.

2. Type Volume VII, Issue 8 in the Header box, as shown in **Figure 5-14**.

3. Click the Switch Between Header and Footer button 🖳 on the Header and Footer toolbar. Word automatically scrolls to the bottom of the page so the Footer box is visible and places the insertion point there.

4. Click the Insert AutoText button [Insert AutoText ▾] on the Header and Footer toolbar. A menu of AutoText entries appears.

5. Click Created by on the menu, and then type Juan Flores to finish the footer text.

6. Select the footer text. Then, click [I] and [☰] on the Formatting toolbar to italicize the footer text and right align it.

7. Click [Close] on the Header and Footer toolbar. In Print Layout View, the footer should like **Figure 5-15**.

8. Save the document.

More

Headers and footers are not always appropriate for every page in a document. For example, the first page of many types of documents will not use a header. To eliminate the header from the first page of a document, or use a different header on the first page, click the Page Setup button 🗐 on the Header and Footer toolbar. The Page Setup dialog box will open to the Layout tab, as shown in **Figure 5-16**. If you activate the Different first page check box in the Headers and Footers section of the tab, you can edit the first page header and footer independently.

By default, headers and footers will always appear on printed pages. However, they will not always be visible when you are working in Word. They are only visible when you are working in Print Layout View or Print Preview mode. To view headers and footers in other views, select the Headers and Footers command from the View menu. If you are already in Print Layout View, you can edit your headers and footers by double-clicking them.

Figure 5-14 Inserting a header

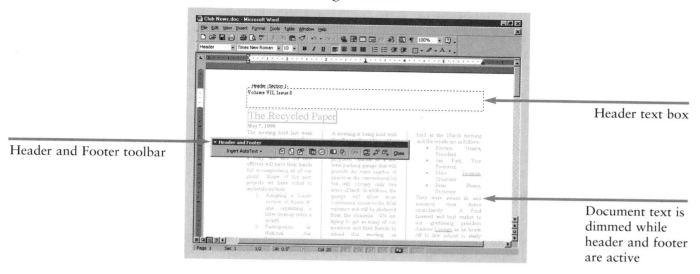

Header text box

Header and Footer toolbar

Document text is dimmed while header and footer are active

Figure 5-15 Finished footer in Print Layout View

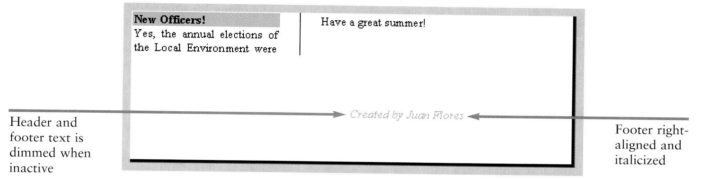

Header and footer text is dimmed when inactive

Footer right-aligned and italicized

Figure 5-16 Layout tab

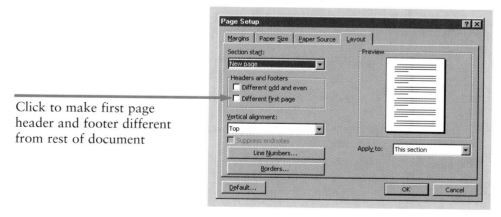

Click to make first page header and footer different from rest of document

Practice

Open the student file **Prac5-6** to practice working with headers and footers.

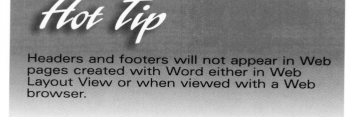

Hot Tip

Headers and footers will not appear in Web pages created with Word either in Web Layout View or when viewed with a Web browser.

Shrinking a Document to Fit

Concept

If a small portion of a document does not fit on a page, Word can systematically revise it to eliminate the extra page. To do this, Word shrinks aspects of the document such as text size and line spacing until text that has spilled over is able to fit on fewer pages.

Do It!

Juan wants to shrink his newsletter so that it fits on a single page.

1. Click the Print Preview button on the Standard toolbar. The Print Preview screen appears with the newsletter displayed on two pages. If you do not see two pages, click the Multiple Pages button and select 1 x 2 Pages.

2. Click the Shrink to Fit button on the Print Preview toolbar. Word reduces elements of the document so that it fits on one page (see **Figure 5-17**). Notice that the section break after the three column section has been preserved.

3. Click Close on the Print Preview toolbar to exit Print Preview.

4. Click on the Standard toolbar to print a copy of Juan's newsletter.

5. Save the final changes to the newsletter.

6. Close the file.

More

When attempting to shrink a document, Word will only change certain aspects of it, and then only to a certain degree. If too much text is on the extra page to allow Word to shrink the document in a practical manner, the program will notify you that it is unable to complete the command. The document will be left unchanged. Sometimes, especially with longer documents, the Shrink to Fit command can remove several pages from the total number of pages in the document.

Figure 5-17 Newsletter shrunk to fit one page

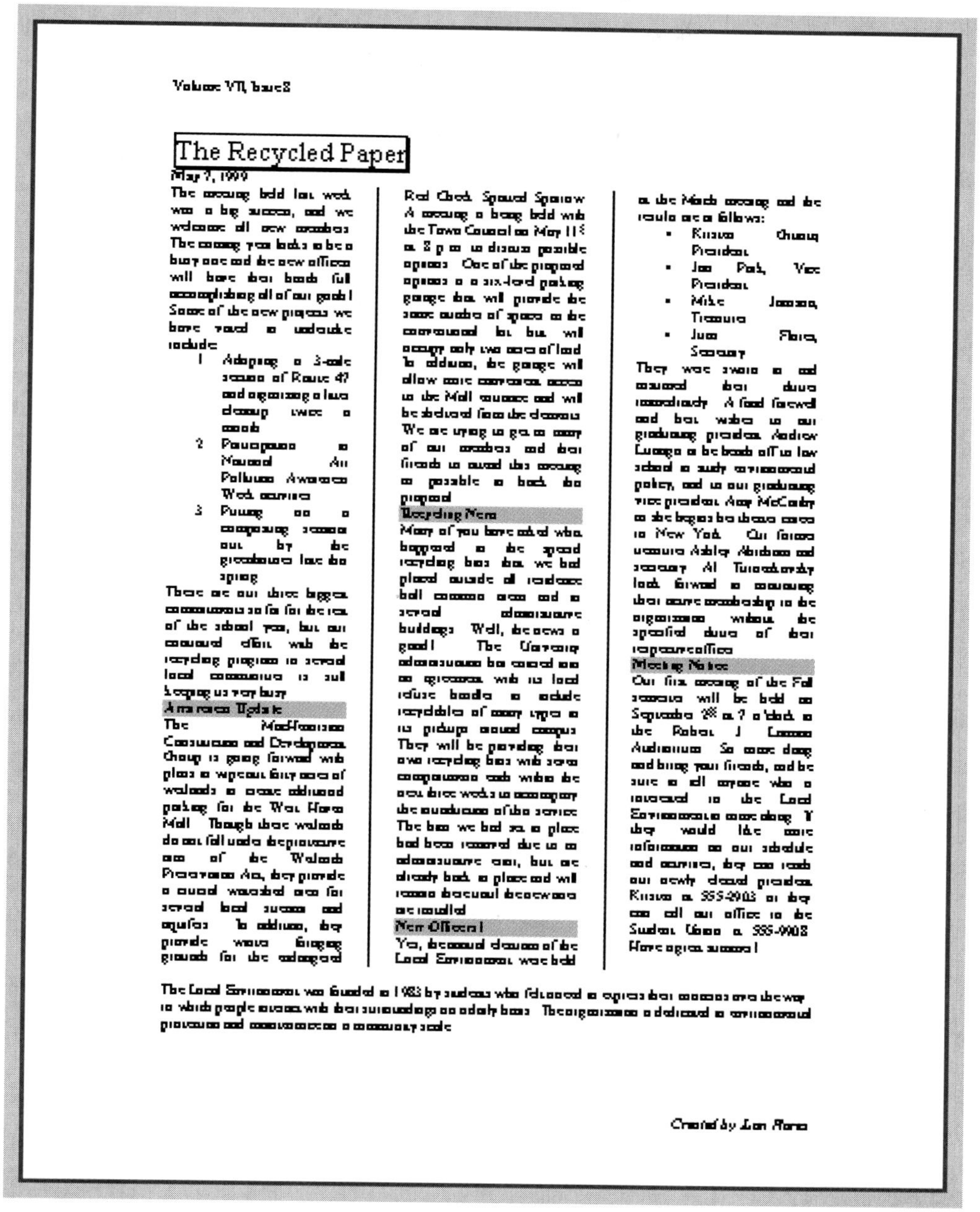

Practice

Open the student file **Prac5-7** to practice shrinking a document to fit a particular space.

Hot Tip

On occasion you may be able to use the Shrink to Fit command more than once to further reduce the length of a document.

Modifying Page Numbers

Concept

In an earlier Lesson, you learned how to insert page numbers in a document. You were also introduced to the idea of formatting page numbers to fit their usage or location in a document. Even after you have already inserted page numbers, you can still modify them to keep in step with changes you have made to a document.

Do It!

Juan needs to change the page numbering scheme in a document he is preparing as a final paper for his Social and Cognitive Psychology course. He wants to start the page numbering over on the last page, and format that page's number differently than the other page numbers because it is in a separate section of the document.

1. Open the file Doit5-8 from your student disk and save it as Psych Final. You will need to work in Print Layout View to complete this exercise.

2. Scroll down to the bottom of the first page. You will see that the document uses standard Arabic numerals centered in the footer as page numbers.

3. Click Edit, then click Go To. The Find and Replace dialog box will open to the Go To tab as shown in Figure 5-18. The Go To tab allows you to jump quickly to a specific place or item in a document.

4. Click Section in the Go to what: scrolling list box to select it. Notice that the label of the text box to the right changes to Enter section number.

5. Click in the Enter section number: box and type 2.

6. Click the Go To button [Go To] . Word takes you directly to Section 2 of the document, which was created when Juan inserted a Next Page section break to place his References section by itself on the last page of the paper.

7. Close the Find and Replace dialog box.

8. Click Insert, then click Page Numbers to open the Page Numbers dialog box.

9. Click the Format button [Format...] to open the Page Number Format dialog box.

10. Click the Number format: drop-down list arrow and select lowercase Roman numerals (i, ii, iii...) from the drop-down list.

11. Click the Start at: radio button in the Page numbering section of the dialog box, and leave the Start at: value set to i.

12. Click [OK] to close the Page Number Format dialog box, and then again to close the Page Numbers dialog box.

13. Scroll down to the bottom of page 5 to view the new page number (shown in Figure 5-19), and then check to see that the previous page is still numbered as 4.

14. Save the document to preserve the new numbering, and then close it.

Figure 5-18 Go To tab

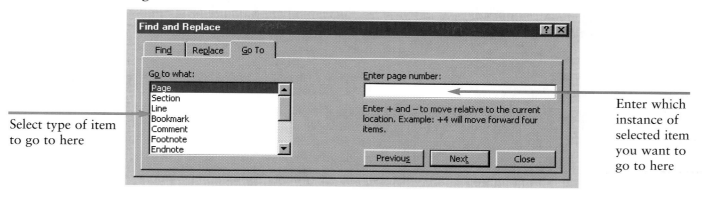

Select type of item to go to here

Enter which instance of selected item you want to go to here

Word 2000

Figure 5-19 Reformatted page number

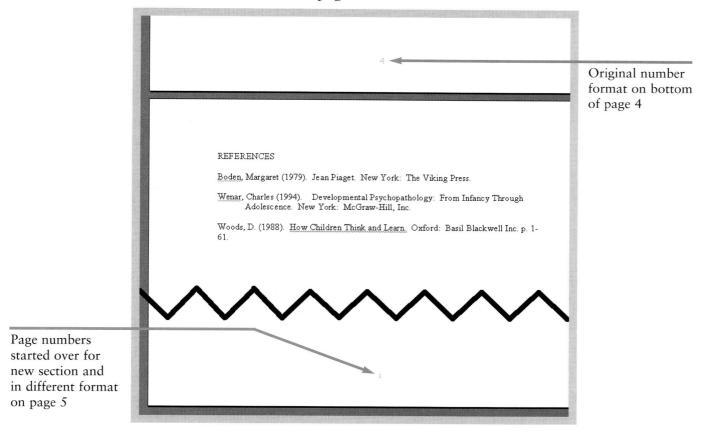

Original number format on bottom of page 4

Page numbers started over for new section and in different format on page 5

REFERENCES

Boden, Margaret (1979). Jean Piaget. New York: The Viking Press.

Wenar, Charles (1994).   Developmental Psychopathology: From Infancy Through Adolescence. New York: McGraw-Hill, Inc.

Woods, D. (1988). How Children Think and Learn. Oxford: Basil Blackwell Inc. p. 1-61.

Practice

Open the student file **Prac5-8** to practice modifying page numbers.

Hot Tip

To change the default font or font size for page numbers, choose the **Style** command from the **Format** menu and select the **Page Number** style. You can also reformat page numbers by selecting them in the header or footer in which they are located.

 # Changing Page Orientation

Concept

You may be accustomed to working with word processing documents that are set up the way you would normally hold a piece of 8½" by 11" paper: with vertical height longer than the horizontal width. This in known as Portrait page orientation because the paper resembles the shape of a portrait that you might see hanging on a wall. Word allows you to change the orientation of a document from Portrait to its opposite, Landscape. In Landscape page orientation, the horizontal width of the page is greater than its vertical height.

Do It!

Juan is creating an electronic greeting card, which he will e-mail to his friend Sabrina to congratulate her on her new job. He has realized that he must change the page orientation to Landscape in order for the card to fit on the page correctly.

1. Open the file Doit5-9 from your student disk and save it as Card.doc.

2. Click the Zoom box `100%` drop-down arrow and select 50% from the drop-down list. You should now be able to see most of the document in the document window without scrolling, and that some of the text does not fit on the page (see **Figure 5-20**).

3. Click File, then click Page Setup. The Page Setup dialog box will open.

4. Click the Paper Size tab to bring it to the front of the Page Setup dialog box.

5. In the Orientation section of the tab, click the Landscape radio button, shown in **Figure 5-21**. The preview will change to show that the width of the page is now greater than its height.

6. Click `OK` to change the page orientation. The document should now look like **Figure 5-22**.

7. Save your changes.

More

The document with which you were working in the above exercise was created using text boxes. You can create a text box by clicking the Text Box button 📰 on Word's Drawing toolbar. The middle text box was formatted with a border while the two outer text boxes were formatted with a No Line border. The text in these two boxes was aligned vertically in the text box using the Change Text Direction button 📖 on the Text Box toolbar, which you can access when a text box is selected. The Text Direction command is also available on the Format menu. Text boxes are useful because they can be formatted and moved independently of the rest of a document.

You can control the vertical alignment of text in relation to a page from the Layout tab in the Page Setup dialog box. The Vertical alignment: drop-down list box allows you to align text with the top, bottom, or center of the page. You can also justify text vertically, spacing it equally between the top and bottom of the page.

Figure 5-20 Card.doc in Portrait orientation at 50%

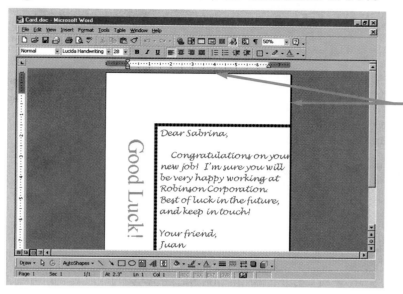

Portrait orientation:
vertical height greater
than horizontal width

Figure 5-21 Selecting Landscape

Figure 5-22 Card.doc changed to Landscape

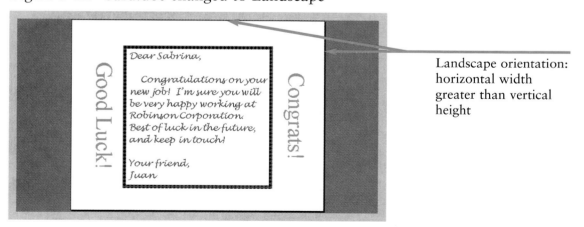

Landscape orientation:
horizontal width
greater than vertical
height

Practice

Open the student file **Prac5-9** to practice
changing the page orientation of a Word
document.

Hot Tip

Page orientation and vertical alignment can
be applied to the whole document or to the
portion of the document beginning where
the insertion point is located.

Using Special Formatting Effects

Concept

You have seen how formatting text can enhance the appearance of documents. Character formats such as bold, italic, and underline can help to emphasize the most important points in an academic or business document. Word offers even more character formats, which may not be appropriate for the types of documents mentioned above, but can contribute greatly to your work when you are using the program as a desktop publishing tool.

Do It!

Juan wants to add special character effects to the electronic card he created for Sabrina.

1. Click the text Good Luck! on the left side of Card.doc to activate its text box.

2. Triple-click (three rapid clicks) inside the text box to select all of its text.

3. Click Format, then click Font. The Font dialog box appears. The Effects section of the dialog box allows you to apply special formatting such as strikethrough marks, small caps, superscript text, and subscript text to your document.

4. Click the Shadow check box to activate it. The Preview window displays the added effect on the selected text, as shown in **Figure 5-23**.

5. Click the Text Effects tab to bring it to the front of the Font dialog box. The Text Effects tab offers a number of animation effects that you can apply to your text.

6. Click Sparkle Text in the Animations: list box to select it. Again, the Preview window demonstrates the added effect.

7. Click [OK] to add both the Shadow and Sparkle Text effects to the text you selected. If your computer has a slower processor, the Sparkle Text effect might take a moment to initiate.

8. Select the right-hand text box that contains the word Congrats! and apply the same two formatting effects.

9. When you are finished, the card should resemble **Figure 5-24**.

10. Save and close the document.

More

E-mailing a Word document with Word 2000 has become a simple operation due to the application's close association with Outlook 2000, a mail and news reader and contact manager that is also part of the Office 2000 suite. To e-mail the active document, simply click the E-mail button 📧 on Word's Standard toolbar. Assuming you have it installed and configured correctly, Outlook 2000 will launch automatically and open a New Message window. The text of your Word document will appear as the body of the message, and the file name will appear as the Subject of the message. All you have to do is enter an e-mail address and click the Send button. You can also use Outlook to attach entire Word files to an e-mail message.

Figure 5-23 Previewing font effects

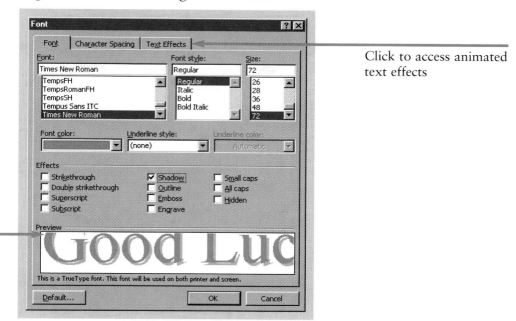

Click to access animated text effects

Preview of selected text with Shadow effect applied

Figure 5-24 Document with Shadow and Sparkle Text effects

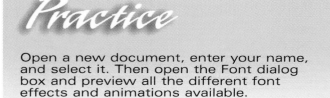

Practice

Open a new document, enter your name, and select it. Then open the Font dialog box and preview all the different font effects and animations available.

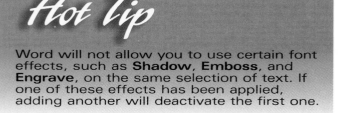

Hot Tip

Word will not allow you to use certain font effects, such as **Shadow**, **Emboss**, and **Engrave**, on the same selection of text. If one of these effects has been applied, adding another will deactivate the first one.

Shortcuts

Function	Button/Mouse	Menu	Keyboard
Save changes to an existing file	💾	Click file, then click Save	[Ctrl]+[S]
Justify text	▤		[Ctrl]+[J]
Left align text	▤		[Ctrl]+[L]
Right align text	▤		[Ctrl]+[R]
Repeat last action	↻	Click Edit, then click Repeat (action name)	[Ctrl]+[Y]
Bold text	**B**	Click Format, then click Font	[Ctrl]+[B]
Italicize text	*I*	Click Format, then click Font	[Ctrl]+[I]
Go To	⊙ ⟶ →	Click Edit, then click Go To	[Ctrl]+[G]

Identify Key Features

Name the items indicated by callouts in **Figure 5-25**.

Figure 5-25 Items in a newsletter

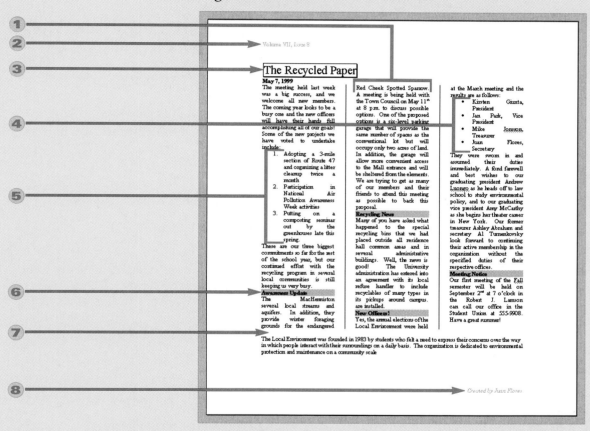

Select The Best Answer

9. A character used to separate items in a list

10. Allows different column formats to exist in one document

11. Trims line spacing, font size, and other formatting characteristics to reduce the amount of space required by a document

12. Format used for sequential or ranked items

13. Contains the Date and Time command

14. Text that appears between the top margin and the main text

15. Text that appears above the bottom margin, but below the main text

16. Allows you to jump to a specific item in a document

17. Allows you to change page orientation

a. Footer

b. Numbered List

c. Page Setup dialog box

d. Header

e. Bullet

f. Go To command

g. Insert menu

h. Shrink to Fit

i. Section break

Quiz (continued)

Complete the Statement

18. Lines of different colors and styles that can be inserted around paragraphs are called:

    a. Margins

    b. Borders

    c. Section breaks

    d. Text boxes

19. The Line between option is available:

    a. On the Standard toolbar

    b. On the Formatting toolbar

    c. In the Borders and Shading dialog box

    d. Columns dialog box

20. The Numbering button can be found on the:

    a. Standard toolbar

    b. Formatting toolbar

    c. Header and Footer toolbar

    d. Vertical alignment drop-down list

21. To insert a different header on the first page of a document, open the Page Setup dialog box to the:

    a. Layout tab

    b. Margins tab

    c. Paper Source tab

    d. Header and Footer tab

22. The Start at: option for beginning a new section with a specific page number is found in the:

    a. Page Number dialog box

    b. Page Setup dialog box

    c. Break dialog box

    d. Page Number Format dialog box

23. To access the Shrink to Fit feature, you must be in:

    a. Normal View

    b. Print Layout View

    c. Print Preview mode

    d. Header and Footer View

24. If you want a document's horizontal width to be greater than its vertical height, change it to:

    a. Print Preview mode

    b. 50% its original size

    c. Landscape page orientation

    d. Portrait page orientation

25. You can control the vertical alignment of text in relation to a page from the Page Setup dialog box's:

    a. Layout tab

    b. Margins tab

    c. Paper Size tab

    d. Paper Source tab

Interactivity

Test Your Skills

1. Format a document with columns:

   a. Open the student file SkillTest5 and save it to your student disk as Test5.

   b. Select all the text in the document.

   c. Format the document into two columns, and include a vertical line between them.

2. Create a bulleted list:

   a. Scroll down the first page of the document until you can see the paragraph that begins No Person shall be a Representative... in the first column (it is the first paragraph after the one that begins Section 2).

   b. Select this paragraph and the remaining paragraphs in Section 2 through ...Power of Impeachment. in the second column.

   c. Convert the selection into a bulleted list.

3. Add borders and shading to text:

   a. Select the first paragraph of the document (We the People...).

   b. Apply a 3 pt, Box border to the selected paragraph.

   c. Apply 15% shading to the same paragraph.

4. Insert a section break:

   a. Use the Go To dialog box to go to page 8 of the document.

   b. Place the insertion point in front of the paragraph that begins In witness whereof... near the bottom of the second column.

   c. Insert a Continuous section break at the insertion point.

   d. Format the portion of the document from the section break through the end into one column.

5. Insert a header, footer, and the date in a document:

   a. Switch to Header and Footer View.

   b. Use the Date and Time command to insert the date in the header using the default date format.

   c. Edit the header so that it reads September 17, 1787 instead of the current date.

   d. Switch the document's footer and enter TYS 5.

   e. Align the footer to the right.

Interactivity (continued)

6. Shrink a document to fit a space:

   a. Switch to Print Preview.

   b. Click the Multiple Pages button and select 2 x 3 Pages.

   c. Click the Shrink to Fit button to reduce the document's length by one page.

   d. Close Print Preview

7. Insert page numbers in a document:

   a. Open the Page Numbers dialog box.

   b. Align the page numbers to the left.

   c. Format the page numbers as lowercase letters.

8. Add special character formatting:

   a. Scroll to the beginning of the document and select the title text The U.S. Constitution.

   b. Open the Font dialog box and change the font color of the selected text to blue.

   c. Add the Emboss effect to the selected text.

   d. Save the changes you have made to the document.

Problem Solving

1. Before heading off to law school next year, you are getting your feet wet with a paid internship at a prestigious law firm. Some of the partners have recognized your ability to be an impartial observer and have asked you to assist them in determining certain company policies. Among the policies in question is that of Internet usage, including e-mail, web browsing, and newsgroup reading. Your assignment is to create a succinct one page document that discusses the pros and cons of allowing employees Internet access. Your document should consist of two columns (one for pro and one for con), with a section break between the title of the document and the columns. Format the title of the document with a border, and the text in the pro and con columns as numbered lists. Also, add a header that includes your name and the date.

2. As the Assistant Principal at a high school, you have decided to try to improve relations among students and between students and faculty by creating a bimonthly school newsletter. This first issue will serve as the template for all future issues, so take care in designing it. Include sections for news from each class, your own column, a guest column, and a calendar of upcoming events. When you insert the date, be sure to set it to update automatically so you will not have have to worry about changing it for each issue. Use the footer to insert an Issue and Volume number. Feel free to shrink the newsletter should it run slightly over onto an extra page.

Interactivity (continued)

Problem Solving

3. Open the student file Problem Solving 5a and save it to your student disk as Solved5a. Then, use the skills you learned in Lesson 5 and previous lessons to format the document so it resembles **Figure 5-26.**

Figure 5-26 Advanced Formatting

THE BILL OF RIGHTS

Amendment I

Congress shall make no law respecting an establishment of religion, or prohibiting the free exercise thereof; or abridging the freedom of speech, or of the press; or the right of the people peaceably to assemble, and to petition the government for a redress of grievances.

Amendment II

A well regulated militia, being necessary to the security of a free state, the right of the people to keep and bear arms, shall not be infringed.

Amendment III

No soldier shall, in time of peace be quartered in any house, without the consent of the owner, nor in time of war, but in a manner to be prescribed by law.

Amendment IV

The right of the people to be secure in their persons, houses, papers, and effects, against unreasonable searches and seizures, shall not be violated, and no warrants shall issue, but upon probable cause, supported by oath or affirmation, and particularly describing the place to be searched, and the persons or things to be seized.

Amendment V

No person shall be held to answer for a capital, or otherwise infamous crime, unless on a presentment or indictment of a grand jury, except in cases arising in the land or naval forces, or in the militia, when in actual service in time of war or public danger; nor shall any person be subject for the same offense to be twice put in jeopardy of life or limb; nor shall be compelled in any criminal case to be a witness against himself, nor be deprived of life, liberty, or property, without due process of law; nor shall private property be taken for public use, without just compensation.

Amendment VI

In all criminal prosecutions, the accused shall enjoy the right to a speedy and public trial, by an impartial jury of the state and district wherein the crime shall have been committed, which district shall have been previously ascertained by law, and to be informed of the nature and cause of the accusation; to be confronted with the witnesses against him; to have compulsory process for obtaining witnesses in his favor, and to have the assistance of counsel for his defense.

Amendment VII

In suits at common law, where the value in controversy shall exceed twenty dollars, the right of trial by jury shall be preserved, and no fact tried by a jury, shall be otherwise reexamined in any court of the United States, than according to the rules of the common law.

Amendment VIII

Excessive bail shall not be required, nor excessive fines imposed, nor cruel and unusual punishments inflicted.

Amendment IX

The enumeration in the Constitution, of certain rights, shall not be construed to deny or disparage others retained by the people.

Amendment X

The powers not delegated to the United States by the Constitution, nor prohibited by it to the states, are reserved to the states respectively, or to the people.

Interactivity (continued)

Problem Solving

4. Open the student file **Problem Solving 5b** and save it to your student disk as **Solved5b**. Then, use the skills you learned in Lesson 5 and previous lessons to format the document so it resembles **Figure 5-27**.

Figure 5-27 Advanced Formatting

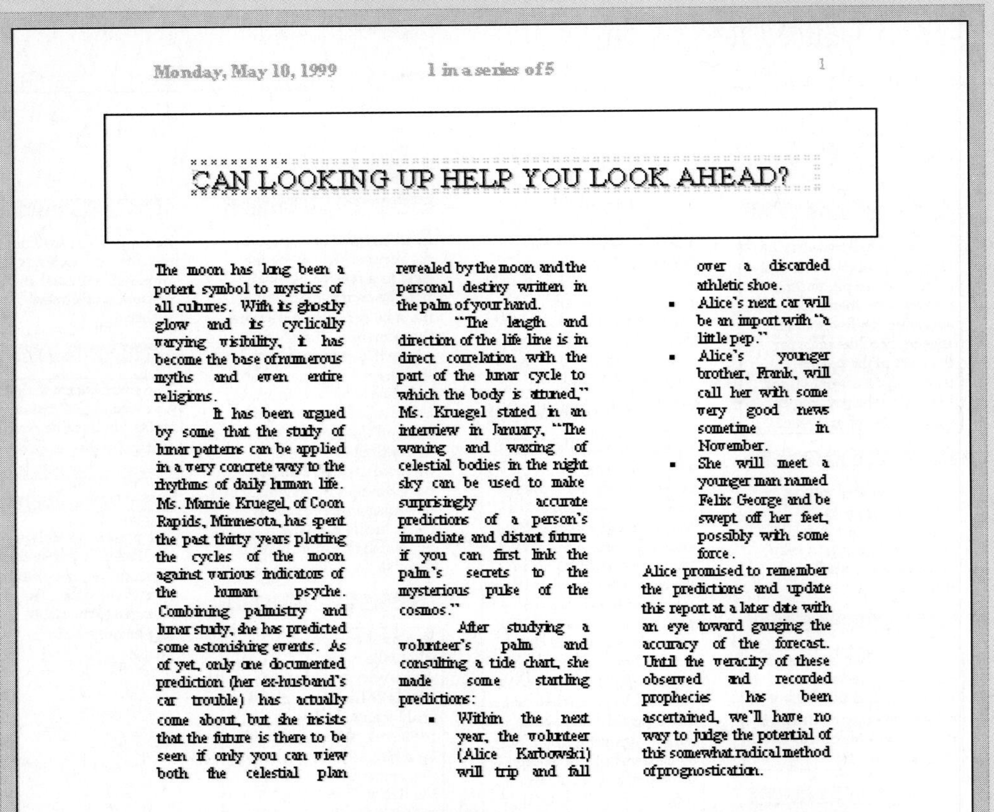

Monday, May 10, 1999 1 in a series of 5 1

CAN LOOKING UP HELP YOU LOOK AHEAD?

The moon has long been a potent symbol to mystics of all cultures. With its ghostly glow and its cyclically varying visibility, it has become the base of numerous myths and even entire religions.

It has been argued by some that the study of lunar patterns can be applied in a very concrete way to the rhythms of daily human life. Ms. Mamie Kruegel, of Coon Rapids, Minnesota, has spent the past thirty years plotting the cycles of the moon against various indicators of the human psyche. Combining palmistry and lunar study, she has predicted some astonishing events. As of yet, only one documented prediction (her ex-husband's car trouble) has actually come about, but she insists that the future is there to be seen if only you can view both the celestial plan revealed by the moon and the personal destiny written in the palm of your hand.

"The length and direction of the life line is in direct correlation with the part of the lunar cycle to which the body is attuned," Ms. Kruegel stated in an interview in January. "The waning and waxing of celestial bodies in the night sky can be used to make surprisingly accurate predictions of a person's immediate and distant future if you can first link the palm's secrets to the mysterious pulse of the cosmos."

After studying a volunteer's palm and consulting a tide chart, she made some startling predictions:

- Within the next year, the volunteer (Alice Karbowski) will trip and fall over a discarded athletic shoe.
- Alice's next car will be an import with "a little pep."
- Alice's younger brother, Frank, will call her with some very good news sometime in November.
- She will meet a younger man named Felix George and be swept off her feet, possibly with some force.

Alice promised to remember the predictions and update this report at a later date with an eye toward gauging the accuracy of the forecast. Until the veracity of these observed and recorded prophecies has been ascertained, we'll have no way to judge the potential of this somewhat radical method of prognostication.

Other than the somewhat mysterious synchronization of the lunar cycle and the human female reproductive cycle, little factual correlation has been found to back up the claims of self-proclaimed lunar-palmist prophets. Much more evidence exists pointing toward a solar connection, however. This makes logical sense, as the primary solar cycle dictates the daily schedule of most plants and animals. Likewise, the secondary (seasonal) solar cycle dictates the fluctuation in locale climates and is therefore easily shown to influence the life of terrestrial organisms. Other than creatures dependent upon tidal fluctuation and those with a certified breeding pattern linked to the lunar cycle (most noticeably in Pacific corals), no concrete evidence has thus far been gathered to support these conclusions. Of course, this ignores entirely the skepticism surrounding palmistry, which has been largely regarded as bogus since the establishment turned from phrenology in the mid nineteenth century.

▷ **Applying a Character Style**

▷ **Creating Your Own Character Style**

▷ **Applying an AutoFormat**

▷ **Using the Style Gallery**

▷ **Editing a Style**

▷ **Applying Styles on the Paragraph Level**

▷ **Displaying a Style Report**

▷ **Browsing by Style**

▷ **Finding and Replacing a Style**

▷ **Using the Tabs Command**

▷ **Using Click and Type**

L E S S O N

USING CHARACTER STYLES AND AUTOFORMAT

All documents have style. This is not to say that all documents are stylish. Style is the manner in which a document is formatted. Stylish is how you use those styles. Word 2000 has many style options available to help make your documents more stylish.

When using the Word program, you have three options: you can accept the default style that Word uses to create documents; you can choose a different, preset style from Word; or you can create your own style and apply it to sentences, paragraphs, or the entire document. Further, using AutoFormat, you can access the Style Gallery and choose from casual, elegant, or professional templates to apply to your document.

Word 2000 also offers features designed to help you keep track of the styles you use in documents. By displaying a Style Report, you can see at a glance how every line is formatted is a document. Using the Find and Replace feature, you can find one example of a style, or all examples of a style, and replace them with different styles.

Becoming familiar with the ways in which Word handles style will give you the power to make the documents you create more effective, more professional, and ultimately, more stylish.

Case Study:
In this lesson, Sabrina, who has begun her work as Assistant to the Director of Public Relations at Robertson Corporation, will create several documents and format various elements within those documents. Along the way, she will examine the AutoFormat feature and the Style Gallery. She will create her own style for use in the document, as well as apply a character style, browse by style, display a Style Report, edit a style, and find and replace styles. Finally, she will discover the uses of Click and Type, and how to format using the Tabs command.

Applying a Character Style

Concept

A character style is a set of stored text format settings. Using character styles, you can format text quickly and consistently.

Do It!

Sabrina will apply a new character style to a portion of her document.

1. Open the student file Doit6-1.

2. Highlight the title of the report, the word by, and Sabrina's name.

3. Click on the Format command in the menu bar.

4. Select Style from the Format menu.

5. When the Styles dialog box opens (see **Figure 6-1**), check the List: box to make sure it is set to All Styles. If not, use the drop-down arrow to do select the All Styles option.

6. Scroll through the Styles list box until you find the Title style. Highlight it by clicking once on it.

7. Click Apply to make the change. Your document should now look like **Figure 6-2**.

8. Save the document as MassMail.doc.

More

Applying a character style using the Format Styles option has one distinct advantage: it can save you time. If you tried to change the title of the document manually, you would have to highlight each word, change the font, change the alignment, change the font size, make the print bold, etc.

Figure 6-1 Style dialog box

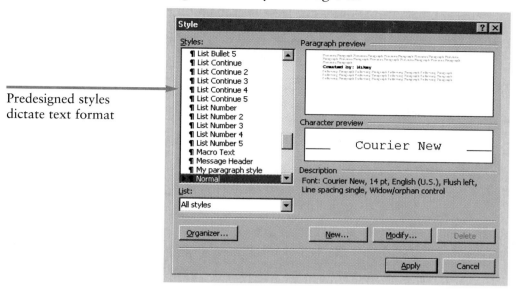

Predesigned styles
dictate text format

Figure 6-2 Document with style change

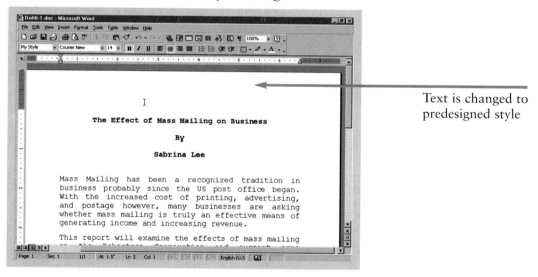

Text is changed to
predesigned style

Practice

Open the student file **Prac6-1** and follow
the instructions.

Hot Tip

An easy way to move in the Style selection
box without using the mouse is to use the
keyboard. Simply press the first letter of
the style you are seeking and Word will
take you immediately to the section of
styles that begin with that letter.

Creating Your Own Character Style

Concept

While Word has many character styles available, they are based on standard usage. Sometimes, you as a user may want a slightly different look than that of a preselected format. Word gives you the option of customizing character styles.

Do It!

Sabrina is not satisfied with the look of the title of her document and will create her own character style and apply it.

1. Open your student file MassMail.doc.

2. Highlight the title of the document: The Effect of Mass Mailing on Business by Sabrina Lee.

3. Click on Format in the menu bar and select Style from the drop-down menu.

4. Click New... in the Style dialog box.

5. The New Style dialog box opens with the Name text box highlighted (see Figure 6-3). Type My Title.

6. Click on the drop-down arrow in the Style Type selection box and select Character.

7. Click Format ▾ button at the bottom of the dialog box. A drop-down list will appear showing the things you can format (see Figure 6-4). Select Font by clicking once on it.

8. The Font dialog box opens (see Figure 6-5) with the Font tab to the front and the current settings highlighted. Scroll through the Font selection window using the scroll arrows until you find the font named Garamond. Click on it to select it.

Figure 6-3 New Style dialog box

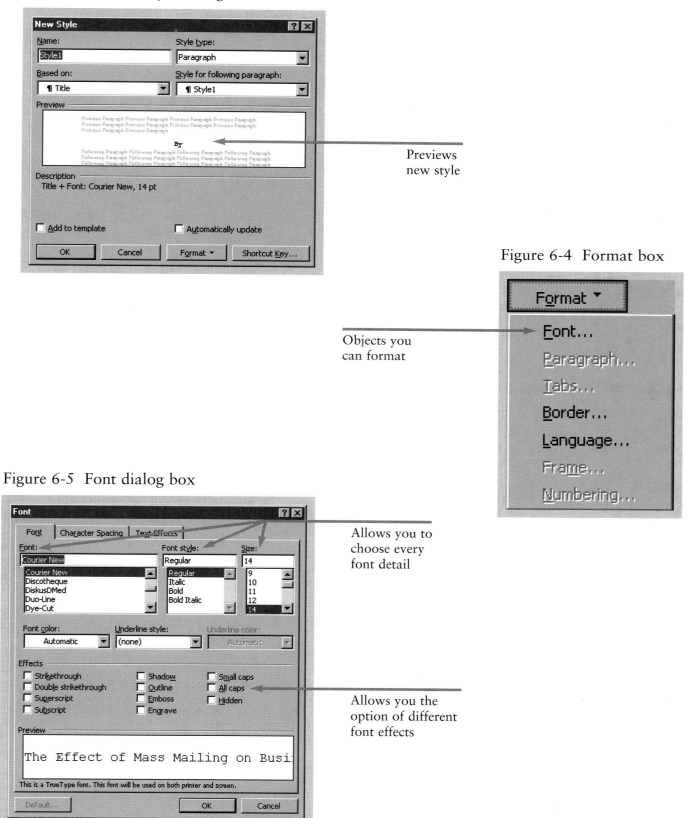

Previews
new style

Figure 6-4 Format box

Objects you
can format

Figure 6-5 Font dialog box

Allows you to
choose every
font detail

Allows you the
option of different
font effects

Word 2000

 # Creating Your Own Character Style (continued)

Do It!

9 Click on Bold Italic in the Font Style selection box. Notice how the Preview window changes to reflect the change in Font style and type.

10 Change the Font Size to 16 by clicking on the number 16 in the Font Size selection box.

11 Click the drop-down arrow in the Underline Style selection box. Select the third line from the top (see **Figure 6-6**).

12 Click [OK]. The New Style dialog box reappears. Select the Add to Template check box. Click [OK].

13 The Style dialog box reappears. Click [Apply]. Your document should now look like **Figure 6-7**.

14 Save your work.

More

Now that you have created and saved this style, you can apply it to any other Word document by highlighting the text and selecting My Style from the Style dialog box.

Figure 6-6 Underline Style box

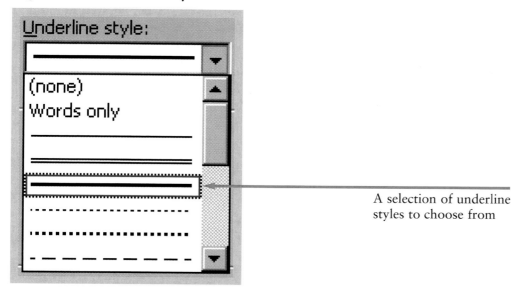

A selection of underline styles to choose from

Word 2000

Figure 6-7 Document with new style

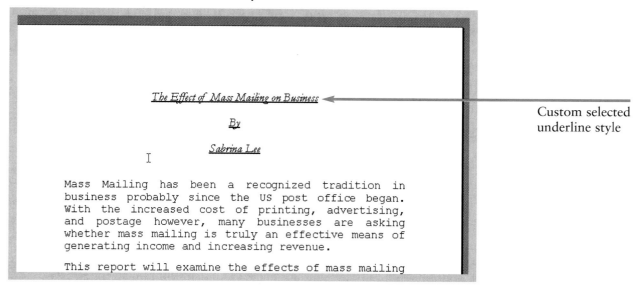

Custom selected underline style

Practice

Open the student file **Prac6-2** and follow the instructions.

Hot Tip

You can change a character style that you have created by clicking on the **Modify** button in the Style dialog box.

WD 6.7

Applying an AutoFormat

Concept

AutoFormat is a convenient tool for applying an entire set of stored formats to a Word document.

Do It!

Sabrina will apply the AutoFormat to her report, and review the changes before accepting the new formatting.

1 Open your file MassMail.doc.

2 Click on Format on the menu bar. If the AutoFormat command does not appear, click on the double set of downward pointing arrows to expand the menu.

3 Select AutoFormat by clicking on it. The AutoFormat dialog box opens (see **Figure 6-8**).

4 Select the radio button for AutoFormat and review each change. Click the Options button [Options...] in the lower-right corner of the dialog box. The AutoCorrect dialog box opens with the AutoFormat tab selected (see **Figure 6-9**).

5 Check to make sure the Preserve Styles option is checked. It must be in order to preserve the formatting of the title.

6 Click [OK] to return to the AutoFormat dialog box.

7 Click [OK] to apply the AutoFormat.

8 After formatting is completed, the AutoFormat dialog box appears giving you the option of accepting, rejecting, reviewing the changes, or selecting from the Style Gallery. Click on [Accept All].

9 Your document should now look like **Figure 6-10**. Save your work as MassMail.doc.

More

If you so choose, you can review each change that the AutoFormat made by clicking on the [Review Changes...] in the AutoFormat dialog box that appears after you apply the AutoFormat. Word will describe each change it made to your document, and give you the option of accepting or rejecting it.

Figure 6-8 AutoFormat dialog box

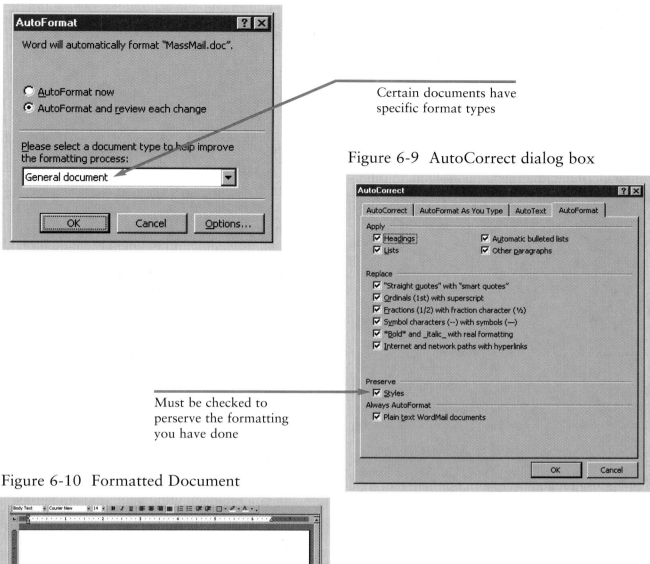

Certain documents have
specific format types

Figure 6-9 AutoCorrect dialog box

Must be checked to
perserve the formatting
you have done

Figure 6-10 Formatted Document

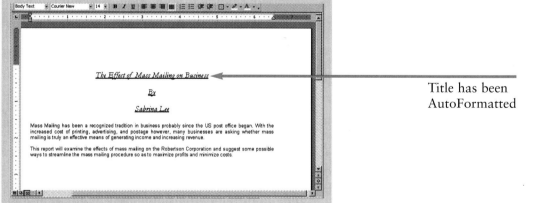

Title has been
AutoFormatted

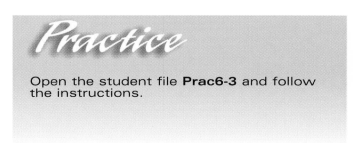

Practice

Open the student file **Prac6-3** and follow
the instructions.

Hot Tip

The drop-down box in the AutoFormat
dialog box allows you to select formatting
for a specific type of document: General
document, Letter, or E-mail.

Using the Style Gallery

Concept

The Style Gallery contains various templates designed to enhance the appearance of documents.

Do It!

Sabrina will use the Style Gallery to give the fax she has written a professional appearance.

1 Open the file Doit6-2.

2 Click on Format in the menu bar.

3 Click on AutoFormat.

4 Select the AutoFormat and review each change radio button.

5 Click ▐ OK ▌.

6 From the AutoFormat dialog box that appears after formatting is completed, click on ▐ Style Gallery... ▌. The Style Gallery dialog box opens (see **Figure 6-11**).

7 From the template selection box on the left side of this box, select the Professional Fax template by clicking on it.

8 Click ▐ OK ▌, and then click ▐ Accept All ▌ in the AutoFormat dialog box.

9 Print the document, and then save it as Fax1.doc.

More

If the template you want to use is not installed on your computer, Word will install it when you ask for it. However, you must have the program disks available for Word to do this.

Figure 6-11 Style Gallery

Previews the
selected template

Lists available
templates

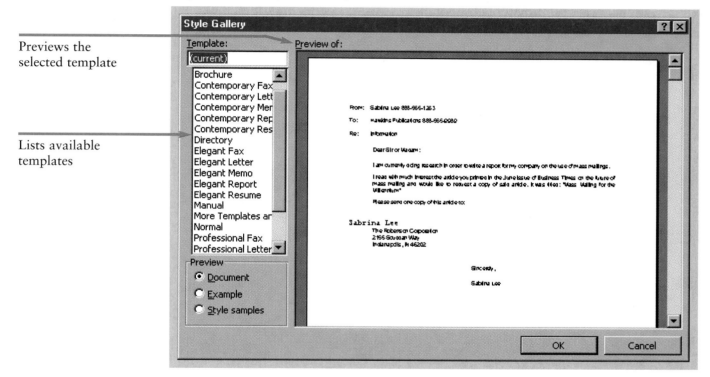

Practice

Open the student file **Prac6-4** and follow
the instructions.

Hot Tip

Another option available in the template
selection box of the Style Gallery is the
Manual template. This feature allows you
to manually configure a template for your
document rather than accepting the
premade templates.

Editing a Style

Concept

Using styles to format text allows you to modify format settings for each occurrence of the style in a document. This is accomplished easily by changing one example of the formatting and applying that change to all others of its type.

Do It!

Sabrina will change a style she has created to make it more useful in the body of her report.

1. Open the file MassMail2.doc and save it on your computer as the same.

2. Find and highlight the first instance of Robertson Corporation in the report. (Hint: check the fourth paragraph)

3. Open the Style box on the Formatting toolbar (see **Figure 6-12**).

4. Scroll and find My Style and click it to apply it to the highlighted text. The text changes to reflect the new style (see **Figure 6-13**).

5. Click on the drop-down arrow in the Font Size box (see **Figure 6-14**).

6. Select font size 12 by clicking once on it.

7. Click the Bold Button once to deselect it.

8. Open the Style box on the Formatting toolbar again, scroll and find My Style, and click on it.

9. A Modify Style dialog box opens (see **Figure 6-15**) asking if you would like to update the current style, or change the highlighted text back to the selected style.

10. Choose Update style to reflect current changes, and then click [OK].

11. Notice that all other text formatted with My Style has changed to reflect the update.

12. Save your work.

More

You can simplify the process for the changes you make to a style by selecting the Automatically update the style from now on selection box in the Modify Style dialog box.

Figure 6-12 Style box

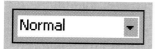

Figure 6-13 Text with new style

Selected text changes
to reflect new style

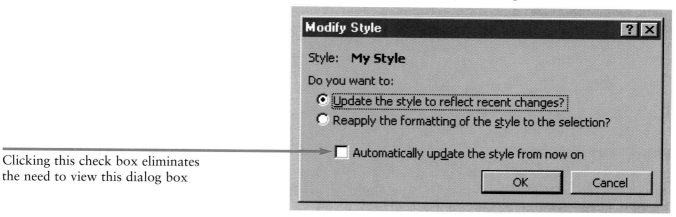

It's not enough to send regular mail. The Internet, through the use of batched addresses, will allow us to reach thousands more potential customers with a cost of just pennies per advertisement. I propose that *Robertson Corporation* take its current mass mailing and send it out to e-mail addresses as well as postal addresses. Using an address service, our company can purchase 10,000 e-mail addresses for as little as $50. To mail 10,000 pieces in the normal manner would cost us $3300 in postage, PLUS the cost of printing.

Figure 6-14 Font Size box

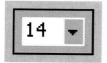

Figure 6-15 Modify Style dialog box

Modify Style

Style: **My Style**

Do you want to:

⦿ Update the style to reflect recent changes?

◯ Reapply the formatting of the style to the selection?

☐ Automatically update the style from now on

OK   Cancel

Clicking this check box eliminates
the need to view this dialog box

Practice

Open the student file **Prac6-5** and follow the instructions.

Hot Tip

You can undo formatting changes to your document by pressing **[Ctrl]+[Z]** immediately after you change the formatting.

 # Applying Styles on the Paragraph Level

Concept

A paragraph style is a set of format settings stored by Word and applied to whole paragraphs. These settings are used to ensure consistent formatting throughout a document.

Do It!

In this lesson, Sabrina will create a new paragraph style and apply it to other paragraphs in her report.

1. Open the student file MassMail3.doc and save it on your computer using the same name.

2. Highlight the first paragraph. Open the Format menu on the menu bar.

3. Click the Style command to open the Style dialog box. Click `New...` in the Style dialog box.

4. In the Name box type: My Paragraph Style. Open the Format menu and select Font. Select Italics from the Font Style selection box. Click `OK` to accept the change.

5. Click `OK` in the Style Dialog box to accept the changes.

6. Click `Apply` in the Style box to accept the changes. The highlighted paragraph should now look like **Figure 6-16**.

7. Highlight paragraph 3. Open the Style box on the formatting toolbar and select My Paragraph Style. Paragraph 3 will change to reflect the new formatting.

8. Reformat paragraph 5 in the same manner. Your report should now look like **Figure 6-17**.

9. Save your work.

More

You can copy styles between documents using the Style organizer, which is available when you are in the Style dialog box. Use the arrows to copy a style from one document to another.

Figure 6-16 Selected paragraph

Mass Mailing has been a recognized tradition in business probably since the US post office began. With the increased cost of printing, advertising, and postage however, many businesses are asking whether mass mailing is truly an effective means of generating income and increasing revenue.

Style is applied to
selected paragraph

Figure 6-17 Reformatted report

Paragraphs may have
styles selectively applied

Mass Mailing has been a recognized tradition in business probably since the US post office began. With the increased cost of printing, advertising, and postage however, many businesses are asking whether mass mailing is truly an effective means of generating income and increasing revenue.

This report will examine the effects of mass mailing on the Robertson Corporation and suggest some possible ways to streamline the mass mailing procedure so as to maximize profits and minimize costs.

It's not enough to send regular mail. The Internet, through the use of batched addresses, will allow us to reach thousands more potential customers with a cost of just pennies per advertisement. I propose that Robertson Corporation take its current mass mailing and send it out to e-mail addresses as well as postal addresses. Using an address service, our company can purchase 10,000 e-mail addresses for as little as $50. To mail 10,000 pieces in the normal manner would cost us $3300 in postage, PLUS the cost of printing.

In a recent article published in Business Times, Arnold Stang proposed that mass mailing would be more cost effective in the future by utilizing the internet. With the advent of the Internet into society in 1990, a whole new avenue of advertising opened up for companies around the world. Not only could companies advertise to local consumers, the Internet allowed them to go global. Going global, according to Business Times, is the hottest trend in marketing.

Looking at it another way, for the same $3300 dollars the Robertson Corporation would spend in the conventional manner, we could purchase over a half million e-mail addresses. And, using a bulk E-mail program, which is readily available for free on the Internet, one person could do the work of 50.

Business Times magazine advises that people begin advertising on the Internet immediately before it becomes glutted with advertisers and consumers become inured to the advertising. I suggest,

Practice

Open the student file **Prac6-6** and follow the instructions.

Hot Tip

You can quickly apply a style by pressing **[Ctrl]+[Shift]+[S]**, typing the name of the style you wish to apply, and pressing **[Enter]** to apply that style.

Displaying a Style Report

Concept

You can view the style of any item in any Word document by placing the insertion point in the item and checking the Style box. However, the easier way to check your document for consistent styling is by using the Style Report.

Do It!

Sabrina will use the Style Report to ensure that her paragraph styles are consistent.

1. Open your MassMail3.doc file. If the MassMail3.doc is not in Normal View, click the Normal View button to the far left of the horizontal scroll bar.

2. Open the Tools menu from the menu bar.

3. Click the Options command. The Options dialog box opens (see **Figure 6-18**).

4. Click the View tab to bring it forward (see **Figure 6-19**).

5. Using the up arrow in the Style area width: box, click until the number in the box is 1".

6. Click [OK]. Your screen should now look like **Figure 6-20**.

More

You can print normally even while the Style area is in view. The Style area is listed in the left margin and will not print. You can also continue to work on your document while the Style area is in view.

Figure 6-18 Options dialog box

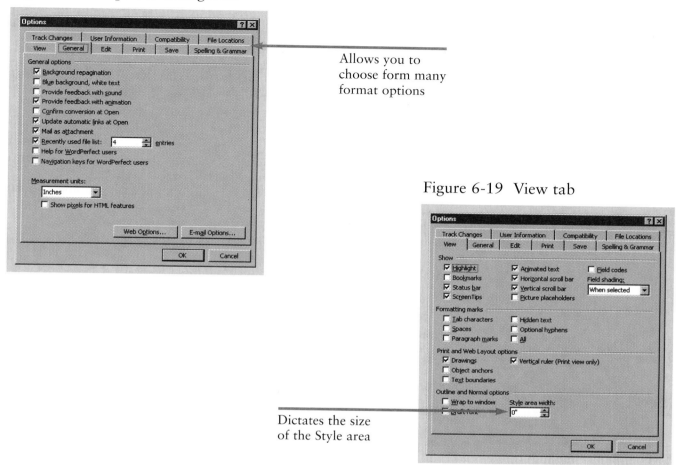

Allows you to choose form many format options

Figure 6-19 View tab

Dictates the size of the Style area

Figure 6-20 Document with Style area

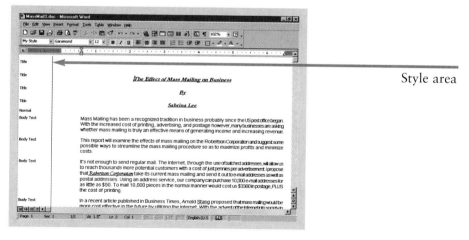

Style area

Practice

Add a Style area to **Malice.doc**.

Hot Tip

To take the Style area away, open the Option dialog box and reset the Style Area width: box to zero inches.

Browsing by Style

Concept

Using Word's Find feature, you can set Word to browse by a particular style thereby allowing you to quickly check your work for consistency.

Do It!

Sabrina will set her Find feature to browse by style, and then will check her report.

1 Press [Ctrl]+[F] to access the Find and Replace feature. The Find and Replace dialog box will open.

2 Click on More ▾ to access more features (see **Figure 6-21**).

3 Click on Format and select Style from the menu. The Find Style dialog box will open (see **Figure 6-22**).

4 Find My Paragraph Style in the selection box and click on it. Click OK to return to the Find and Replace box.

5 Click Find Next . Word will highlight the first paragraph in the report that is formatted in My Paragraph Style.

6 Click Find Next again, and the third paragraph of the report is highlighted.

7 Click Find Next one more time, and the fifth paragraph is highlighted.

8 Click Find Next one last time, and a dialog box appears stating that Word has finished checking the document. Click OK .

9 Leave the Find and Replace dialog box on the screen for the next skill.

More

You should notice that the Previous Page and Next Page buttons below the vertical scroll bar are now blue. This indicates that Word is now programmed to browse by something other than page, which is the default setting. Clicking these buttons will allow you to browse your document by the last object you searched for, in this case, style. In fact, the ScreenTips for these buttons will have changed from Previous Page and Next Page to Previous Find/GoTo and Next Find/GoTo.

Figure 6-21 Find and Replace dialog box

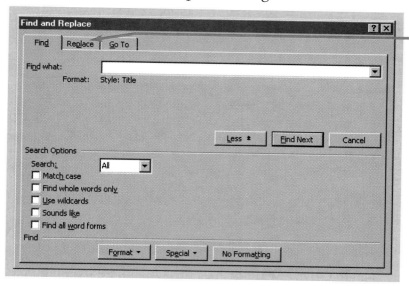

Allows you to find style instances and replace them

Word 2000

Figure 6-22 Find Style dialog box

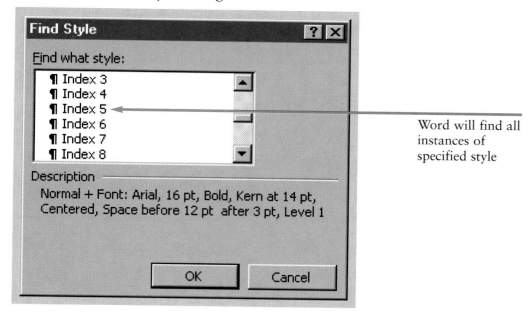

Word will find all instances of specified style

Practice

Using the Find and Replace dialog box, reset it to search by **Body Text** style, and search the document for instances of this style.

Hot Tip

An easy way to change the browse buttons back to normal is to click on the center button and select **Browse by Page** which is represented by a single sheet of paper.

Finding and Replacing a Style

Concept

Using the Find and Replace dialog box, you can find certain formatting types, and replace them with different formatting.

Do It!

Sabrina will use the Find and Replace feature to reformat parts of her document.

1. The Find and Replace dialog box should be on the screen from the last lesson. If it is not, press [Ctrl]+[F] to access it.

2. Click on the Replace tab to bring it forward. (see **Figure 6-23**).

3. While the insertion bar is blinking in the Find what? box, click on Format, and select Style.

4. From the Find Style box, select My Paragraph Style, and click OK .

5. Click once in the Replace With box, and click on Format, and select Style.

6. Find Body Text Style in the Find Style box, select it, and click OK .

7. Click Replace All in the Find and Replace dialog box.

8. Close the Find and Replace dialog box. Your document should now look like **Figure 6-24**.

9. Save your work.

More

While [Ctrl]+[F] is the easiest way to access the Find and Replace feature, there are two other, more standard ways that you should know. The Find feature is available on the edit menu. You can also access it by clicking on the Select Browse Object button on the vertical scroll bar.

Figure 6-23 Find and Replace dialog box

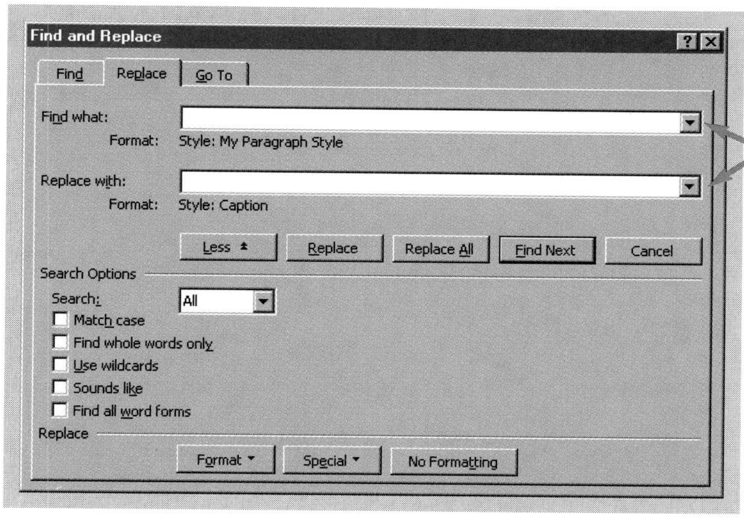

Allows you to specify what is to be replaced by what

Figure 6-24 Document with styles replaced

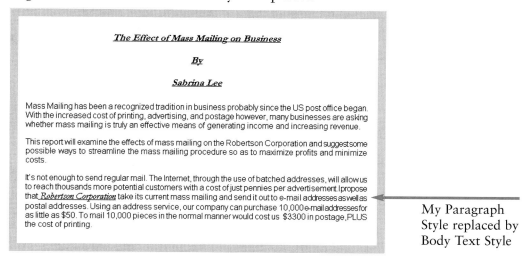

My Paragraph Style replaced by Body Text Style

Practice

Find and Replace all examples of **Title** with **Body Text** in the **MassMail3 Document**.

Hot Tip

You can add a Find button to the Standard toolbar by clicking on the down pointing arrow at the right end of the toolbar, selecting add or remove buttons, and then clicking on the Find button.

Using the Tabs Command

Concept

The Tabs command allows the user to format tab stops to enhance the appearance of documents.

Do It!

Sabrina will use the Tabs command on a section of her report.

1 Open Doit6-3.doc.

2 Highlight all text from History of the Internet1 through Call to Action8.

3 Open the Format menu.

4 If the Tabs command is not visible when the menu opens, click on the double arrows at the bottom of the menu to expand it and then click once on Tabs.

5 The Tabs dialog box (see **Figure 6-25**) will open with the insertion point in the Tab Stop position box. Type 5.5 in this box.

6 Click on the radio button for 2 in the Leader section of the Tab dialog box. Click OK .

7 Place the insertion bar between Internet and 1 in the document. Press the [Tab] key once.

8 Place the insertion bar between Internet and 3 in the document and press the [Tab] key once.

9 Follow the above procedure with the rest of the topics. Your document should look like **Figure 6-26**.

10 Save your work as TitlePage.doc.

More

In order to clear the tab stops you have created, access the Tabs dialog box, and click on the Clear All button. This will return the tabs to the default setting.

Figure 6-25 Tabs dialog box

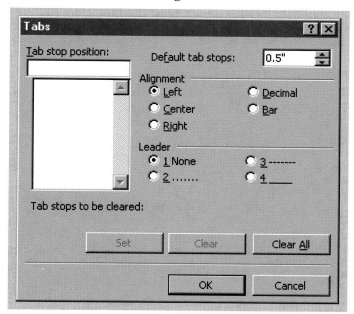

Figure 6-26 Document with tabs

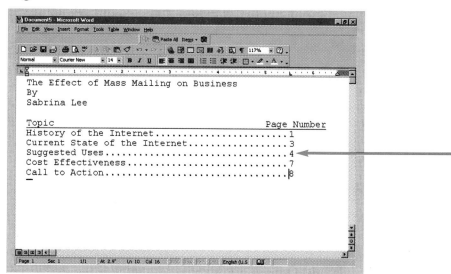

Tabs create the alignment of this text

Practice

Open the student file **Prac6-7** and follow the instructions.

Hot Tip

You can permanently change the tab stops in Word using the Tabs dialog box. Select a new default tab stop by using the arrow keys in the Default tab stops selection box, and then click **OK**.

Using Click and Type

Concept

The Click and Type feature is used to insert text, graphics, tables or other items in any blank area of a document, regardless of where the insertion point is currently placed. Click and Type gives you the ability to add text or objects to a document without creating blank lines or tab stops.

Do It!

Sabrina will create a title page for her report using Click and Type.

1. Click on New document.

2. Click the Print Layout View button to the left of the horizontal scroll bar (see **Figure 6-27**).

3. Position the I-beam two inches from the top of the new document and in the center of the page.

4. Double-click the left mouse button.

5. Type The Effect of Mass Mailing on Business.

6. Position the I-beam in the center of the page, two inches below the title. Double-click the left mouse button.

7. Type By.

8. Position the I-beam in the center of the page, two inches below the word By. Double-click the left mouse button.

9. Type Sabrina Lee.

10. Save your work as TitlePage.doc.

More

The floating icons attached to the I-beam (see **Figure 6-28**) change as you move it across the page into different formatting zones to indicate what type of formatting will be used when you utilize the Click and Type feature. You will recognize these icons as being similar to those found on the Align Left, Center, and Align Right buttons on the Formatting toolbar.

Figure 6-27 View buttons

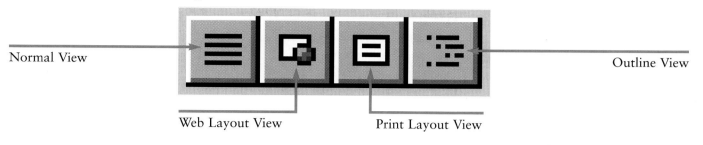

Normal View

Outline View

Web Layout View

Print Layout View

Figure 6-28 I-beam position indicators

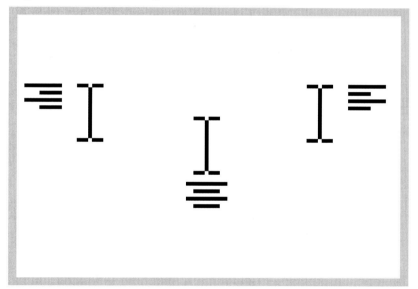

Practice

Create a title page for **Prac 6-1A.doc**.

Hot Tip

Click and Type is only available in Print Layout View and Web Layout View. The feature cannot be used in areas with certain types of formatting including multiple columns and bulleted and numbered lists.

Shortcuts

Function	*Button/Mouse*	*Menu*	*Keyboard*
AutoFormat		Click Format, then click AutoFormat	
Format Paragraph		Click Format, then click Paragraph	
Format Font		Click Format, then click Font	
Bold Text			[Ctrl]+[B]
Italicize Text			[Ctrl]+[I]
Underline Text			[Ctrl]+[U]

Identify Key Features

Name the items indicated by callouts in Figure 6-29 and 6-30

Figure 6-29 Word report

① ② ③ ④ ⑤

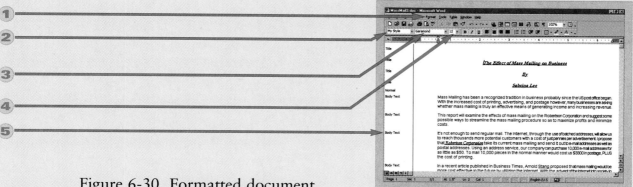

Figure 6-30 Formatted document

⑥ ⑦ ⑧ ⑨

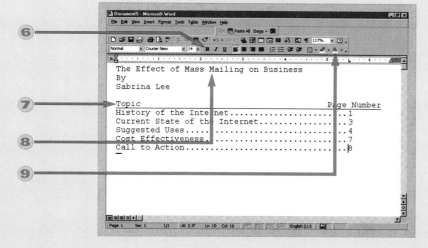

Select The Best Answer

10. Use this dialog box to alter the style of selected text

11. Use this dialog box to create your own style for text

12. This feature applies a set of stored formats

13. Templates are stored here

14. Use this option to permanently change a style you have created

15. A set of format settings applied to whole paragraphs

16. Shows you, on screen, the style of every element of a document

17. Allows you to search for types of style and substitute other styles

a. Paragraph Style

b. Style Report

c. AutoFormat

d. Style Gallery

e. Find and Replace Feature

f. Styles dialog box

g. New Styles dialog box

h. Update style to reflect current changes

Quiz (continued)

Complete the Statement

18. To change the Styles: box to reflect every style, set the List: box below it to:

    a. Styles in Use

    b. Delete Style

    c. All Styles

    d. User Defined Styles

19. In order to create a new style, you must access the:

    a. Tabs Command

    b. Delete Format dialog box

    c. New Styles dialog box

    d. User Defined Styles command

20. In order to make sure that previously selected styles do not change when using AutoFormat, select the:

    a. Keep Styles option

    b. Reject all changes

    c. Accept all changes

    d. Preserve Styles option

21. Before you can access the Style Gallery, you must first use the:

    a. Delete Command

    b. AutoFormat Command

    c. Insert Tables Command

    d. Preserve Styles Option

22. You can copy styles between documents using the:

    a. Style Organizer

    b. Clipboard

    c. Format Painter

    d. Spell Checker

23. In order to make sure that the Style Report does not print the styles in your document when you print your document, you must:

    a. Delete the Style Report.

    b. Change the settings on the printer.

    c. Do nothing. The Style Report never prints.

    d. Change the formatting.

24. When you change the default setting of the Find feature, the Browse Object buttons turn:

    a. Communist

    b. Red

    c. Black

    d. Blue

25. Click and Type cannot be used with all views. The view it can be used with is:

    a. Normal View

    b. Print Preview

    c. Print Layout View

    d. Outline View

Interactivity

Test Your Skills

1. Apply a character style to a document:

   a. Open MassMail3.doc.

   b. Highlight the title only.

   c. Access the Style dialog box.

   d. Select Document Map from the Styles: list box.

   e. Apply the style.

2. AutoFormat a document:

   a. Open MassMail2.doc.

   b. Select AutoFormat from the Format menu.

   c. Do not select to review each change.

   d. Click OK.

3. Display a Style Report:

   a. Open MassMail3.doc and put it in Normal View.

   b. Open the Options dialog box and click the View tab.

   c. Set the Style area width: box to 1".

   d. Click OK.

4. Finding and Replacing a style:

   a. Open the MassMail3.doc and press [Ctrl]+[F].

   b. Click the Replace tab, click on Format and select Style.

   c. Choose Body Text and click OK.

   d. Place the insertion bar in the Replace window, click on Format and select Style.

   e. Choose My Paragraph Style and click OK.

   f. Replace all.

Interactivity (continued)

Problem Solving

1. Create a new document of your choice. Said document must contain a title and a byline. Apply at least three new formatting changes to the document.

2. Create a new document of your choice. Highlight one of the paragraphs. Create a new paragraph style and apply it to at least two paragraphs in your document.

3. Create a memo to other employees of a company you own outlining company procedures for evacuating the building in the event of fire. Format your document using the AutoFormat and the Professional Memo template.

4. Create a table of contents for a fictional book containing chapter headings and page numbers. Use the Tab command to link the chapter headings with their page numbers.

▶ **Creating a Main Document**

▶ **Creating a Data Source**

▶ **Adding Information to a Data Source**

▶ **Adding Merge Fields to a Main Document**

▶ **Editing Individual Merged Documents**

▶ **Printing Merged Documents**

▶ **Preparing and Printing Labels**

▶ **Preparing and Printing Envelopes**

L E S S O N

7

MERGING DOCUMENTS

S ometimes it is necessary to create a large number of similar documents, such as form letters or billing statements. Instead of forcing you to create these documents individually, Word allows you to create a single document plus a separate file containing the information that will be unique to each copy when it is printed. This powerful feature, known as Mail Merge, makes large-scale mailings and other similar chores as simple as creating a letter and an address list. Even if you have used a mail merge to produce a document, you can still edit it individually.

Once you have made a list of recipients' names and addresses, called a data source, you can use it again for a different form letter, or to create addressed envelopes and mailing labels. Alternatively, you can simply print the information out as a table.

Case Study:
In this Lesson, you will follow Sabrina as she creates a from letter for her company, which she will then send to the company's shareholders. She will create a main document and a data source, and then add merge fields to the main document. Once these items are completed she will be able to use the Mail Merge function to create a form letter that is customized for each shareholder. Finally, Sabrina will edit individual documents and use Word to create mailing labels and envelopes for her letters.

Creating
a Main Document

Concept

Before documents can be merged, a main document must be created. This document, called boilerplate text, contains all the elements of the letter that will be common to the customized copies. It can be created with any standard Word document.

Do It!

Kay will create a main document from a letter she has written.

1. Open the student file Doit7-1 and save it as MainDoc on your computer. This file contains the letter that Sabrina has written.

2. Click Tools, then click Mail Merge. The Mail Merge Helper dialog box opens (see Figure 7-1).

3. Click [Create ▾], then click Form Letters. Another dialog box appears (see Figure 7-2) asking if you want to get the text for the form letter from the active window or from a new document.

4. Click [Active Window]. The dialog box disappears and the document name is displayed in the Main Document section of the Mail Merge Helper dialog box. The letter is now the boilerplate text. The Mail Merge Helper dialog box will remain open.

More

A mail merge document consists of several basic elements. You have already learned about boilerplate text, which is the text common to all copies of a merged document. A data source is the table-like document created to hold all the fields that will be inserted into a merged document, such as name, address, date, salary, or any other kind of information that you would like to include. Records are the information contained in the fields for ONE individual. For example, the data source for a merged document from a politician to his or her constituents would contain one record for each person on the mailing list, and each record would contain several fields for each person. The header row in a data source contains the name of the fields.

Figure 7-1 Mail Merge Helper dialog box

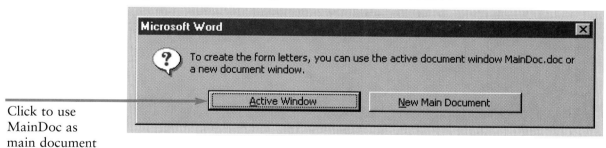

Click to choose type
of document you
will create

Figure 7-2 Choosing a main document source

Click to use
MainDoc as
main document

Practice

There is no Practice file for this Skill, as an
additional Word file will not open while the
Mail Merge Helper dialog box is open.

Hot Tip

It does not matter if your main document
does not fill an entire page. Word inserts a
section break after each merged copy to
force it to print on its own page.

Creating a Data Source

Concept

Once a main document has been created, you can select a data source and link it to the main document. You may use an existing data source, such as a table of addresses, or create a new one. Before entering records into a new data source, you must define its fields.

Do It!

Sabrina will create a data source for her form letter.

1. In the Mail Merge Helper dialog box, click [Get Data ▾], then click Create Data Source. The Create Data Source dialog box appears, as shown in **Figure 7-3**. Word offers many common field titles, so you must delete the fields you do not need.

2. You will notice that the first field, Title, is already highlighted in the Field Names in Header Row text box. Click the Remove Field Name button [Remove Field Name]. The field is removed and placed temporarily in the Field name: text box.

3. Using the same procedure as you used in step 2, remove the following fields: JobTitle, Company, Address2, Country, HomePhone, and WorkPhone (when necessary, click a field name to select it).

4. Now that you have removed the extraneous fields, you can add a field that was not provided by Word. Since Sabrina's company classifies all stockholders as one of two types (Blue Chip or Common), she would like to add a field to designate this. Type MemberYear in the Field name: text box, replacing its current contents, and click the Add Field Name button [Add Field Name ▸▸].

5. Since the new field should go just below the LastName field, click the Move Up button [▴] four times slowly to move the field to the correct place.

6. Click [OK]. The Save As dialog box appears with the insertion point in the File name: box.

7. Type MergeData as the file name. Make sure you save into the same folder that contains MainDoc.

8. Click [🖫 Save]. A message box appears telling you that no records are in the data source (see **Figure 7-4**). Do not click anything yet. You will add records in the next Skill.

More

A data source can consist of a single record or it may contain hundreds of records. The fields in a data source can be anything that will differ in each version of the final merged document, whether it is a single word, such as a salutation, or an entire paragraph. The flexibility of Word's Mail Merge feature is what makes it so useful for creating large numbers of similar documents.

Figure 7-3 Create Data Source dialog box

Add your own
field names here

Click arrows to
move selected
field up or down
in field order

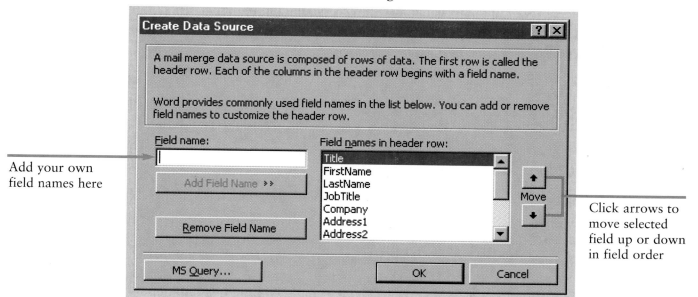

Word 2000

Figure 7-4 Microsoft Word message box

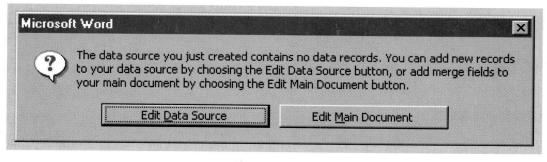

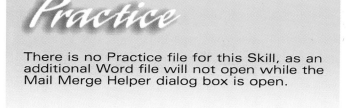

Practice

There is no Practice file for this Skill, as an
additional Word file will not open while the
Mail Merge Helper dialog box is open.

Hot Tip

A data source may be used to create a mail
merge with more than one document.

Adding Information to the Data Source

Concept

Once you have created a data source, and specified the fields to be in that data source, adding records is easy using the data form. Using the data form is a very convenient way of entering records compared to typing each one on an actual letter.

Do It!

Sabrina wants to add records to the data source.

1 Click Edit Data Source in the Word message box. The Data Form dialog box appears with the insertion point in the FirstName field (see **Figure 7-5**).

2 Type William, and then press [Enter] to move the insertion point to the next field.

3 Type Smither into the LastName field box and press [Enter].

4 Type 88 in the MemberYear field and press [Enter].

5 Type 125 Wellington Way in the Address1 field.

6 Type Briarcliff Manor in the City field.

7 Type NY in the State field.

8 Type 13562 in the PostalCode field.

9 Click OK to accept the data and close the data form. (To add more records, click Add New instead.) The main document is now left in the document window with the Mail Merge toolbar, shown in **Figure 7-6**, appearing below the Formatting toolbar.

More

When the last field of a particular record has been filled, you can add a blank record by pressing [Enter] instead of clicking the Add New button. If you need to undo a change to a record, click the Restore button Restore . The record will revert to its original state. In addition, fields may be left blank without affecting the mail merge process. For example, if you include a middle name field, and one of your records does not have a middle name, Word will simply leave a blank space where the missing data should have appeared in the merged document.

Figure 7-5 Data Form dialog box

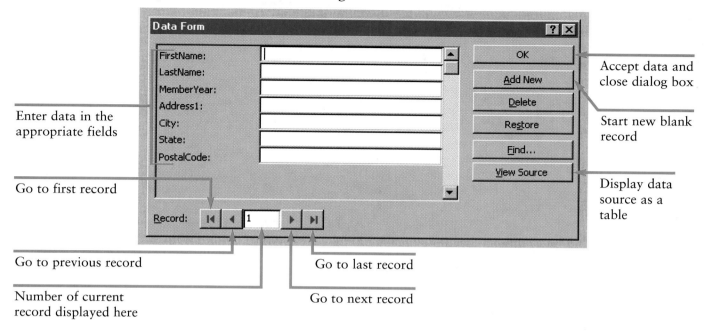

Enter data in the appropriate fields

Go to first record

Go to previous record

Number of current record displayed here

Go to last record

Go to next record

Accept data and close dialog box

Start new blank record

Display data source as a table

Figure 7-6 Mail Merge toolbar

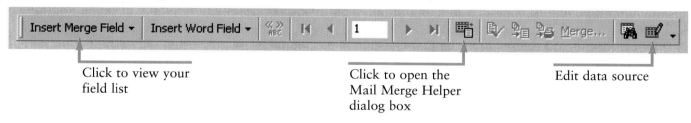

Click to view your field list

Click to open the Mail Merge Helper dialog box

Edit data source

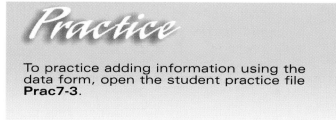

Practice

To practice adding information using the data form, open the student practice file **Prac7-3**.

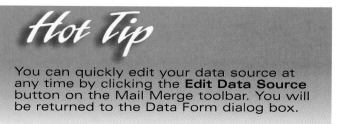

Hot Tip

You can quickly edit your data source at any time by clicking the **Edit Data Source** button on the Mail Merge toolbar. You will be returned to the Data Form dialog box.

Adding Merge Fields to a Main Document

Concept

A merge field tells Word what data to insert and where to insert it in a main document when you merge documents. A merge field appears as the field name that will be inserted enclosed in chevrons (see **Figure 7-7**). When inserting merge fields, you must include punctuation, returns, and spaces where necessary.

Do It!

Sabrina wants to designate data from an existing data source for use with her form letter. She will also insert the merge fields into her main document.

1. Open the student file MainDoc if it is not already open.

2. Click the Mail Merge Helper button ▣ to open the Mail Merge Helper dialog box.

3. Click the Get Data button Get Data ▾ , then click Open Data Source.

4. Select the student file Doit7-4. This is the data source containing the names and addresses on Sabrina's mailing list for the form letter.

5. Click ☞ Open to open the file. A message box appears saying that the file MergeData has not been saved and asks you if you want to save it.

6. Click No . A preexisting data source will be used in the final merge instead. A dialog box appears saying that no merge fields have been inserted into the main document.

7. Click Edit Main Document . The dialog boxes close, and the main documents is left alone on the screen.

8. Select the words Recipient's Address underneath the letterhead graphic.

9. Click Insert Merge Field ▾ . A drop-down list appears (see **Figure 7-8**) showing the fields that you can insert. Click FirstName. The field replaces the selected text.

10. Press [Space]. Click Insert Merge Field ▾ again. As you can see, inserting merge fields requires a combination of merge fields from the drop-down list and keystrokes. Click LastName to add it to the letter at the insertion point after the space.

11. Insert the rest of the fields and keystrokes as follows: [Space]['']MemberYear [Enter] Address1 [Enter] City [,] [Space] State [Space] [Space] Postal Code.

12. Double-click the word recipient below the fields you have just entered to select it.

13. Click Insert Merge Field ▾ , then click FirstName. Refer back to **Figure 7-7** to see how your merge fields should appear in the document.

14. Click the Save button on the Standard toolbar to save the main document with the merge fields that have been inserted.

More

When the document is merged, the information specified by each merge field will be added to replace the name of the field as it appears in the main document. Merge fields can be inserted anywhere in a main document, and may be formatted in any way that the text can be formatted. For example, formatting the merge field in italics will italicize the inserted data in the final merged document.

Figure 7-7 Inserted merge fields

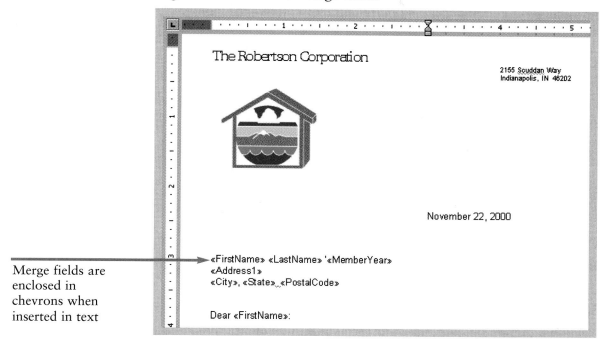

Merge fields are enclosed in chevrons when inserted in text

Figure 7-8 Insert Merge Field drop-down list

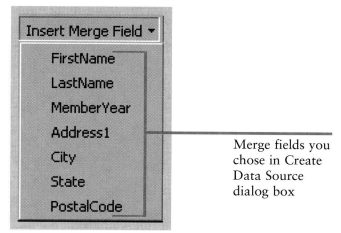

Merge fields you chose in Create Data Source dialog box

Practice adding merge fields to a main document by opening the student file **Prac7-4** and following the instructions.

Hot Tip

Merge fields can also be used effectively within the main body of the letter. For example, Sabrina could have added a field for **SharesHeld** and then written, "Your <<**SharesHeld**>> shares should be worth much more after the acquisition."

Editing Individual Merged Documents

Concept

Merged documents based on a single main document and containing the same fields of information can still be personalized. Once the document has been merged, different copies of the document can be easily edited to meet the user's needs.

Do It!

Sabrina wants to merge the documents and personalize one of them further.

1. With the file MainDoc open in the document window, click the Merge to New Document button ▣ on the Mail Merge toolbar. The main document and data source are merged into a new document called Form Letters 1 that consists of several pages, each page a letter based on the main document with one record's data inserted into the merge fields.

2. Place the insertion point after the end of the third paragraph (see **Figure 7-9**). There is a copy of the letter on every page, so make sure you are on the copy for William Smither, which is the first page.

3. Type Your personal holdings increased $750. The paragraph should now look like **Figure 7-10**.

4. Save the newly created form letters using the name Form Letters 1 for the file.

5. Save any changes you made to the other files as well.

More

Once the files have been merged, they are transformed into one long document consisting of all copies of the letter that will eventually be printed. At this point the new document may be treated like any other Word document, and each letter may be modified as you like.

If you have a large number of records to be used, it may be inappropriate and a waste of your hard drive space to create a single file containing all the documents. Instead, you can print all the documents directly by clicking the Merge to Printer button ▣ on the Mail Merge toolbar. This will print all copies of the merged information. However, you will not have the opportunity to edit or preview individual documents.

To merge only specified records with the main document instead of merging all the records in the data source, click the Start Mail Merge button Merge... on the Mail Merge toolbar. This will open the Merge dialog box, in which you can specify a range of records to include in the merge.

Figure 7-9 Editing a merged document

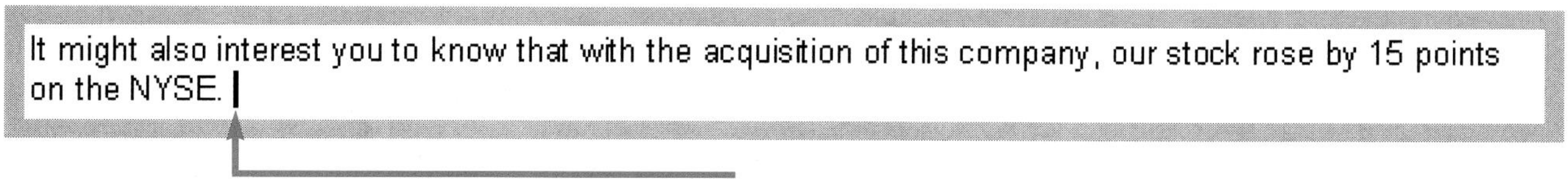

> It might also interest you to know that with the acquisition of this company, our stock rose by 15 points on the NYSE. |

Place insertion point as you would
for normal document editing

Figure 7-10 Edited paragraph

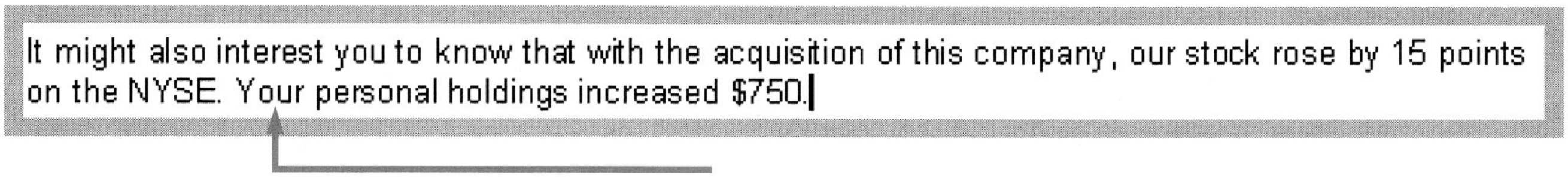

> It might also interest you to know that with the acquisition of this company, our stock rose by 15 points on the NYSE. Your personal holdings increased $750.|

New sentence will appear only
in this particular document

Practice

To practice editing individual merged documents, open the student file **Prac7-5**.

Hot Tip

You can see how the merge fields will look when they are replaced with the specified data by clicking the **View Merged Data** button on the Mail Merge toolbar.

 # Printing Merged Documents

Concept

A merged document can be previewed and printed just like any other Word document. Previewing allows you to be sure your documents have merged correctly.

Do It!

Sabrina would like to preview her letters , and then print them.

1 Open the student file Doit7-6.doc.

2 Click the Print Preview button 🔍 on the Standard toolbar. The Print Preview window appears with six pages showing (see **Figure 7-11**). (If six pages are not showing, click the Multiple Pages button 🔳 on the Print Preview toolbar and drag all the way down and to the right to select all pages.)

3 Notice that the second page is blank, and therefore there are only five copies of the letter on the screen. Click on the blank page to magnify it. The page fills the screen.

4 Click the Magnifier button 🔍 on the Print Preview toolbar to deselect the Magnifier tool. The mouse pointer will become an I-beam when it is over the page so that the page can be edited.

5 Scroll to the top of the blank page and you will see the blinking insertion point. Press the [Back Space] key four times. This will place the insertion point after the last line of the first page.

6 Select the Magnifier tool and click the page to zoom out again so that you can see all six pages. Now, there is one letter on each page and you are ready to print (see **Figure 7-12**).

7 Click the Print button 🖨 on the Print Preview toolbar after making sure that your computer is properly connected to a working printer.

8 Click Close on the Print Preview toolbar to exit Print Preview mode.

9 Click the Save button 💾 on the Standarad toolbar. The Save As dialog box appears.

10 Save the document as MergeDoc and then close it.

More

Using the Print Preview screen makes it possible to quickly spot unwanted variations between different copies of the merged document or to find at a glance such problems as blank pages. If you merged to a new document as in the example above, you may not want to save the newly merged document. If many records were merged or the main document contains graphics and the final merged document is exceedingly long, it may be a better idea to discard the final merged document and save only the main document and the data source. If you need to print it again or modify it later, it only takes the click of a button to merge the document again.

Figure 7-11 Print Preview mode

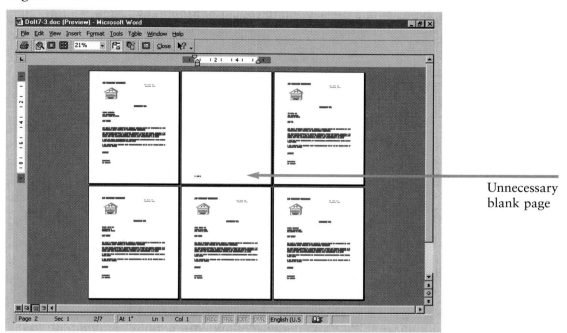

Unnecessary
blank page

Word 2000

Figure 7-12 Document ready for printing

Blank page replaced
by copy of letter

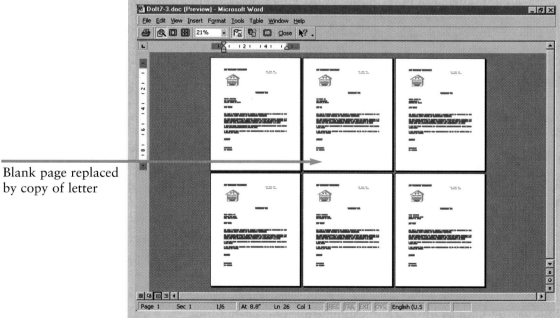

Practice

For more practice previewing and printing a merged document, open the student file **Prac7-6** and follow the instructions

Hot Tip

When previewing merged documents, be especially observant of extra lines being added or removed from adjacent pages; spotting these problems before you print will save a lot of time and paper.

Preparing and Printing Labels

Concept

Word's Mail Merge function can create a variety of document types other than form letters. For example, to mail the form letter that was created in the previous skill, you might want to create mailing labels with the same data source you used for each of the six letter recipients.

Do It!

Sabrina wishes to create mailing labels to disseminate quarterly reports to stockholders. She will use the same data source she used to create the form letters.

1. Click Tools, then click Mail Merge to bring up the Mail Merge Helper dialog box.

2. Click Create ▾, then click Mailing Labels. A dialog box appears asking whether you want to use the active document window or a new document window.

3. Click New Main Document. The dialog box disappears and the document's temporary name is displayed in the Main Document section of the Mail Merge Helper dialog box.

4. Click Get Data ▾, then click Open Data Source. The Open Data Source dialog box appears. You will be using the same data source you used to merge the form letter.

5. Select Doit7-4 and click 🗁 Open. A dialog box appears saying that Word needs to set up the main document.

6. Click Set Up Main Document. The Label Options dialog box appears, as shown in **Figure 7-13**. Mailing labels come in sheets ready to print; and in this dialog box you must specify what type of labels you will be using.

7. Scroll down through the Product number: box and select 5262-Address.

8. Click OK. The Create Labels dialog box opens, allowing you to insert merge fields just as you did in the form letter.

9. Insert the fields in the following manner: FirstName [Space] LastName [Enter] Address1 [Enter] City [,][Space] State [Space][Space] Postal code (see **Figure 7-14**).

10. Click OK to accept the inserted merged fields and return to the Mail Merge Helper dialog box.

Figure 7-13 Label Options dialog box

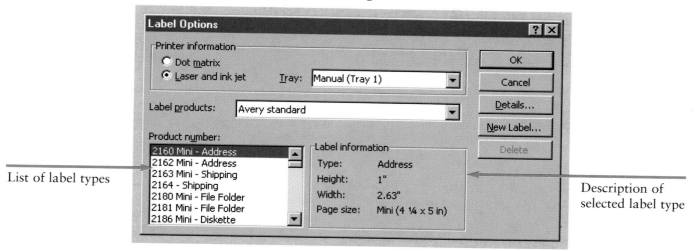

List of label types

Description of
selected label type

Figure 7-14 Inserted merge fields for mailing labels

Click to select from
menu of available
merge fields

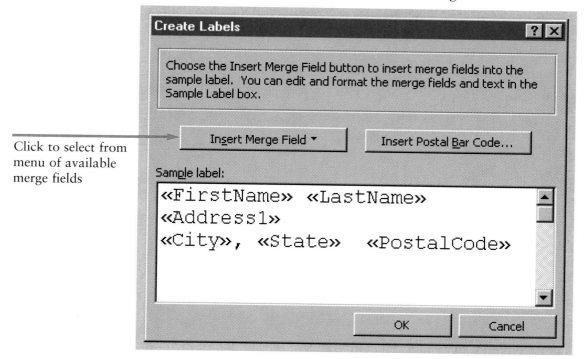

Preparing and Printing Labels (continued)

Do It!

11 Click [Merge...]. The Merge dialog box appears (see **Figure 7-15**).

12 Click [Merge]. The document will merge and should look like **Figure 7-16**.

13 Click the Print button 🖨 on the Standard toolbar after making sure that your computer is properly connected to a working printer. The labels print on plain paper, formatted as they would appear on Avery 5262 Address label sheets.

14 Close the merged labels document, and save it to your student disk as Merged Labels. The unmerged label document reappears in the active window.

15 Close this document, saving it to your student disk as Unmerged Labels.

More

To view the formatting changes you have made to a merged label document, you can use the Print Preview command as you did with the form letters. This makes it easier to spot formatting errors, such as a name that spreads over two lines due to its length or an increased font size. As with the form letter, each record in the final merged document may be edited to fix any individual problems. The Merge dialog box allows you to control whether Word will insert blank lines in an address when data is not available for a merge field in a particular record.

Figure 7-15 Merge dialog box

Click to select destination for merge

Select to create a partial merge using only the records you specify

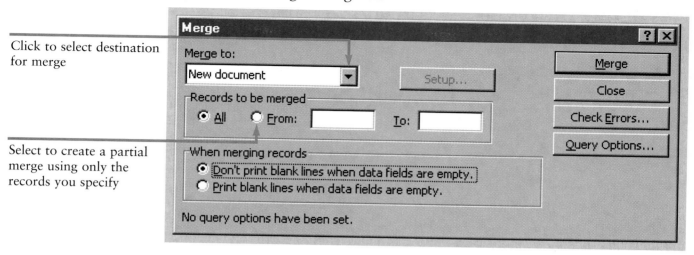

Figure 7-16 Merged labels document

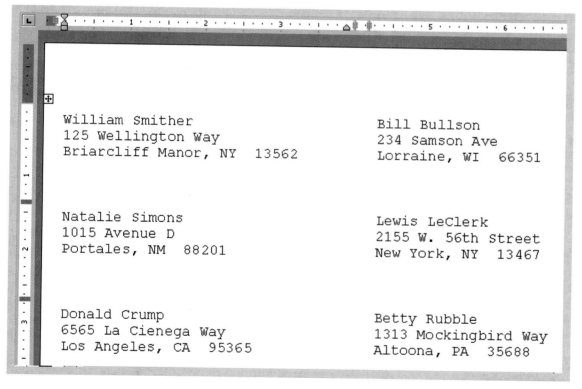

William Smither
125 Wellington Way
Briarcliff Manor, NY   13562

Bill Bullson
234 Samson Ave
Lorraine, WI   66351

Natalie Simons
1015 Avenue D
Portales, NM   88201

Lewis LeClerk
2155 W. 56th Street
New York, NY   13467

Donald Crump
6565 La Cienega Way
Los Angeles, CA   95365

Betty Rubble
1313 Mockingbird Way
Altoona, PA   35688

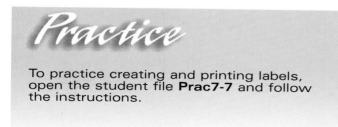

Practice

To practice creating and printing labels, open the student file **Prac7-7** and follow the instructions.

Hot Tip

If the information in your data source cannot be made to fit a given label, it may be wise to pick an alternate label type from the Product numbers list that will better suit your needs.

Preparing and Printing Envelopes

Concept

Along with mailing labels, Word gives you the ability to create envelopes for use with your form letters. By printing addresses directly on envelopes, you can save the time it takes to apply mailing labels.

Do It!

Sabrina has decided to save her labels for another mailing. She will print envelopes for her form letters instead.

1. Click Tools, then click Mail Merge to open the Mail Merge Helper dialog box.

2. Click ⟨ Create ▾ ⟩, then click Envelopes. A dialog box appears asking whether you want to use the active document window or a new document window.

3. Click ⟨ New Main Document ⟩. The dialog box disappears and the document's temporary name is displayed in the Main Document section of the Mail Merge Helper dialog box.

4. Click ⟨ Get Data ▾ ⟩, then click Open Data Source. The Open Data Source dialog box appears. You will be using the same data source you used to merge the mailing labels.

5. Select Doit7-4 and click ⟨ 🗁 Open ⟩. A dialog box appears saying that Word needs to set up the main document.

6. Click ⟨ Set Up Main Document ⟩. The Envelope Options dialog box appears, as shown in Figure 7-17.

7. Click ⟨ OK ⟩ to accept the default envelope options. The Create Envelopes dialog box opens, allowing you to insert merge fields just as you did for the mailing labels.

8. Insert the fields in the following manner: FirstName [Space] Last Name [Enter] Address1 [Enter] City [,][Space] State [Space][Space] PostalCode (see Figure 7-18).

9. Click ⟨ OK ⟩ to accept the inserted merged fields and return to the Mail Merge Helper dialog box.

Figure 7-17 Envelope Options dialog box

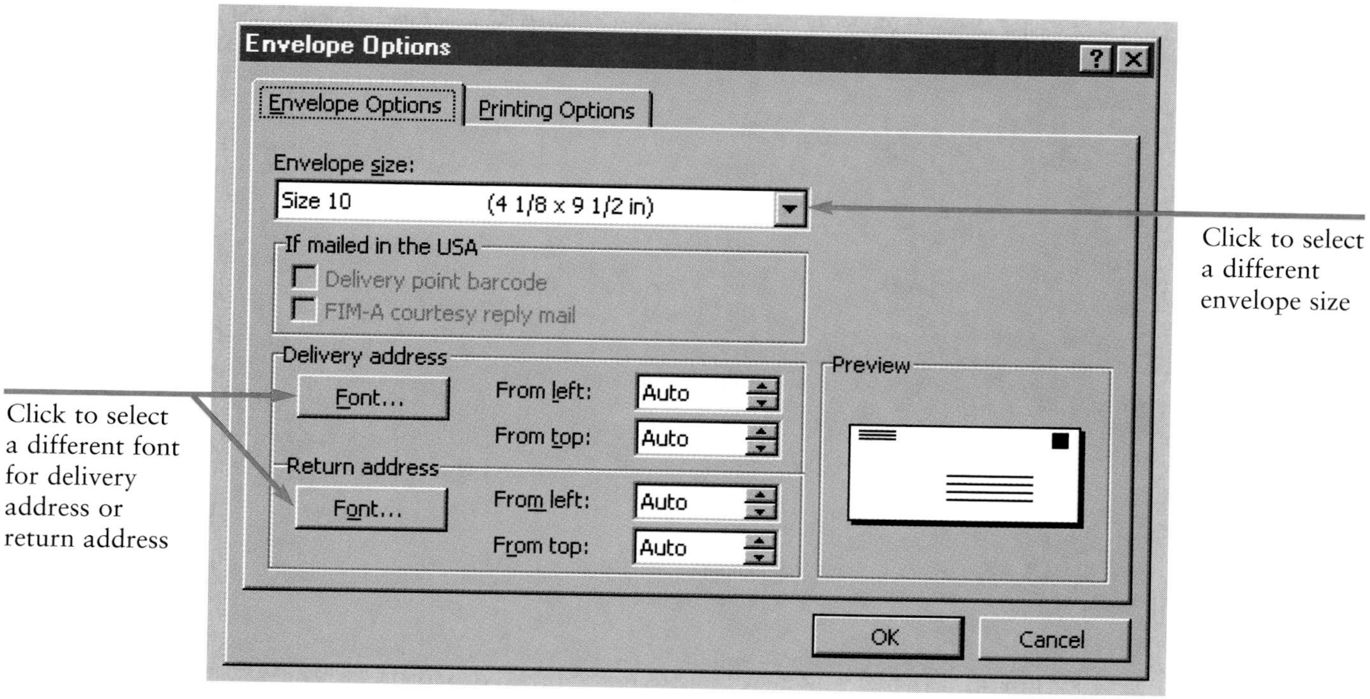

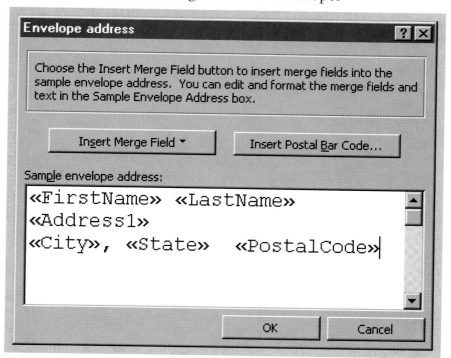

Figure 7-18 Inserted merge fields for envelopes

Preparing and Printing Envelopes (continued)

Do It!

10 Click [Merge...] . The Merge Dialog box appears.

11 Click [Merge] to merge the envelopes to a new document. The document will merge and should look like **Figure 7-19**.

12 Click the Print Preview button 🔍 on the Standard toolbar.

13 Before you print, check to see how the envelopes should be aligned in the manual feed tray of the printer by clicking Tools, and then selecting Envelopes and Labels. In the lower-right corner of the dialog box that opens, you will see how to align the envelopes (see **Figure 7-20**). If this illustration conflicts with the feed method illustrated on your printer, you might want to print a test envelope before printing the entire envelope merge.

14 After aligning the envelopes properly in the printer tray, click the Print button 🖨️. Close the Print Preview window.

15 Save the envelopes as Merged Envelopes and close the document.

16 The unmerged letter document appears in the active window. Save this as Unmerged Envelopes and close this document as well.

More

Word provides a method for printing a single mailing label or envelope quickly and easily. When you select the Envelopes and Labels command after starting a new document, the Envelopes and Labels dialog box will appear containing two tabs: one for envelopes and one for labels. Both tabs provide text boxes in which you can type the delivery address, and for an envelope, the return address. You also have options such as omitting the return address or printing an entire sheet of the same mailing label. If you select text in a document before choosing the Envelopes and Labels command, the selected text will be used in the dialog box automatically.

Word can also create main documents in Catalog format, which essentially lists the records one after the other, each formatted according to the placement of its merge fields. Catalog formatting is useful for parts lists, membership directories, and other such data compilations.

Figure 7-19 Merged envelopes document

Figure 7-20 Envelopes and Labels dialog box

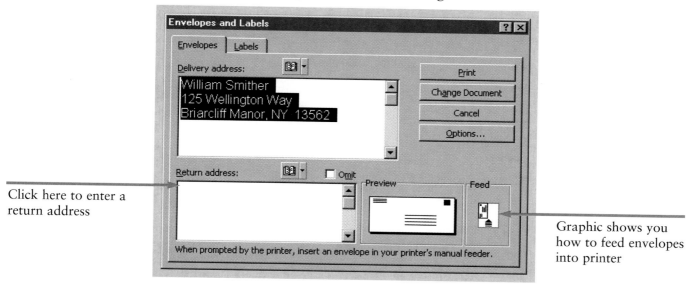

Click here to enter a
return address

Graphic shows you
how to feed envelopes
into printer

Practice

To practice creating and printing envelopes,
open the student file **Prac7-8** and follow
the instructions.

Hot Tip

If you are creating envelopes to be mailed
within the United States, Word can print a
delivery point of address bar code based
on the ZIP code of each record.

Shortcuts

Function	Button/Mouse	Menu	Keyboard
Display Mail Merge Helper dialog box		Click Tools, then click Mail Merge	[Alt]+[T], [R]
Edit a data source			[Alt]+[Shift]+[E]
Insert a merge field	Insert Merge Field ▾		[Alt]+[Shift]+[F]
Merge documents to a new document			[Alt] +[Shift]+[N]
Merge documents to a printer			[Alt]+[Shift]+[M]
Check merge for errors			[Alt]+[Shift]+[K]
Find record (in field)			

Identify Key Features

Name the items indicated by callouts in **Figure 7-21**.

Figure 7-21 Features of the Mail Merge toolbar

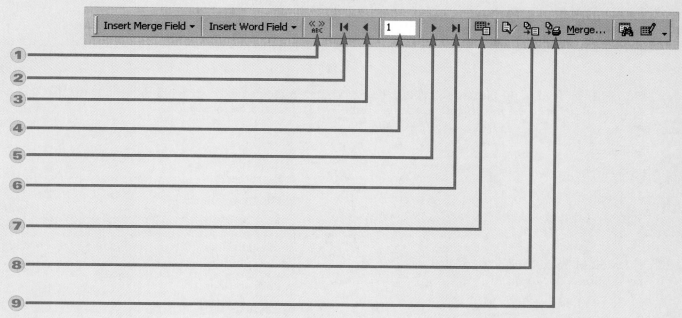

Select The Best Answer

10. Text that is the same for each version of a merged document

11. The place in a main document where data is inserted when the document is merged

12. A command that creates one long document consisting of all versions of a merged document

13. The data pertaining to a single recipient

14. A command that prints merged documents without first creating a document containing all versions

15. The command which allows you to see the document before printing

16. The place from which you select label type

17. The main command used to create merged documents

a. Merge Field

b. Boilerplate text

c. Merge to New Document

d. Merge to Printer

e. Data Record

f. Product Number Box

g. Mail Merge

h. Print Preview

Quiz (continued)

Complete the Statement

18. To move to the next field in the Data Form dialog box, press:

    a. [Esc]

    b. The right arrow key

    c. [Enter]

    d. [Ctrl]+[Q]

19. When the last field of the current record has been filled, you can open the next blank record by pressing:

    a. [Enter]

    b. The right arrow key

    c. [Tab}

    d. [Ctrl]+[Alt]+[R]

20. The Mail Merge command that allows you to personalize a document is:

    a. Merge to Printer

    b. Edit Data Source

    c. Merge to New Document

    d. Find Record

21. To merge only specified records with the main document, use the:

    a. Merge to Printer command

    b. Start Mail Merge button

    c. Merge to New Document Command

    d. Edit Data Source command

22. All the information contained in the fields for ONE individual is called a:

    a. Document

    b. Record

    c. Data Form

    d. Field report

23. A merge field appears as the field name that will be inserted enclosed in:

    a. Chevrons

    b. Cognito

    c. Parentheses

    d. Quotation marks

24. Besides envelopes, letters, and mailing labels, Word can also create:

    a. Presentations

    b. Catalogs

    c. Databases

    d. Worksheets

25. To add records to a data source, you should use the:

    a. Mail Merge command

    b. Edit command

    c. [Tab] key

    d. Data Form

Interactivity

Test Your Skills

1. Create a business letter and turn it into a **main document**:

    a. Use the Letter Wizard to create a letter to be sent to a mailing list.

    b. Click **Create**, then **Form Letters** in the Mail Merge Helper dialog box.

    c. Click **Edit**, then the form letter to edit it.

    d. Replace the body text with: **The product you ordered is currently on backorder and will be available in 4-6 weeks. Thank you for your patience.**

2. Open a **data source** and insert **merge fields** for your letter:

    a. From the Mail Merge Helper dialog box, click **Get Data** and select the student file **Doit7-4**. This is the same source you used for Sabrina's form letter.

    b. From the Mail Merge Helper dialog box, click **Edit Main Document**.

    c. Insert merge fields in the letter in the appropriate places.

3. **Merge** the document and examine the results in **Print Preview** mode:

    a. Click the **Merge to New Document** button on the Mail Merge toolbar.

    b. Open the Print Preview screen to view the merged document.

    c. Close Print Preview to return to your open Word documents. Save the final merged document to your student disk as **Test 7**.

4. Create **mailing labels** for your form letter.

    a. In the Mail Merge Helper dialog box, click **Create** and select **Mailing Labels**. Click **Get Data** and select the student file **Doit7-4**.

    b. Select **Labels 5262**, and insert the appropriate merge fields.

    c. Finish merging the document and print a copy of the mailing labels.

5. Create a single envelope:

    a. Open a new blank document.

    b. Select the **Envelopes and Labels** command from the **Tools** menu.

    c. Address the envelope to a friend and use your address as the return address.

    d. Preview your envelope with **Print Preview**.

    e. **Print** the envelope either on an actual envelope or on a regular sheet of paper if an envelope is not available.

Interactivity (continued)

Problem Solving

1. Open the student file Problem Solving 7 and save it as Solved 7. Open the Mail Merge Helper dialog box and create a main document from the active window. Create a data source with at least three records for people to whom you want to send the letters, with the following fields: FirstName, LastName, Title (Mr./Mrs./Ms.), Address1, City, State, and PostalCode. Insert the merge fields into the main document in the appropriate places. Near the bottom, insert your name where indicated. After you have inserted the merge fields, add another record to the data source. Then, merge the documents to a new document and preview the result. From the Print Preview screen, add a personal note to one of the letters. Finally, print the merged documents.

2. Using the data source that you created for problem 1, create envelopes using the Mail Merge Helper. Do not include the Title field in the envelopes. Preview the envelopes using Print Preview, and then print them.

3. Using the data source that you created for problem 1, create mailing labels using the Mail Merge Helper. Include all the fields. Preview the envelopes using Print Preview, and then print the envelopes.

4. Using the data source NewDataSource from your student disk, and the file Problem Solving 7, create envelopes using the Mail Merge Helper. Preview the envelopes using Print Preview, and then print the envelopes.

Creating a Web Page with a Template

Saving a Document as a Web Page

▶ **Inserting Clip Art**

▶ **Formatting Clip Art**

▶ **Drawing AutoShapes**

▶ **Formatting Drawn Objects**

▶ **Inserting a Picture from a File**

▶ **Using WordArt**

▶ **Inserting Hyperlinks**

▶ **Previewing and Editing a Web Page**

L E S S O N

CREATING WEB PAGES AND GRAPHICS

One of the most important features of Word 2000 is its improved compatibility with the World Wide Web. Word 2000 allows you to convert any of your documents into Web pages by simply using the File menu's **Save as Web Page** command. This command translates your document into **HTML** (HyperText Markup Language), the standard programming language used to write Web pages. The formatting and functionality of your original Word document will be carried over to the Web page. Once you have a file stored as HTML, it can be published on the Web by uploading it to a Web server. Anyone with an Internet connection and a Web browser will then be able to view your Word documents. If you are new to the concepts of layout and page design, Word provides several Web page templates that you can use to get you started.

Two of the greatest advantages of the Web are that it makes documents available to a worldwide audience and it allows you to update documents as often as necessary to keep them current. Most Web browsers include an edit function. If you use your browser's edit function on a Web page created in Word, the Word program will be launched so you can edit the document with its original application. Once you save your changes, you can then "round-trip" the document back to the Web.

Many of your Word documents can benefit from the inclusion of graphics. Word provides a number of methods for inserting different types of images. For example, you can add a premade **Clip Art** drawing from the **Microsoft Clip Gallery**. Or, you can draw your own figures using tools available on Word's Drawing toolbar. If you have graphic design experience and have created your own images, or simply have images on file, you can insert those images into a Word document as well.

Case Study:
Sabrina will use a Web template to create a simple Web page for her department. She will enhance the page by incorporating various graphical elements and hyperlinks.

 **Creating a Web Page with a Template**

Concept

Web pages can serve a variety of functions. The design of a page should complement its purpose. For example, a page that is intended to provide information will generally be text oriented without a lot of graphics and animations. These can be distracting, and they take longer to load, both of which interfere with the goal of the page. If you are new to the Web, you will probably want some guidance when you design your first Web pages. Word provides a number of Web page templates that allow you to focus on the content of the page without having to worry about its layout. As mentioned earlier, Web pages must be saved in a particular file format in order to function properly on the Web.

Do It!

Sabrina will create a new document from a template and save it as a Web page.

1. Click File, then click New. The New dialog box will open to the General tab.

2. Click the Web Pages tab to bring it to the front of the dialog box. The Web Pages tab contains a number of templates and a Wizard that will walk you through the process of creating a Web page (see **Figure 8-1**).

3. Double-click the Left-aligned Column icon. The dialog box will close, and a new Word application window with the Left-aligned Column Web page in its document window will open.

4. Templates provide placeholder text so that you will know where on the page to place your own text.

5. Position the mouse pointer directly in front of the text Main Heading Goes Here, and then click and drag over the text to highlight it.

6. Type Robertson Corporation to replace the placeholder text.

7. Select the first occurrence of the text Section Heading Goes Here and replace it with Our Goal.

8. Select the two paragraphs of text below the first section heading and replace them with To promote environmental issues and awareness in all corners of the Earth. The document should now resemble the one shown in **Figure 8-2**.

9. Close the document. You do not need to save it.

More

If you prefer to design a Web page on your own, Word provides a blank Web page template on the General tab in the New dialog box. This template is analogous to the NORMAL.DOT template used for standard word processing documents.

Figure 8-1 New dialog box's Web Pages tab

Web page templates use the icon of your default Web browser, in this case Internet Explorer

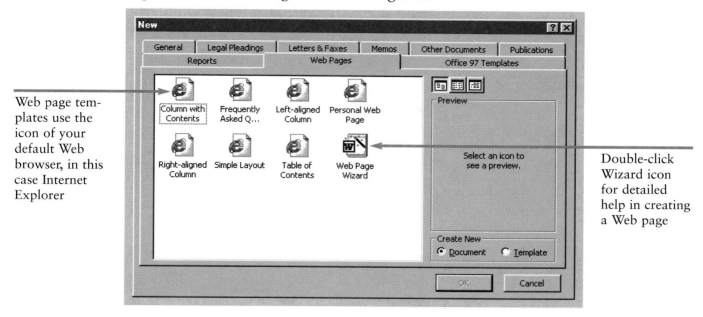

Double-click Wizard icon for detailed help in creating a Web page

Word 2000

Figure 8-2 Left-aligned Column Web page template

New Web Page button

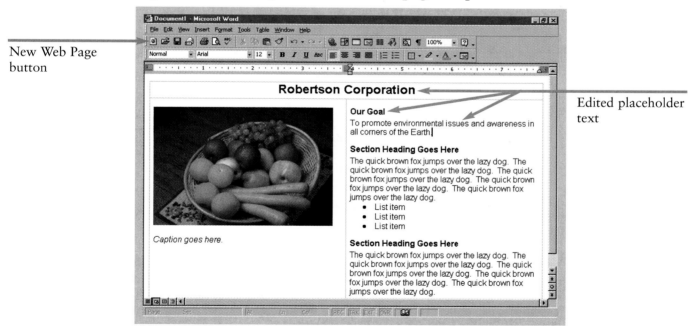

Edited placeholder text

Use the Personal Web Page template to create a home page for yourself.

The placeholder text in a template is already formatted with certain text characteristics, but you can change the formatting to suit your own needs and preferences.

Saving a Document as a Web Page

Concept

Converting a Word document to a file format that is readable on the World Wide Web is a simple process that does not require the knowledge of a programming language like HTML. If you use the Save As dialog box, you can save any Word document as a Web page by selecting Web Page in the Save as type: box. For a more direct approach, simply choose the Save as Web Page command from the File menu, which will cause the Save as type: box to default to the Web Page setting.

Do It!

Sabrina wants to save the document she created as a Web page.

1. Open the Word document file Doit8-2 from your student disk. This is a completed version of the document you created but did not save in the previous Skill.

2. Click File, then click Save as Web Page. The Save As dialog box will appear.

3. Use the Save in: box and the contents window to open the folder in which you will be saving Web page.

4. Click the Change Title button [Change Title...] to open the Set Page Title dialog box, shown in **Figure 8-3**. This dialog box allows you to set the title of the page as it will appear in the title bar of a browser window when the page is viewed on the Web.

5. Since the default title Left-aligned Column is already highlighted, type Robertson Corporation to replace it.

6. Click [OK] to set the new title.

7. Change the default file name given by Word, Doit8-2.htm, to robertson.htm, as shown in **Figure 8-4**.

8. Click the Save button [Save] to save the document as a Web page with its new name and file type.

More

If you have access to your organization's Web server, and it supports Web folders (shortcuts to the Web server), you can save your Web pages directly to a Web folder to publish them on a the Web. To create a Web folder, select Web Folders from the Save As dialog box's Save in: drop-down list and then click the Create New Folder button. This will activate the Add Web Folder Wizard. You should consult your system administrator before attempting to save any documents directly to a Web server.

When you save a Word document as a Web page, Word creates a folder in the same directory in which you stored the page for the files associated with it. This folder is for items such as image files and linked files, and it must be uploaded to a Web server with the actual page in order for the page to function properly on the Web.

Figure 8-3 Set Page Title dialog box

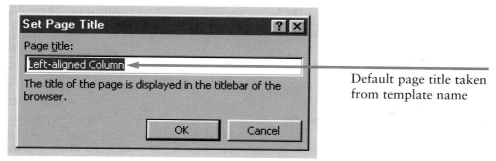

Default page title taken
from template name

Word 2000

Figure 8-4 Saving as a Web page

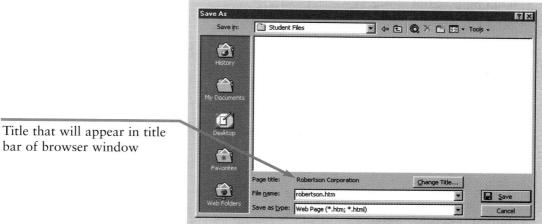

Title that will appear in title
bar of browser window

Figure 8-5 Web page formatting help

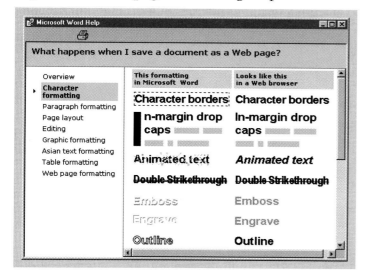

Save the Personal Web Page document you
created in the last Practice as a Web page
with the page title **Home Page** and the file
name **MyPrac8-2.htm**.

Hot Tip

Not all of the formatting you apply to a
standard Word document can be carried
over to a Web page successfully. Read the
help topic **What happens when I save a
document as a Web page? (Figure 8-5)** for
more information.

Inserting Clip Art

Concept

Word processing programs have evolved from electronic typewriters into full desktop publishing tools. Word gives you the ability to add a variety of graphic types to any kind of document, including Web pages. One of the easiest ways to add graphics is though the Microsoft Clip Gallery, accessible from the Insert Clip Art dialog box, which contains pictures that you can insert in a document.

Do It!

Sabrina wants to replace the fruit basket photo included in the Web page template she chose with a more appropriate Clip Art picture.

1. Click the photograph in the left column of robertson.htm to select it.

2. Press [Back Space] on the keyboard to delete the picture. A blinking insertion point will remain where the picture resided, and the caption text will move up.

3. Click Insert, then highlight Picture, then click Clip Art. The Insert Clip Art dialog box will open, giving you access to the Microsoft Clip Gallery. If the Picture tab is not at the front of the dialog box, click it to bring it forward.

4. Scroll down the Picture tab until you see the category Symbols, and then click its icon. Icons for all of the Clip Art pictures in the category will appear.

5. Place the mouse pointer over the fourth icon in the first row (if your dialog box has been resized, the rows may be configured differently). A ScreenTip will appear stating the picture's name (recycling), file size (22.4 KB), and file type (wmf, or Windows metafile).

6. Click the recycling picture icon. A menu with four buttons will pop up beside the icon, as shown in **Figure 8-6**.

7. Click the first button, Insert clip ▨, then close the Insert Clip Art dialog box to view the picture inserted in the Web page (see **Figure 8-7**).

8. Click ▤ to save the changes you have made to the document.

More

The Insert Clip Art dialog box is a powerful tool that includes browsing capabilities, a search mechanism, and its own help facility. You can drag and drop Clip Art pictures directly from the gallery to a document, or copy and paste them into and out of the gallery. Click the Clips Online button [🗐 Clips Online] to connect to a special Web site for Office 2000 users that provides more clips that you can download directly to your gallery. The Microsoft Clip Gallery Live offers Clip Art, photographs, sound files, and video files. The Sounds and Motion Clips tabs in the Insert Clip Art dialog box will be empty until you add clips yourself.

Figure 8-6 Using the Insert Clip Art dialog box

Type keywords in text box and press [Enter] to search for a clip

Click to collapse dialog box to a smaller version

Click to add clip to Favorites or other category

Click to preview clip at full size

Click to locate similar clips

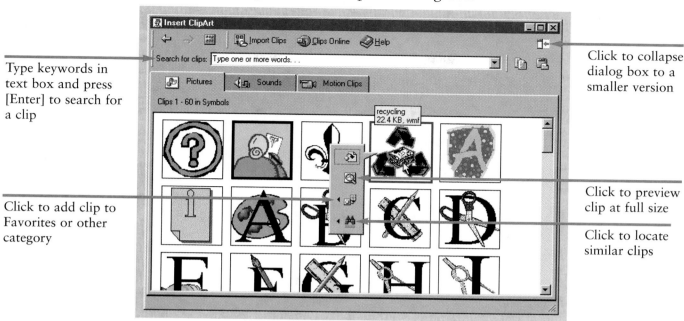

Word 2000

Figure 8-7 Clip Art inserted in document

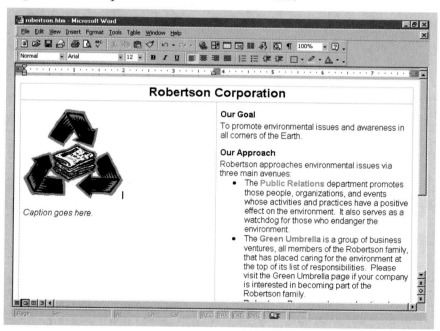

Practice

Open the student file **Prac8-3** and follow the instructions given in the document.

Hot Tip

To add your own files to the Clip Gallery, click the **Import Clips** button. The **Add clip to Clip Gallery** dialog box that appears acts as a gateway between any disk drive you can access and the Clip Gallery.

 **Formatting Clip Art**

Concept

Even though a Clip Art picture is a finished piece of artwork, you may find that it is necessary or desirable to adjust certain aspects of a picture. Various techniques will allow you to change a picture's dimensions, position, and alignment. You can also adjust a picture's contrast, brightness, line style, and background color.

Do It!

Sabrina will increase the size of her Clip Art picture and then change its alignment on the page. She will also adjust the picture's brightness with the Picture toolbar.

1. Click the recycling Clip Art picture you inserted in the previous Skill. A border and sizing handles will appear to indicate that the picture has been selected.

2. Place the mouse pointer over the sizing handle on the bottom-right corner of the picture's border. The mouse pointer will change to a diagonal double-headed arrow.

3. Click and drag down and to the right until the temporary dashed border of the picture is extended approximately an inch past the original border (see **Figure 8-8**).

4. Release the mouse button. The picture expands to fill the new, larger frame.

5. Click the Center button ≣ on the Standard toolbar. The recycling picture is realigned so that it is spaced evenly between the borders of its column.

6. Click View, then highlight Toolbars, and then click Picture on the submenu. The Picture toolbar will appear, floating over the window.

7. Click the More Brightness button ☼↑ twice to increase the brightness of the picture.

8. Select the text **Caption goes here.**, center it, and replace it with Please recycle! The document should now resemble **Figure 8-9**.

9. Save your changes.

More

If you require more precise control over the formatting changes you make to a picture, you can use the Format Object dialog box, accessible by choosing the Format Object command from the Format menu when the picture is selected. Each tab in the dialog box allows you to control a different aspect of an object by entering exact values. For example, on the Size tab, shown in **Figure 8-10**, you can set the dimensions of an object by changing its measurements in inches. Or, you can expand or shrink the objective by a percentage of its original size.

If you insert a picture into an area of a document that also contains text, you can control how the picture and text interact by using the Layout tab in the Format Object dialog box or the Text Wrapping button on the Picture toolbar.

Figure 8-8 Resizing Clip Art

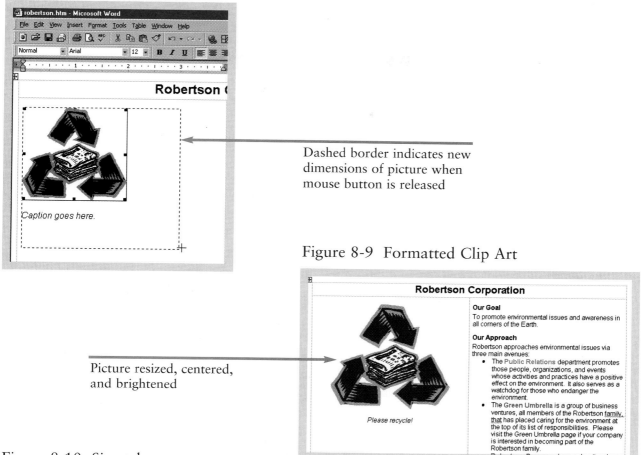

Dashed border indicates new dimensions of picture when mouse button is released

Figure 8-9 Formatted Clip Art

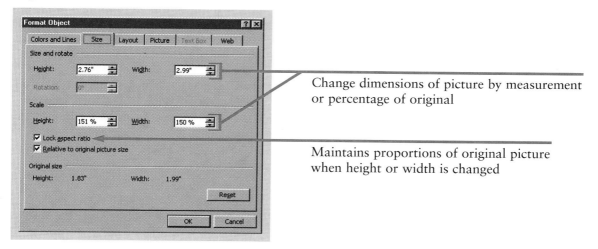

Picture resized, centered, and brightened

Figure 8-10 Size tab

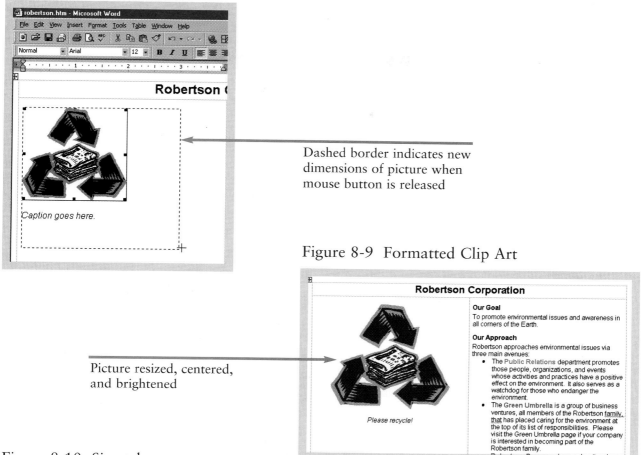

Change dimensions of picture by measurement or percentage of original

Maintains proportions of original picture when height or width is changed

Practice

Open the student file **Prac8-4** and follow the instructions in the document.

Hot Tip

If you are working with a standard Word document rather than a Web page, the Format Object command and Format Object dialog box will be called Format Picture.

Drawing AutoShapes

Concept

Word's Drawing toolbar allows you to add lines, shapes, pictures, and other graphical objects to your documents. Some of these objects are functional, while others can be used simply for decorative purposes. You have complete control over where these items, called AutoShapes, are placed and how much space they will occupy. Once you draw an AutoShape you can change its layer order so that interacts with other elements on the page more effectively.

Do It!

Sabrina will use the Drawing toolbar to add an AutoShape to her Web document.

1. Click View, then highlight Toolbars, then click Drawing to activate the Drawing toolbar if it is not already visible.

2. Click the AutoShapes button AutoShapes ▾ on the Drawing toolbar. The AutoShapes menu will appear.

3. Point to Stars and Banners on the AutoShapes menu to highlight it. A submenu will open that contains a variety of star and banner shapes.

4. Click the Down Ribbon button , as shown in **Figure 8-11**. The menus will close and the shape you clicked is activated. As you move the mouse pointer over the document, the pointer will change to + .

5. Position the mouse pointer just below the recycling Clip Art and approximately one inch to the left of the text Please Recycle! Then click and drag down and to the right. As you drag, the banner you are drawing will begin to take shape. Release the mouse button when the center part of the banner is large enough to accommodate the text. As soon as you release, the banner will conceal the text.

6. Click the Draw button Draw ▾ on the Drawing toolbar. A menu of commands will appear. Highlight the Order command, and then click Send Behind Text on the submenu. The selected banner will move behind the text, making the phrase Please Recycle! visible. The document should now look like **Figure 8-12**.

7. Save the changes you have made.

More

After you have drawn an AutoShape, you can still alter its structure. AutoShapes have sizing handles, represented by small, white rectangles, like other objects. They also have adjustment handles, represented by yellow diamonds, that allow you to change certain aspects of the shape. The number of adjustment handles available is specific to each AutoShape.

Figure 8-11 Selecting an AutoShape

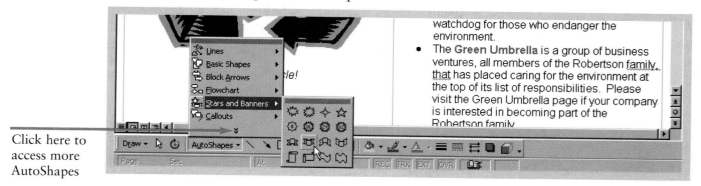

Word 2000

Click here to
access more
AutoShapes

Figure 8-12 Down Ribbon AutoShape

AutoShape moved
behind text

Adjustment handle

Practice

Open the student file **Prac8-5** and follow
the instruction in the document.

Hot Tip

Use the **Send to front**, **Send to Back**,
Send Forward, and **Send Backward** commands on the Order submenu to layer
AutoShapes with other AutoShapes and
objects.

Formatting Drawn Objects

Concept

Objects such as AutoShapes that you add to a document can be formatted in a variety of ways. Among the formatting options you can apply to a drawn object are fill color, line color, textures, shadows, and 3-D effects.

Do It!

Sabrina wants to add a texture and a shadow to the Down Ribbon AutoShape she drew previously.

1. Click the Down Ribbon AutoShape to select it if it is not already selected.

2. Click the arrow on the right edge of the Drawing toolbar's Fill Color button. A color palette that also contains two commands at the bottom will appear. You can click any of the color squares to apply a color to the selected object.

3. Click the Fill Effects command at the bottom of the palette. The Fill Effects dialog box will open.

4. Click the Texture tab to bring it to the front of the dialog box. On the Texture tab, you will see a grid of images that can be applied to objects as textures.

5. Drag the scroll bar box on the Texture tab to the bottom of the scroll bar to bring a different set of textures into view.

6. Click the second texture in the second row of the visible grid to select it as shown in **Figure 8-13**. The name of the texture, Paper bag, will appear below the grid.

7. Click ⬚ OK ⬚ to close the Fill Effects dialog box and apply the texture. The AutoShape is filled with the Paper bag texture.

8. With the Down Ribbon still selected, click the Shadow button 🔲 on the Drawing toolbar. A menu of shadows will appear.

9. Click the button for Shadow Style 14 🔲 (each button's name will appear in a ScreenTip when you point to it). A drop shadow is added to the shape.

10. Select the text inside the Down Ribbon and make it bold and yellow. Compare your work to **Figure 8-14** for accuracy, and then save your changes.

More

A gradient is a fill color effect that causes a color to fade from dark to light, or intensify from light to dark. You can use the Gradient tab in the Fill Effects dialog box to create a one color or two color gradient. Options for shading style and directional variants for the gradient are also available. If none of the colors on the Fill Color palette satisfies your needs, you can create custom colors by clicking the More Colors command near the bottom of the palette.

Figure 8-13 Texture tab in Fill Effects dialog box

Selected texture

Click to create a
texture from your
own image file

Figure 8-14 AutoShape formatted with texture and shadow

Our Goal

To promote environmental issues and awareness in all corners of the Earth.

Our Approach

Robertson approaches environmental issues via three main avenues:

- The Public Relations department promotes those people, organizations, and events whose activities and practices have a positive effect on the environment. It also serves as a watchdog for those who endanger the environment.
- The Green Umbrella is a group of business ventures, all members of the Robertson family, that has placed caring for the environment at the top of its list of responsibilities. Please visit the Green Umbrella page if your company is interested in becoming part of the Robertson family.
- Robertson Press produces educational

Practice

Open the student file MyPrac8-5, which should now contain two AutoShapes. Fill one shape with the color blue, and the other with the texture called **Purple mesh**. Add a shadow to each shape and save the resulting document as **MyPrac8-6**.

Hot Tip

If you are having difficulty selecting an object in a document, make sure the **Select Objects** button on the Drawing toolbars is indented.

Inserting a Picture from a File

Concept

Sometimes you may want to include images in a document that are independent of the Word program. Word can handle several image file formats, allowing you to place almost any image file you have on disk in a document. This flexibility is highly beneficial to organizations that make use of logos and photographs that could not possibly be replicated by Clip Art of AutoShapes.

Do It!

Sabrina needs to include a logo for an upcoming environmental symposium in her document. The file is stored on her hard drive.

1. Scroll down to the bottom of the document robertson.htm and click below the Down Ribbon AutoShape to place the insertion point there.

2. Press [Enter] five times to insert several blank lines below the AutoShape.

3. Click Insert, then highlight Picture, and then click From File on the submenu. The Insert Picture dialog box will appear.

4. Use the Look in: box and the contents window to display contents of your Student Files folder.

5. Select the file Doit8-7.jpg in the contents window, as shown in **Figure 8-15**. A preview of the picture will appear in the right half of the dialog box (if you do not see the preview, click the Views button 🔳 until it appears).

6. Click the Insert button [Insert ▾] to place the picture file in the Word document.

7. Click the picture to select it on the page.

8. Click 🔳 to center the picture in the column, as shown in **Figure 8-16**.

9. Save your document.

More

The Insert button includes a drop-down arrow that you can click to obtain a menu of options for inserting the selected picture. The first option, Insert, is simply the equivalent of clicking the button itself as you did above. If you choose Link to File, the image you insert is not actually embedded in the document with which you are working. Instead, Word creates a link to the image's source file that allows it to appear in the second, or destination, file as well. Any changes made to the source file will be updated in the linked version of the image automatically. The last option, Insert and Link, allows you to include all of the data for the image file in the destination while also maintaining a link to the source image for automatic updating.

Figure 8-15 Insert Picture dialog box

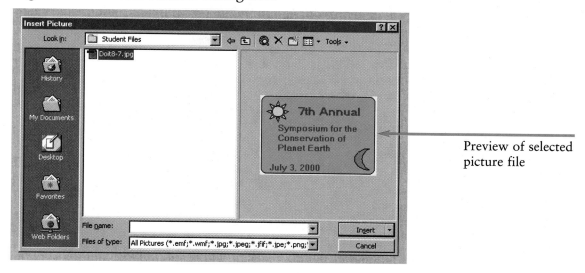

Preview of selected picture file

Figure 8-16 Picture inserted from file

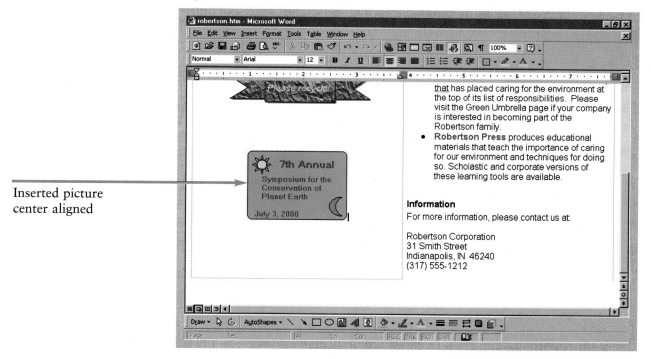

Inserted picture center aligned

Practice

Open a blank document and insert the picture file **Prac8-7.bmp**. Save the new Word file as **MyPrac8-7**.

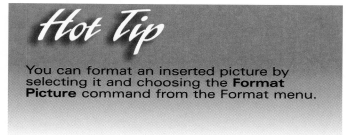

Hot Tip

You can format an inserted picture by selecting it and choosing the **Format Picture** command from the Format menu.

Using WordArt

Concept

WordArt is a versatile tool that enables you to improve your documents visually by combining text and graphics into one object. A piece of WordArt can consist of any text that you choose, structurally altered with a style from the WordArt Gallery. Since this text becomes an object, its size, shape, and color can be manipulated easily.

Do It!

Sabrina wants to convert the main heading text on her Web page into WordArt.

1. Select the text Robertson Corporation at the top of robertson.htm.

2. Click ✂ to remove the text and place a copy of it on the Clipboard.

3. With the insertion point still in the row, use the Font Size box on the Standard toolbar to change the point size of the row to 36.

4. Click the Insert WordArt button 📄 on the Drawing toolbar. The WordArt Gallery dialog box will open.

5. Click the fourth WordArt style from the left in the third row of the gallery to select it, as shown in **Figure 8-17**.

6. Click OK . The WordArt Gallery dialog box closes and is replaced by the Edit WordArt Text dialog box. In this dialog box, you type the text that you want to turn into WordArt. You can also select a font, font size, and text style. Word has already highlighted its default text, Your Text Here.

7. Press [Ctrl]+[V] on the keyboard to paste the text you cut earlier over the default text.

8. Use the Font Size box in the dialog box to change the size of the WordArt text to 28 pt, as shown in **Figure 8-18**.

9. Click OK to close the dialog box. The WordArt you have created will appear in the center of the document. The WordArt toolbar will also appear.

10. Place the mouse pointer over the WordArt so that the pointer changes to ✛.

11. Click and drag the WordArt straight up and drop it in the row at the top of the document (see **Figure 8-19**).

Figure 8-17 WordArt gallery dialog box

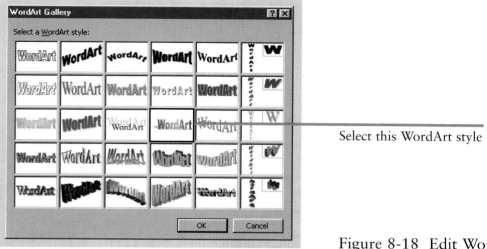

Select this WordArt style

Figure 8-18 Edit WordArt Text dialog box

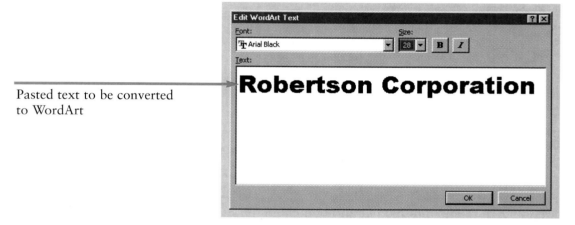

Pasted text to be converted to WordArt

Figure 8-19 Repositioned WordArt

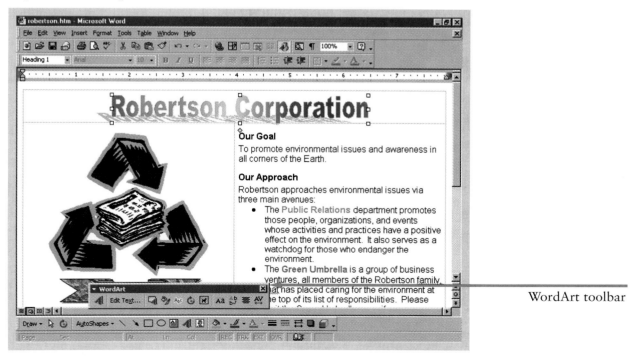

WordArt toolbar

Using WordArt
(continued)

Do It!

12 Click the WordArt Character Spacing button ⊞ on the WordArt toolbar. A menu of spacing options will open. The current spacing setting is Normal.

13 Click Tight on the Character Spacing menu. The letters in your WordArt will be pushed closer together.

14 Click the WordArt Shape button 📶 on the WordArt toolbar. An extensive menu of WordArt shape choices will appear.

15 Click the shape called Inflate Top (it is the fifth shape in the fourth row) as shown in **Figure 8-20**. The WordArt will reform itself with the new shape.

16 When you change the shape of WordArt, its position on the page can be affected. If necessary, use the arrow keys on the keyboard to nudge the WordArt back into position.

17 Click a blank part of the document to deselect the WordArt. **Figure 8-21** shows its completed form.

18 Save the changes you have made to your document.

More

Table 8-1 Other WordArt toolbar buttons

BUTTON	COMMAND	FUNCTION
🔲	WordArt Gallery	Opens the WordArt Gallery
📝	Format WordArt	Opens the Format WordArt dialog box
🔄	Free Rotate	Allows you to rotate the selected WordArt
🔲	Text Wrapping	Controls how WordArt interacts with surrounding text
Aa	WordArt Same Letter Heights	Makes all letters in selected WordArt equal in height
🔡	WordArt Vertical Text	Arranges text vertically, top to bottom
≣	WordArt Alignment	Opens a menu of text alignment choices

Figure 8-20 Selecting a WordArt shape

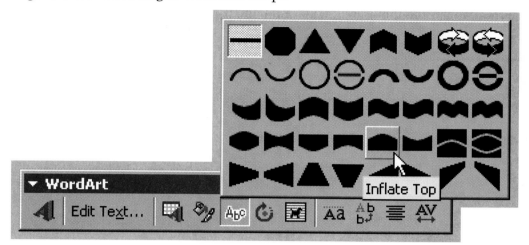

Figure 8-21 WordArt with new spacing and shape

Practice

Open a new document and create a piece of WordArt that uses **Loose** character spacing and the shape **Wave 2**. Save the file as **MyPrac8-8**.

Hot Tip

Double-clicking a piece of WordArt opens the Edit WordArt Text dialog box.

Inserting Hyperlinks

Concept

One of the greatest strengths of the World Wide Web as an informational tool is that it does not require you to access resources in a linear fashion. You can go directly from a page of hockey statistics stored on a server in Toronto to an online music store operating in Florida with one click of the mouse. Hyperlinks provide the key to exploring Web. Since each file on the Web has a particular storage location, and all of the computers on the Web are connected as part of a network, you can insert a link to any file on the Web in your Web page.

Do It!

Sabrina will insert a link to Robertson's Public Relations Web page in the page she has been designing.

1. Click and drag with the mouse to select the words Public Relations in the first bulleted paragraph under Our Approach (do not highlight the space between Relations and department – see **Figure 8-22**).

2. Click the Insert Hyperlink button 🔗 on the Standard toolbar. The Insert Hyperlink dialog box will appear with a blinking insertion point in the Type the file or Web page name: text box. The Existing File or Web page button should be depressed in the Link to: bar on the left side of the dialog box. The text you selected in the document has been inserted in the Text to display: text box. This box will be empty if you execute the Insert Hyperlink command without selecting text first.

3. Type http://www.domain.org/~robertson/pr.htm (this is a fictional Web address) in the Type the file or Web page name: box, as shown in **Figure 8-23**.

4. Click the ScreenTip button ScreenTip... to open the Set Hyperlink ScreenTip dialog box. In this dialog box, you can set a customized ScreenTip that will appear when a Web user rests the mouse pointer over the hyperlink you are creating. As noted in the dialog box, only users of the Internet Explorer 4.0 browser or later will be able to receive the ScreenTip.

5. Type Robertson Public Relations and then click OK to set the ScreenTip.

6. Click OK in the Insert Hyperlink dialog box to insert the Public Relations hyperlink. The hyperlinked text is now underlined, which is a standard identifier and a Word default setting for hyperlinks. It is also blue, which is Word's default color for unvisited links (and fairly standard on the Web as well). When you place the pointer over the link, the pointer will change to a hand, and the customized ScreenTip you created will appear (see **Figure 8-24**).

More

The Link to: bar in the Insert Hyperlink dialog box allows you to create three other kinds of links. If you want to create a link to a target in the same document, click the Place in this Document button. The Create New Document button allows you to insert a link to a document that does not yet exist. You will then have the option of creating the new document immediately or later. The E-mail Address button creates a link that will open the user's mail writing client to a new message window. The address field will be filled out with the address you embedded in the link.

Figure 8-22 Selecting text for a hyperlink

Our Goal
To promote environmental issues and awareness in all corners of the Earth.

Our Approach
Robertson approaches environmental issues via three main avenues:
- The Public Relations department promotes those people, organizations, and events whose activities and practices have a positive effect on the environment. It also serves as a watchdog for those who endanger the environment.

Highlighted text will be converted to hyperlink

Figure 8-23 Insert Hyperlink dialog box

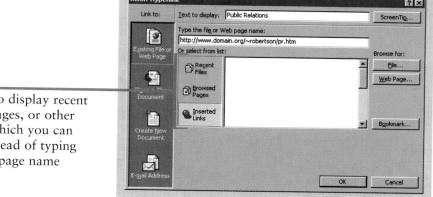

Click a button to display recent files, browsed pages, or other inserted links, which you can choose from instead of typing in a file or Web page name

Figure 8-24 Inserted hyperlink

Our Approach
Robertson approaches environmental issues via three main avenues: Robertson Public Relations
- The **Public Relations** department promotes those people, organizations, and events whose activities and practices have a positive effect on the environment. It also serves as a watchdog for those who endanger the environment.

Customized ScreenTip

Link Select pointer

Practice

In the document robertson.htm, change the text **Green Umbrella** in the second bulleted paragraph to a hyperlink aimed at the following fictional address:
http://www.domain.org/~robertson/gu.htm

Hot Tip

You can modify the default formatting style for hyperlinks by choosing the Style command from the Format menu. You can also format individual links in any manner you wish. Objects such as pictures can also be made into hyperlinks.

Previewing and Editing a Web Page

Concept

One of the greatest problems that novice Web page designers encounter is that their pages look nothing like they thought they would when viewed on the Web with a browser. To combat this problem, Word provides the Web Page Preview command, which permits you to view your page as it will appear when viewed on the Web. You can then edit your page accordingly. As mentioned at the beginning of this Lesson, Word's editing capabilities are extremely convenient. You can bring an HTML document created with Word right back into the program for editing. When you have made the necessary adjustments, you are free to round-trip the document right back to the Web, where anyone with a Web browser can view it.

Do It!

Sabrina wants to preview her document as a Web page, and then bring it back into Word for editing.

1. Click File, then click Web Page Preview. Word will launch your default Web browser (Microsoft Internet Explorer 5.0 in this example), and load the page into the browser window. As you can see in **Figure 8-25**, some of the elements of the page have not translated correctly.

2. Notice that the Edit button on the Standard Buttons toolbar includes the Word icon. This signifies that the default editor for this document is Microsoft Word. You can click on the arrow on the right edge of the button to select a different editing tool such as Windows Notepad. Using Notepad requires that you know HTML.

3. Click (click the button itself, not the arrow). The Word window reappears with the document. This window was, of course, already open. However, if you had actually been viewing this document on the Web instead of reading it from a local disk, the document would have been opened in Word as well.

4. Click in the top-left corner of the page's left column to place the insertion point there. Then press [Enter] three times. Everything in the column will move down the page.

5. Click just in front of the text Please Recycle! inside the Down Ribbon AutoShape to move the insertion point there. Press [Enter] once to move just that text down one line.

6. Click in the top-left corner of the right column to place the insertion point directly in front of Our Goal. Then press [Enter] twice.

7. Save the changes you have made to the document. If you do not save the document, Web Page Preview cannot access the most recent version of your work.

8. Run Web Page Preview again. The items that were aligned incorrectly before should now be placed properly, as shown in **Figure 8-26**.

Figure 8-25 Previewing a Web page with Internet Explorer

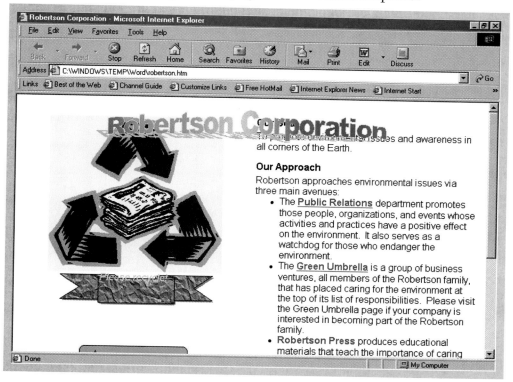

Figure 8-26 Preview of corrected Web page

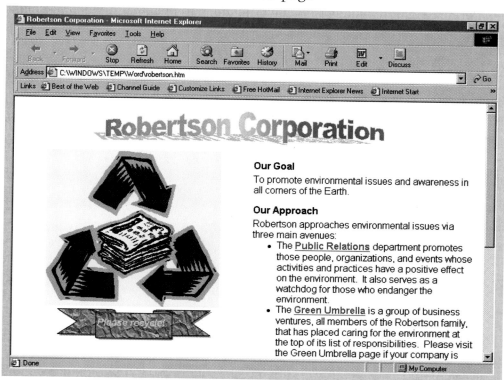

Word 2000

Shortcuts

Function	Button/Mouse	Menu	Keyboard
Insert Clip Art		Click Insert, then highlight Picture, then click Clip Art	[Alt]+[I], [P], [C]
Center selected object		Click Format, then click Format Object (AutoShape, etc.)	[Ctrl]+[E]
Insert Hyperlink		Click Insert, then click Hyperlink	[Ctrl]+[K]
Insert WordArt		Click Insert, then highlight Picture, then click WordArt	[Alt]+[I], [P], [W]

Identify Key Features

Name the items indicated by callouts in **Figure 8-27**.

Figure 8-27 Graphics and Web related elements

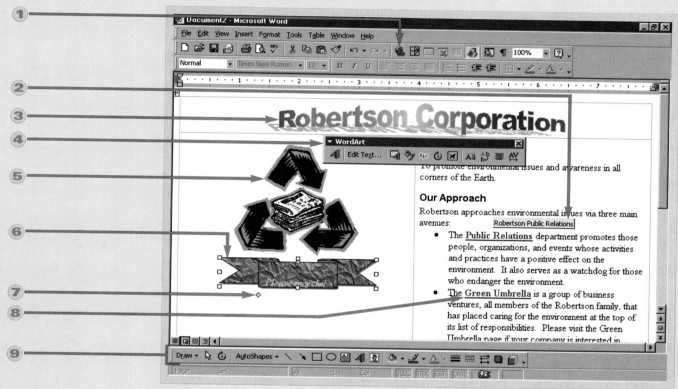

Select The Best Answer

10. Creates an HTML document

11. Pictures included with Word that you can insert in a document

12. Found on the Picture toolbar

13. A category of AutoShapes

14. Contains the Order command

15. A fill effect consisting of colors that fade or intensify

16. Allows you to place graphics you have on file in a document

17. Text that you can click to connect to another target, document, or file

18. Allows you to view a document as it will appear on the Web

a. Draw menu

b. Web Page Preview

c. Insert Picture dialog box

d. Save as Web Page

e. Stars and Banners

f. Hyperlink

g. Clip Art

h. More Brightness button

i. Gradient

Quiz (continued)

Complete the Statement

19. If you want to make changes to a Web page that you are viewing in your browser, click the browser's:

    a. Home button

    b. Back button

    c. Refresh button

    d. Edit button

20. Text that is underlined and blue is most likely:

    a. WordArt

    b. A hyperlink

    c. Selected

    d. A placeholder

21. To change the text used in WordArt, you need to access the:

    a. WordArt Gallery

    b. Edit WordArt Text dialog box

    c. Microsoft Clip Gallery

    d. Style Gallery

22. The Texture tab can be found in the:

    a. Fill Effects dialog box

    b. WordArt Gallery

    c. AutoShape dialog box

    d. Insert Hyperlink dialog box

23. Text that you enter in the Set Page Title dialog box will appear in the:

    a. Document's file name

    b. Title bar of the Word window

    c. Title bar of the browser window

    d. First line of the Web page

24. The AutoShapes button is found on the:

    a. Picture toolbar

    b. Formatting toolbar

    c. Drawing toolbar

    d. WordArt toolbar

25. The WordArt toolbar contains all of the following buttons except:

    a. Free Rotate

    b. WordArt Character Spacing

    c. Text Wrapping

    d. More Contrast

26. Inflate Top is an example of:

    a. A WordArt Style

    b. A WordArt Shape

    c. An AutoShape

    d. Web page template

Interactivity

Test Your Skills

1. Create a Web page using a Word template:

   a. Create a new document by choosing the Simple Layout template from the Wep Pages tab in the New dialog box.

   b. Replace the main heading placeholder text with the name of a fictional company.

   c. Change the Section 1 placeholder text to Who We Are, Section 2 to What We Do, and Section 3 to Where You Can Contact Us.

   d. Replace the placeholder text under each section heading with appropriate text about your fictional company.

   e. Save the document as a Web page named TYS8.htm. Set the page title to be the name of the company.

2. Insert Clip Art into a document:

   a. Insert a piece of Clip Art from the Business category at the top of the page's left column.

   b. Insert a piece of Clip Art from the People at Work category at the top of the page's right column.

   c. Resize both pieces of Clip Art so that they are approximately half their original sizes.

   d. Center both pieces of Clip Art in their respective columns.

3. Draw and format an AutoShape:

   a. Draw a Curved Up Ribbon below the Clip Art in the left column.

   b. Draw a Curved Down Ribbon below the Clip Art in the right column.

   c. Fill one of the ribbons with the texture Recycled paper and the other with Canvas.

   d. Type a short slogan for your company on top of each of the ribbons.

   e. Apply a shadow style to each ribbon.

4. Add WordArt to a document:

   a. Replace the name of your company at the top of the page with WordArt.

   b. Make the text for the WordArt 20 pt, Times New Roman.

   c. Once inserted, move the WordArt to its proper position, centered at the top of the page.

   d. Change the shape of your WordArt to Chevron Up.

5. Convert selected text to a hyperlink:

   a. Select the Section 1 heading, Who We Are, and open the Insert Hyperlink dialog box.

   b. Link the selected text to http://www.wordl8.com/tys.

   c. Set a ScreenTip for the hyperlink that reads Click here for more info.

Interactivity (continued)

6. Preview and edit a Web page:

   a. Use the Web Page Preview command to view your document in a Web browser.

   b. Edit the document based on what you saw in the Web Page Preview.

   c. Save the finished document

Problem Solving

1. As the Assistant to the Director of Communications at a large educational publishing firm, you have been put in charge of all of the company's internal communications. You have decided that your colleagues would benefit from receiving a bimonthly newsletter. This will ensure that each department is aware of developments throughout the company on a regular basis. One of the featured items in the premiere edition of your newsletter is the adoption of Word 2000 by your company. You have dedicated yourself to making the newsletter lively so that people will not view it as just another piece of paper piling up on their desks. To that end, use Clip Art, AutoShapes, and WordArt in the newsletter. In addition, your boss has informed you that your newsletter may eventually appear on the company's Web site. Therefore, you should save your newsletter as a standard Word document and as a Web page. Be sure to preview the document as a Web page to ensure that the HTML version functions properly. Save the documents as Solved8-1.doc and Solved8-1.htm.

2. Having worked in the Customer Service department of a health insurance company for several years, you know that customers have plenty of questions about their health care plan and coverage. You have decided to provide an extra source of information for customers by adding a Frequently Asked Questions page to the company's Web site. Use Word's Frequently Asked Questions Web page template to create the page. You may add visual enhancements to the page, but use them sparingly as the purpose of the page is to inform. Save the document as Solved8-2.htm.

3. Use Word's Personal Web Page template to design a home page for yourself. Illustrate the points you make about yourself with Clip Art, and use AutoShapes and WordArt to call attention to particular items. In the Favorite Links section, insert hyperlinks for your favorite Web pages. If you are not familiar with the Web, use the following addresses as hyperlinks: http://www.whitehouse.gov, http://www.usps.gov, http://www.loc.gov. Save your home page as Solved8-3.htm.

4. You have recently started working in the newsroom at a city newspaper, which is owned by a larger conglomerate. Most of your coworkers have been with the station for many years, and are still resisting the switch from typewriters to word processing. You know that word processing will make their jobs much easier, and Word's graphic capabilities will even allow them to do mock layouts. Use Word to design an illustrated guide to word processing with Microsoft Word 2000. Explain how to insert objects like Clip Art, AutoShapes, WordArt, pictures from file, and hyperlinks. Include of examples of these items in the guide. Save the document as Solved8-4.

Glossary

A

Alignment
The horizontal position of text within a line or between tab stops. Word's alignment options are right, left, centered, and justified.

Application
See *program.*

Arrow keys
The [↑], [↓], [←], and [→] keys on the keyboard. Used to move the insertion point, select from a menu or a list of options, or in combination with other keys to execute specific commands.

Automatic save
A feature that automatically saves document changes in a temporary file at specified intervals. If power to the computer is interrupted, the changes in effect from the last save are retained. Enabled by default, you can turn off this feature from the Save tab of the Options dialog box on the Tools menu.

AutoCorrect
A feature that automatically corrects misspelled words as they are entered. Word provides many entries for commonly misspelled words, but you may also add your own.

AutoFormat
A feature that improves the appearance of a document by applying consistent formatting and styles based on a default document templates or a document template that you specify. The AutoFormat feature can also add bullets or numbers to lists and symbols for trademarks and copyrights where necessary.

AutoShapes
An object from the drawing toolbar which allows you complete control over every aspect of that object.

AutoText
Text that Word is programmed to recognize. When you begin to type a word or phrase that Word recognizes, the program offers to complete it for you.

B

Browser
An application that allows you to find and view information on the World Wide Web. Major browsers include Netscape Navigator and Microsoft Internet Explorer.

C

Case
Refers to whether or not a letter is capitalized. Some search features are case-sensitive; that is, they will differentiate between words that are spelled the same but have different capitalization.

Cell
The basic unit of a table, separated by gridlines. In a table, the intersection of a row and a column forms one cell.

Cell reference

A code that identifies a cell's position in a table. Each cell reference contains a letter indicating its column and a number indicating its row.

Character style

A combination of character formats from the Font dialog box that is identified by a style name. Changing an element (such as the font size) of a character style changes all text that has been formatted with that style.

Chart

A graphical representation of data.

Click

To press and release a mouse button in one motion; usually refers to the left mouse button.

Click and Type

A method of placing the insertion point somewhere in a document to precisely choose where to add text.

Clip art

A precreated, usually copyright-free, graphic image that can be inserted into a document to illustrate a point or to add visual interest. Clip art often comes in large collections.

Clip Gallery

A Microsoft Office facility that acts as a library of clip art, pictures, sounds and videos. It allows you to import, store, and reuse these objects in Word documents and in other Office applications.

Clipboard

A temporary storage area for cut or copied text or graphics. You can paste the contents of the Clipboard into any Word document or into a file of another Microsoft Windows program. The Office Clipboard differs from the Windows Clipboard in that it can hold up to twelve items at once. You can view the contents of the Office Clipboard by activating its toolbar from the View menu.

Custom dictionary

A document containing all the words that have been "learned" by Word's spell checker. More that one custom dictionary can be created and referenced by a single copy of Microsoft Word.

Cut

To remove selected text or a graphic from a document to the Clipboard so that it may be reinserted elsewhere in the document or in another document.

D

Data Source

Where the data from a mail merge comes from, a dialog box assists you in finding the neccessary data to complete the merge.

Defaults

Predefined settings for variable items such as page margins, tab spacing, and shortcut key assignments; these can be changed when necessary.

Dialog box

A box that displays the available command options for you to review or change.

Document window

The window on the screen in which a document is viewed and edited. When the document window is maximized, it shares its borders and title bar with the Word application window.

Drag
To hold down the mouse button while moving the mouse.

Draw Table tool
Allows you to create the borders and gridlines of a table freehand.

Drive
The mechanism in a computer that reads recordable media (such as a disk or tape cartridge) to retrieve and store information. Personal computers often have one hard disk drive labeled C, a drive that reads floppy disks labeled A, and a drive that reads CDs labeled D.

E

Edit
To add, delete, or modify text or other elements of a file.

Effects
Text formats such as small caps, all caps, hidden text, strikethrough, subscript, or superscript.

Envelopes
A mail merge may also be used to create merge fields which would be used for addressing envelopes.

Extend selection
To increase the selected area. When a selection is extended, it grows progressively larger each time [F8] is pressed. To shrink the selection, press [Shift]+[F8]. The arrow keys may also be used with the [Shift] key to enlarge or shrink the selection.

F

Field
The place in a main document where a specific portion of a record, such a a postal code, will be inserted when the document is merged. Also known as a merge field.

File
A document that has been created and saved under a unique file name. In Word, all documents and pictures are stored as files.

Find
Command that locates whatever is specified – font, style, word, format, etc.

Find and Replace dialog box
Locates specified items in your document and replaces them with another specified item.

Folders
Subdivisions of a disk that work like a filing system to help you organize files.

Font
A name given to a collection of text characters at a certain size, weight, and style. Font has become synonymous with typeface. Arial and Times New Roman are examples of font names.

Font size
Refers to the physical size of text, measured in points (pts). The more points, the larger the appearance of the text on the page.

Font style
Refers to whether text appears as bold, italicized, or underlined, or any combination of these formats.

Format

The way text appears on a page. In Word formats comes from direct formatting or the application of styles. The four formatting levels are character, paragraph, section, and document.

Formula

An expression that performs a calculation in a table.

G

Global template

In Word, a template named NORMAL.DOT that contains default menus, AutoCorrect entries, styles and page setup settings. Documents use the global template unless a custom template is specified. See also *template*.

Gridlines

The lines that separate cells in a table. Gridlines do not print. You can alternately hide and display gridlines with the Gridlines command on the Table menu.

H

Hanging indent

A paragraph format in which the first line of a paragraph extends farther to the left than subsequent lines.

Header/footer

A header is an item or group of items that appears at the top of every page in a section. A footer appears at the bottom of every page. Headers and footers often contain page numbers, chapter titles, dates, and author names.

Hidden text

A character format that allows you to show or hide designated text. Word indicates hidden text by underlining it with a dotted line. You can select or clear the Hidden Text option with the Options command on the Tools menu. Hidden text may be omitted when printing.

Horizontal ruler

A bar displayed across the top of the document window in all views. The ruler can be used to indent paragraphs, set tab stops, adjust left and right paragraph margins, and change column widths in a table. You can hide this ruler by clicking View, then clicking Ruler.

HTML

An acronym for HyperText Markup Language, which is the language that defines the way information is presented on a Web page. Word can automatically convert the formatting you have given a document into HTML, which functionally turns your document into a Web page.

HTTP

An acronym for HyperText Transfer Protocol; appears at the beginning of a URL to notify the browser that the following information is a hypertext Web document.

Hyperlink

Originated as an element of Web page design; usually text, clicking a hyperlink brings you directly to a predefined location within a document or to a specific page on the World Wide Web.

I

Indent
The distance between text boundaries and page margins. Positive indents make the text area narrower than the space between margins. Negative indents allow text to extend into the margins. A paragraph can have left, right, and first-line indents.

Insertion point
A vertical blinking line on the Word screen that indicates where text and graphics will be inserted. The insertion point also determines where Word will begin an action.

L

Labels
Mailing labels may be crated by using the same type of merge fields used when you are creating a mail merge. They can be created using a mail merge.

Landscape
A term used to refer to horizontal page orientation; opposite of "portrait," or vertical, orientation.

Line break
A mark inserted where you want to end one line and start another without starting a new paragraph. A line break may be inserted by pressing [Shift]+[Return].

Line spacing
The height of a line of text, often measured in lines or points.

M

Mail Merge
A function which allows you to create a single document plus a seperate file containing the information that will be unique to each copy when it is printed.

Margin
The distance between the edge of the text in the document and the top, bottom, or side edges of the page.

Maximize
To enlarge a window to its maximum size. Maximizing an application window causes it to fill the screen; maximizing a document window causes it to fill the application window.

Menu bar
Lists the names of menus containing Word commands. Click a menu name on the menu bar to display a list of commands.

Merge cells
Command that combines two or more cells in a table into one cell.

Merge Fields
Fields which tell Word what data to insert, and where to insert it when you merge documents.

Minimize
To shrink a window to its minimum size. Minimizing an application window reduces it to a button on the Windows taskbar; minimizing a document window reduces it to a short title bar in the application window.

N

Nonprinting characters

Marks displayed on the screen to indicate characters that do not print, such as paragraph marks or spaces. You can control the display of these characters with the Options command on the Tools menu, and the Show/Hide ¶ button on the Standard toolbar.

Normal View

Used for most editing and formatting tasks. Normal View shows text formatting but simplifies the layout of the page so that you can type and edit quickly.

Note pane

A special window in which the text of all the footnotes in a document appears. The note pane can be accessed by double-clicking a note reference mark.

O

Object

A table, chart, graphic, equation, or other form of information you create and edit with a program other than Word, but whose data you insert and store in a Word document.

Office Assistant

An animated manifestation of the Microsoft Office 2000 help facility. The Office Assistant provides hints, instructions, and a convenient interface between the user and Word's various help features.

Options

The choices available in a dialog box.

Overtype

An option for replacing existing characters one by one as you type. You can select overtype by selecting the Overtype option on the Edit tab with the Options command on the Tools menu. When you select the Overtype option, the letters "OVR" appear in the status bar at the bottom of the Word window. You can also double-click these letters in the status bar to activate or deactivate overtype mode.

P

Page Break

The point at which one page ends and another begins. A break you insert is called a hard break; a break determined by the page layout is called a soft break. In Normal View, a hard break appears as a dotted line and is labeled Page Break, while a soft break appears as a dotted line without a label.

Paragraph style

A stored set of paragraph format settings.

Paste

To insert cut or copied text into a document from the Clipboard.

Path

The address of a file's location. It contains the drive, folder and subfolders, and file name. For example, the complete path for Microsoft Word might be C:\Program Files\Microsoft\Office\Winword.exe.

Point size

A measurement used for the size of text characters. There are 72 points per inch.

Portrait

A term used to refer to vertical page orientation; opposite of "landscape," or horizontal, orientation.

Position

The specific placement of graphics, tables, and paragraphs on a page. In Word, you can assign items to fixed positions on a page.

Print Layout View

A view of a document as it will appear when you print it. Items such as headers, footnotes, and framed objects appear in their actual positions, and you can drag them to new positions.

Print Preview

Allows you to view a document as it will appear when printed. Includes a magnifier tool and the ability to view multiple pages at once.

Program

A software application that performs specific tasks, such as Microsoft Word or Microsoft Excel.

Program window

A window that contains the running program. The window displays the menus and provides the workspace for any document used within the application. The application window shares its borders and title bar with maximized document windows.

R

Read-Only

A file setting that allows a file to be opened and read, but not modified.

Redo

Counteracts the Undo command by repeating previously reversed actions or changes, usually editing or formatting commands. Only actions that have been undone can be reversed with the redo command.

Repeat

Command that performs your most recent operation again.

Resize

To change the size of an object (such as framed text or a graphic) by dragging sizing handles located on the sides and corner of the selected object, or by adjusting its dimensions in a dialog box.

Right-click

To click the right mouse button; often necessary to access specialized menus and shortcuts. The designated right and left mouse buttons may be reversed with the Mouse control panel to accomodate user preferences.

S

Sans serif font

A font whose characters do not include serifs, the small strokes at the ends of the characters. Arial and Helvetica are sans serif fonts.

ScreenTip

A brief explanation of a button or object that appears when the mouse pointer is paused over it. Other ScreenTips are accessed by clicking What's This from the Help menu and then clicking a particular item, or by clicking the question mark button in the title bar of dialog boxes.

Scroll bar

A graphical device for moving vertically and horizontally through a document with the mouse. Scroll bars are located along the right and bottom edges of the document window.

Section

A part of a document separated from the rest of the document by a section break. By separating a document into sections, you can use different page and column formatting in different parts of the same document.

Selection bar

An invisible column at the left edge of a column of text used to select text with the mouse. In a table, each cell has its own Selection bar at the left edge of the cell.

Serif font

A font that has small strokes at the ends of the characters. Times New Roman and Palatino are serif fonts.

Soft return

A line break created by pressing [Shift]+[Enter]. This creates a new line without creating a new paragraph.

Spreadsheet program

A software program used for calculations and financial analysis.

Standard toolbar

A row of buttons that perform some of the most frequently used commands, such as Open, Print and Save. Usually located under the menu bar.

Status bar

Located at the bottom of the Word window, it displays the current page number and section number, the total number of pages in the document, and the vertical position of the insertion point. It also indicates whether certain options are active.

Style

A group of formatting instructions that you name and store, and are able to modify. When you apply a style to selected characters and paragraphs, all the formatting instructions of that style are applied at once.

Style dialog box

A feature that allows you to examine the overall formatting and styles used in a document template. You can also preview your document formatted in the styles from a selected template.

Style Gallery

Contains various templates designed to enhance the appearance of your documents.

T

Tab stop

A measured position for placing and aligning text at a specific distance along a line. Word has four kinds of tab stops, left-aligned (the default), centered, right-aligned, and decimal. Tab stops are shown on the horizontal ruler.

Tabs command

A command which allows you to establish a style which is attached to the Tab key, every time it is pressed the style is activated.

Table

One or more rows of cells commonly used to display numbers and other data for quick reference and analysis. Items in a table are organized into rows and columns. You can convert text into a table with the Insert Table command on the Table menu.

Template

A special kind of document that provides basic tools and text for creating a document. Templates can contain styles, AutoText items, macros, customized menu and key assignments, and text or graphics that are the same in different types of documents.

Text wrap

Automatic placement of a word on the next line when there is not enough room for it on the current line.

Title bar

The horizontal bar at the top of a window that displays the name of the document or application that appears in that window.

Toolbar

A graphical bar containing several buttons that act as shortcuts for many common Word commands.

U

Undo

A command that lets you reverse previous actions or changes, usually editing or formatting actions. Actions from the File menu cannot be reversed. You can undo up to 100 previous actions from the time you opened the document.

URL

An acronym for Uniform Resource Locator; an address specifying where a particular piece of information can be found. A Web address is a kind of URL.

V

Vertical alignment

The placement of text on a page in relation to the top, bottom, or center of the page.

Vertical ruler

A graphical bar displayed at the left edge of the document window in Print Preview. You can use this ruler to adjust the top and bottom page margins, and change row height in a table.

View

A display that shows certain aspects of the document. Word has seven views: Normal, Print Layout, Outline, Web Layout, Master Document, Full Screen, and Print Preview.

View buttons

Appear in the horizontal scroll bar. Allow you to display the document in one of four views: Normal, Print Layout, Web Layout, and Outline.

W

Window

A rectangular area on the screen in which you view and work on documents.

Wizard

A helpful program you use to create documents. When you use a wizard to create a document, you are asked a series of questions about document preferences, and then the wizard creates the document to meet your specifications.

WordArt

A versatile tool which allows you to improve your documents by combining text and graphics into one object.

Word processing program

Software used to create documents efficiently. Usually includes features beyond simple editing, such as formatting and arranging text and graphics to create attractive documents.

World Wide Web

A major component of the Internet, which is a vast global network of smaller networks and personal computers. Web pages include hyperlinks and present information in a graphical format that can incorporate text, graphics, sounds, and digital movies.

WYSIWYG

An acronym for What You See Is What You Get; indicates that a document will print out with the same formatting that is displayed in the document window.

A

Active window, WD 3.14-3.15

Alignment in tables, WD 4.6

Alignment of tabs, WD 3.9

Alignment of text, WD 1.14-1.15, 5.2, 5.8

Antonyms, finding, WD 3.24-3.25

Application window, WD 1.4-1.5

Application window Control icon, WD 1.9

Arrow keys, WD 1.12

AutoCorrect Exceptions dialog box, WD 3.24-3.25

AutoCorrect feature, WD 3.22-3.25, 6.8-6.9

AutoFormat, WD 6.1, 6.8-6.9

AutoFormatting tables, WD 4.16-4.17

Automatic Spell Checking, WD 1.6, WD 3.20-3.23

AutoNumber option for footnotes, WD 3.6

AutoShapes, WD 8.10-8.11

AutoText, WD 5.12

B

Backspace key, WD 1.12

Bolding text, WD 1.14, 5.10

Borders, in tables, WD 4.26-4.29

Borders, in text, WD 5.6-5.7

Borders and Shading dialog box, WD 5.6-5.7

Break dialog box, WD 3.12-3.13

Bulleted lists, WD 5.4-5.5

Bullets, WD 5.4-5.5

Bullets and Numbering dialog box, 5.4-5.5

C

Calculating data in tables, WD 4.12-4.15

Centered text, WD 1.15

Changing page orientation, WD 5.18-5.19

Character effects, WD 5.20-5.21

Character Styles:
applying, WD 6.2-6.3
creating your own, WD 6.4-6.7
editing, WD 6.12-6.13
find and replace, ED 6.18-6.21
general, WD 6.1-6.30
paragraphs and, WD 6.14-6.15

Charts, WD 4.18-4.21

Click and Type, WD 6.24-6.25

Clip Art:
formatting, WD 8.8-8.9
inserting, WD 8.6-8.7

Clipboard, WD 2.6-2.7, 3.14

Close button, WD 1.9

Closing documents, WD 1.8-1.9

Color, changing, WD 1.14

Columns, WD 5.2-5.3

Commands, WD 1.4

Continuous section break, WD 3.12-3.13

Copy button, WD 2.6, 2.18

Copying and moving text, WD 2.8-2.9

Copying and pasting text, WD 3.14

Copying formats, WD 3.16-3.17

Copying text, WD 2.6-2.7

Create New Folder button, WD 1.9

Cut button, WD 2.6, 2.18

Cutting-and-Pasting text, WD 2.6-2.7

D

Data Source:
adding information to, WD 7.6-7.7
creating, WD 7.4-7.5

Date and Time dialog box, WD 5.10-5.11

Deleting rows and columns, in tables, WD 4.8-4.9

Deleting text, WD 1.12-1.13, 2.7

Destination files, WD 4.4

Document window, WD 1.4-1.5

Document window
Control menu, WD 1.9
Documents:
closing, WD 1.8-1.9
editing, WD 2.1-2.17
e-mailing, WD 5.20
footnotes and endnotes
in, WD 3.6-3.7
formatting, WD 1.14-
1.15, 3.1-3.29
indents in, WD 3.8-3.9
line spacing in,
WD 3.8-3.9
moving through,
WD 1.4, 1.13
multiple, WD 3.14-3.15
new, WD 1.6
opening, WD 1.10-1.11
page breaks in,
WD 3.12-3.13
page numbers in,
WD 3.4-3.5
saving, WD 1.8-1.9
saving as Web pages,
WD 8.4-8.5
section breaks in,
WD 3.12-3.13
setting margins in,
WD 3.2-3.3
tables in, WD 4.1-4.17
Drag-and-drop method,
WD 2.6, 2.8-2.9
Draw Table tool,
WD 4.22-4.26
Drawing, autoshapes,
WD 8.10-8.11
Drawing toolbar, 8.10-
8.11

E

Edit menu, WD 2.6
Editing:
with AutoCorrect,
WD 3.22-3.25

character style, 6.12-
6.13
documents, WD 2.1-
2.17
merged documents,
7.10-7.11
tables, WD 4.6-4.7
Web pages, WD 8.22-
8.23
E-mailing documents,
WD 5.20
Embedded objects,
WD 4.4
End key, WD 1.12-1.13
Endnotes, inserting,
WD 3.6-3.7
Enter key, WD 1.6-1.7
Entering text, WD 1.6-1.7
Envelope Options dialog
box, WD 7.18-7.19
Envelopes, printing, and
preparing, 7.18-7.21
Envelopes and Labels
dialog box, WD 7.20-
7.21
Eraser button, WD 4.24
Excel worksheets, insert-
ing in Word documents,
WD 4.4
Extensions, file name,
WD 1.8

F

File names, WD 1.8
Files:
destination and source,
WD 4.4
opening different for-
mats, WD 1.10
searching for, WD 2.2-
2.3
Find command, WD 2.2,
3.28, 6.18-6.19

Finding and Replacing
text, WD 3.28-3.29
styles, 6.18-6.21
First line indent marker,
WD 3.8
Font, defined, WD 1.14
Font box, WD 1.4
Font effects, WD 5.20-
5.21
Font Color button,
WD 1.14
Font size drop-down list,
WD 1.14-1.15, 6.12-
6.13
Footers, WD 5.12-5.13
Footnote and Endnote
dialog box, WD 3.6-3.7
AutoNumbering, WD 3.6
Format Painter, using,
WD 3.16-3.17
Formatting:
Clip art, WD 8.8-8.9
drawn objects, WD
8.12-8.13
general, WD 1.14-1.15,
3.1-3.29, 6.1-6.30
tables, WD 4.4, 4.16-
4.17
text with columns, WD
5.2-5.3
Formatting toolbar,
WD 1.4-1.5, 1.14-1.15,
6.12-6.14
Formulas, in tables,
WD 4.12-4.15

G

Go To command, WD
5.16-5.17
Grammar checking,
WD 3.18-3.21
Graphics, WD 8.6-8.28
Graphs, creating,
WD 4.18-4.21

H

Hanging indents, WD 3.8-3.9

Hard page break, WD 3.12

Header and Footer toolbar, WD 5.12-5.13

Header and Footer View, WD 5.12-5.13

Headers, WD 5.12-5.13

Headers and footers, switching between, WD 5.12, 5.13

Help button, WD 2.12

Help facility, WD 2.10-2.13

Highlight button, WD 1.14

Home key, WD 1.12-1.13

Horizontal ruler, WD 1.4-1.5

Horizontal scroll bar, WD 1.4-1.5

HTML, WD 8.1, 8.4-8.5

Hyperlinks, inserting, WD 8.20-8.21

I

I-beam, WD 1.4

Inactive windows, WD 3.14-3.15

Insert Table button, WD 4.2-4.4

Inserting clip art, WD 8.6-8.7

Inserting date and time, WD 5.10-5.11

Inserting headers and footers, WD 5.12-5.13

Inserting hyperlinks, WD 8.20-8.21

Inserting a picture, WD 8.14-8.15

Inserting rows and columns in tables, WD 4.8-4.9

Inserting symbols, WD 5.10

Inserting text, WD 1.12-1.13

Insertion point, WD 1.4-1.5, 1.12, moving, WD 1.13

Italic button, WD 1.14, 4.24, 5.12

J

Justified text, WD 1.15, 5.2

K

Keyboard, WD 1.12

L

Label Options dialog box, WD 7.14-7.15

Labels, printing and preparing, 7.14-7.17

Landscape orientation, WD 5.18-5.19

Left-aligned text, WD 1.15, 5.8

Line spacing, changing, WD 3.10-3.11

Linked objects, WD 4.4

M

Magnification tool, WD 1.16-1.17, 7.12-7.13

Magnifier button, WD 1.16

Mail Merge, WD 7.1-7.26

Mail Merge Helper dialog box, WD 7.2-7.4

Mail Merge toolbar, WD 7.6-7.7

Main Document: adding Merge Fields to, WD 7.8-7.9 creating, WD 7.2-7.3

Manual page break, WD 3.12, 4.2

Margins, setting in documents, WD 3.2-3.3

Maximize button, WD 1.9

Menu bar, WD 1.4-1.5

Merged Documents: editing, 7.10-7.11 printing, 7.12-7.13

Merge Fields, 7.8-7.9

Merging cells, WD 4.24

Merging Documents, WD 7.1-7.26

Microsoft Clip Gallery, WD 8.1

Microsoft Graph, WD 4.18-4.21

Minimize button, WD 1.9

Mirror margins, WD 3.3

Modifying page numbers, WD 5.16-5.17

Mouse: drag-and-drop with, WD 2.8-2.9 Selecting text with, WD 2.5

Moving around documents, WD 1.13

Moving text, WD 2.6-2.7

Multiple Pages button, WD 5.14

N

New dialog box, WD 1.6-1.7, 2.14-2.15
New Document button, WD 1.5, 1.18
Nonprinting characters, WD 1.6
Normal template, WD 2.14, 2.17
Normal View, WD 3.4
Note pane, WD 3.6-3.7
Numbered lists, WD 5.4-5.5
Numbering button, WD 5.4-5.5
Num Lock key, WD 1.12, 2.4

O

Office Assistant, WD 1.2, 1.5, 1.9, 2.10-2.11, 2.18
Office Assistant dialog box, 2.10-2.11
Outline View, WD 3.4
Open button, WD 1.18, 2.2
Open Data Source dialog box, WD 7.14-7.15
Open dialog box, WD 1.10-1.11, 2.2-2.3
Opening existing files, WD 1.10-1.11
Options dialog box, WD 3.20-3.21
Outline style lists, WD 5.4
Outline View, WD 3.4
Outlook 2000, WD 5.20
Overtype mode and button, WD 1.5, 1.12

P

Page breaks, inserting, WD 3.12-3.13
Page layout, defining, WD 3.2
Page Layout View, WD 3.4, 3.6
Page numbers:
inserting, WD 3.4-3.5, 5.16-5.17
formatting, WD 5.16-5.17
Page Numbers dialog box, WD 3.4-3.5, 5.16
Page orientation, WD 5.18-5.19
Page Setup dialog box, WD 3.2-3.3, 5.12, 5.18
Page Up, Page Down keys, WD 1.12-1.13
Paper size, selecting, WD 3.2
Paper source, selecting, WD 3.2
Paragraph:
dialog box, WD 3.8-3.11
formatting, WD 3.10
indents, WD 3.8-3.9
Paragraph mark, WD 1.6
Paste button and command, WD 2.6, 2.18
Placeholders, WD 2.16
Points, for type size, WD 1.14
Portrait orientation, WD 5.18-5.19
Print button, WD 1.16, 5.14
Print dialog box, WD 1.16-1.17
Print Layout View, WD 5.12, 6.25
Print Preview, WD 1.16-1.17, 5.12, 7.12-7.13
Printing:
envelopes, WD 7.18-7.21
general, WD 1.16-1.17
labels, WD 7.14-7.17
merged Documents, 7.12-7.13
Programs menu, WD 1.2-1.3

R

Redo button, WD 2.4, 2.18
Redo command, WD 2.4
Repeat command, WD 4.28-4.29, 5.6
Replace command, WD 3.28-3.29, 6.19-6.21
Restore button, WD 1.9
Résumé Wizard, WD 2.14-2.17
Right-aligned text, WD 1.15, 5.12
Rows and columns, in tables, WD 4.6-4.9
Ruler, WD 1.4-1.5
and indents, WD 3.8-3.9

S

Save As dialog box, WD 1.8-1.9
Save command, WD 1.8
Saving documents, WD 1.8-1.9
as Web pages, WD 8.4-8.5
ScreenTips, WD 1.4, 2.10-2.11, 2.18

Scroll bar arrows, WD 1.5
Scroll bar boxes, WD 1.5
Search the Web button, WD 2.2
Searching for files, WD 2.2-2.3
Section breaks, WD 3.12-3.13, 5.8-5.9
Selecting documents, WD 1.14
Selecting text, WD 2.4-2.5
Shading, WD 4.26-4.29, 5.6-5.7
Shading Color button, WD 4.28
Show/Hide button, WD 1.6, 5.9
Shrink to Fit, WD 5.14-5.15
Size box, WD 1.4
Sizing buttons, WD 1.9
Soft page break, WD 3.12
Sort dialog box, WD 4.10-4.11
Sorting data in tables, WD 4.10-4.11
Source files, WD 4.4
Spacing in documents, WD 3.10-3.11
Spell checking, WD 1.6, 3.18-3.21
Spelling and Grammar dialog box, WD 3.18-3.21
Standard toolbar, WD 1.4-1.5
Start button, WD 1.2
Status bar, WD 1.4-1.5
Style box, WD 1.4, 6.12-6.13
Style command, WD 3.17
Style dialog box, WD 6.2-6.6

Style Gallery, WD 3.17, 6.10-6.11
Style Report, WD 6.16-6.17
Switching between header and footer, WD 5.12-5.13
Symbols, WD 5.10
Synonyms, finding, WD 3.26-3.27

T

Tab key:
    indenting with, WD 3.8
    and Tables, WD 4.6-4.7
Table AutoFormat dialog box, WD 4.16-4.17
Table Shortcut menu, WD 4.8-4.9
Tables:
    calculating data in, WD 4.12-4.15
    and Columns, WD 4.8-4.10
    creating, WD 4.1-4.5
    editing, WD 4.6-4.7
    formatting, WD 4.4, 4.16-4.17
    formulas in, WD 4.12-4.15
    inserting and deleting rows, WD 4.8-4.9
    sorting data in, WD 4.10-4.11
Tables and Borders toolbar, WD 4.4-4.5, 4.22-4.28
Tabs command, WD 6.22-6.23
Templates, using, WD 2.14-2.17
    web page, WD 8.2-8.3
Text:
    alignment of, WD 1.15

boxes, WD 5.18
centered, WD 1.15
cutting, copying, moving, WD 2.6-2.7
deleting, WD 1.12-1.13
entering, WD 1.6-1.7
finding and replacing, WD 3.28-3.29
fonts, WD 1.14
in columns, WD 5.2-5.3
inserting, WD 1.12-1.13
justified, WD 1.15, 5.2
selecting, WD 2.4-2.5
size of, WD 1.14
typing over, WD 1.12
Text Direction button, WD 4.24, 5.18
Thesaurus feature, using, WD 3.26-3.27
Title bar, WD 1.4-1.5
Toolbars submenu, WD 3.4
Typeface, WD 1.14

U

Underline button, WD 1.14, 4.24
Undo button, WD 2.4, 2.18
Undoing actions, WD 2.4
Update automatically (date), WD 5.11
Update Fields command, WD 4.14

V

Vertical alignment, WD 5.18-5.19
Vertical scroll bar, WD 1.4-1.5
View buttons, WD 1.4-1.5, 3.4, 6.24-6.25

W

Web, searching, WD 2.2
Web Layout View,
   WD 3.4, 5.13, 6.25
Web page,
   ceating, WD 8.1-8.5
   editing, WD 8.22-8.23
   from a template, WD
   8.2-8.3
   previewing, WD 8.22-
   8.23
   saving a document as,
   WD 8.4-8.5
What's This? command,
   WD 2.12
Windows Clipboard,
   WD 2.6-2.7, 3.14
Windows desktop,
   WD 1.3
Windows Frequently
   Asked Questions
   (FAQS) file, WD 2.2
Windows Start menu,
   WD 1.2-1.3
Wizards, using, WD 2.14-
   2.17
Word:
   commands, WD 1.4
   screen, WD 1.2-1.5
   starting, WD 1.2-1.3
   wrap, WD 1.6
WordArt, WD 8.16-8.19
Word Count dialog box,
   WD 3.26-3.27
WYSIWYG, WD 1.17

Z

Zoom Control selection
   box, WD 1.16, 5.18